IN THE RED

IN THE RED

THE 2001 SEASON WITH DALE EARNHARDT JR.

jade gurss

octane press

octane ◊ press

First Edition, February 26, 2012

Copyright © *2012*

ISBN-10: 0-9829131-8-4
ISBN-13: 978-0-9829-1318-5

Cover design by Michael Snell of Shade
of the Cottonwood LLC.

Front cover photo by Rick Meoli,
and remaining photos by Harold Hinson Photography.

Book design by Tom Heffron.

www.octanepress.com

Printed in the United States of America.

"Danger? Well, of course. But you're missing a very important point. I think if any of us imagined, really imagined, what it would be like to go into a tree at 150 miles an hour, we would probably never get into the cars at all, none of us. So it has always seemed to me that to do something very dangerous requires a certain absence of imagination.

"When I see something really horrible, I put my foot down. *Hard.* Because I know that everyone else is lifting his."

"What a terrible way to win."

"No. There is no terrible way to win. There is only *winning.*"

—Dialogue from the film *Grand Prix*, 1966
Screenplay by Robert Alan Aurthur

"I can't say that I was ever personally concerned about my own safety in the car, even after Walt [Hangsen's fatal] accident, perhaps because I am something of a fatalist. I figure that no two accidents are ever quite the same, and even if you've prepared for every contingency—something else is going to get you someday. It's not that I'm *opposed* to safety gear, it's just that I don't *worry* about it."

—Mark Donohue
Winner, Indianapolis 500, 1972
Winner, NASCAR Winston Cup Series, Riverside, 1973
Champion, inaugural International Race of Champions (IROC) series, 1974
Died from injuries suffered in a Formula One testing accident, 1975
From his autobiography, *The Unfair Advantage*, 1975

"Launch is . . . acceptance of the risk."
—Story Musgrave, astronaut
"NOVA: Space Shuttle Disaster," PBS, 2008

"I don't wanna die. But I *like* the fact that it's dangerous. It's treacherous. The possibility of hittin' the wall is exciting. That's some of the draw for me. I'm ballsy enough to do it. When I'm in the car, I feel macho, like I can bench press 350 pounds."

—Dale Earnhardt Jr.
Rolling Stone, July 5, 2001

Contents

Contents

preface

Huntersville, North Carolina

As the publicist for Dale Earnhardt Jr. from 1999 through the end of the 2007 season, the entire duration of what us old-timers call "the Budweiser Years," I had a front-row seat for some of the most compelling auto racing stories of all time. Many of the most dramatic moments—the highest highs and lowest lows—took place during the 2001 season.

During Junior's rookie season in NASCAR's Winston Cup Series, I kept a massive amount of detailed notes from the racetrack and his many personal appearances. The original idea was to develop a documentary film or reality-based program to chronicle his first season, but Dale Jr. and I concluded a book would be the best outlet for the material. With the blessing of his father and his sponsor, Anheuser-Busch (makers of Budweiser), Junior and I created the book *Driver No. 8*, which detailed the 2000 season.

As the 2001 season began, I continued documenting days that were soon filled with tragedy after Junior's father was killed on the final lap of the Daytona 500. The rest of the season was infused with daily drama as Dale Jr. and his race team persevered under tremendous pressure, winning races and finishing eighth in the championship standings. This book is the story of those days.

Dale Jr. and I discussed the possibility of collaborating on another book in the years since, but he decided the time and effort needed to undertake and promote such a project didn't fit with his ever-expanding business endeavors. He had also grown weary of the constant demand to talk about his father's death. Out of respect to him, I chose to wait until the time seemed right to tell these stories. With the 10-year anniversary of Dale Earnhardt's death past, that time has arrived.

If you're hoping this tome will expose deep family secrets or dish dirt on conflicts within the Earnhardt family, you will be disappointed. Rather, it is about the struggle of a young man to find his place in the world after the loss of the man that meant the most to him. I trust you'll find it compelling and fascinating.

History tells us winners get to write the books, and I hope this one is a winner. I humbly believe it to be finest work I've ever done. It wasn't easy, but the end result was worth it. I hope you agree.

I am grateful you chose to invest the time to give it a read, and hold great hope you will enjoy the ride.

jade gurss
August 1, 2011

chapter 1

the dream

Winston-Salem, North Carolina

"**I**'m going to win the Daytona 500," Dale Earnhardt Jr. proclaimed.

This simple, confident declaration was a delight to the reporters gathered in the room. Pens scratched and clawed while computer keyboards clicked and clacked with urgency. Sometimes headlines write themselves, especially a claim like this from a young man entering his second season in the NASCAR Winston Cup Series.

"I'm pretty confident I'm going to win because I dreamed about it," he continued, drawing a smattering of laughs from his audience. But no one in the room was more surprised than me, his publicist, as it was the first I had heard of this fantastic dream.

Dale Jr. had them where he wanted, hanging on his every word at the 2001 Winston Cup Preview in Winston-Salem, North Carolina. The annual preseason charitable event is named for the late T. Wayne Robertson, who had been a huge force in the motorsports world as president of Sports Marketing Enterprises, the sports marketing division of R.J. Reynolds Tobacco Company. Starting in 1971, mass infusions of cash from Reynolds' Winston cigarette brand helped propel the National Association of Stock Car Auto Racing from a regional sport with crimson-necked appeal to a thriving business and entertainment juggernaut throughout the country.

The Winston Cup season was the longest of any professional sports league in the world, running from early February through late November. (Known today as the Sprint Cup Series, it remains so.) Yet race fans still suffer withdrawal symptoms during the few weeks considered to be the offseason. The Preview helps soothe spring fever by allowing race teams and their sponsors to unveil the colorful, logo-filled paint schemes they will carry during the coming season. It's as if your favorite football team gets new colors and uniforms each fall, and this is your first glimpse.

More importantly, fans have an opportunity to stand in line, often for many hours at a time, to grab a moment and an autograph from their favorite NASCAR drivers. Under significant pressure from NASCAR and Winston executives, each driver is expected to attend, sign autographs, and meet with the motorsports media for a look ahead at the new season.

Earnhardt Jr. and his Budweiser-sponsored team had won three races the previous season, his rookie year in the premier auto racing series in the United States. But the second half of 2000 saw both driver and team falter badly as their youthful confidence began to erode midseason. In his only previous start in the Daytona 500, Junior finished 13th—hardly earth-shattering. Yet, here he was, boldly staking his claim to victory lane at the biggest and richest event in the stock car world. As the son and namesake of seven-time NASCAR champion Dale Earnhardt, he was accustomed to the rapt attention of journalists wherever he went, but this brash prediction was something new for the usually humble, self-effacing 26-year-old.

"You can all call me crazy," he said, lest anyone think he was joking, "but I've dreamed about it so much. I'll be talking to you at the post-race interview, talking about how I did it. It was so real it's crazy. I woke up with a lot of confidence that it was going to happen, that it was going to come true, that I was going to win the Daytona 500.

"I was out in front all day," he continued. "I remember I kept telling myself I won it in my second try. That's why I'm convinced."

"Where was your dad in the dream?" someone asked.

Dale Jr. paused slightly.

"He wasn't there."

chapter 2

just dale

Mooresville, North Carolina

Missing from the Preview that day was Dale Earnhardt. For the second consecutive year, Dale Sr. was the only no-show among the top drivers.

In 2000, Earnhardt missed the Preview while recovering from surgery to repair a broken neck that had hampered his 1999 season. Despite the injury, most likely suffered several years earlier and then aggravated in a vicious crash at the Atlanta Motor Speedway, Earnhardt hadn't missed a race, giving further credence to one of his many nicknames: Ironhead. He needed help to take off his uniform after every race, but he never missed a start.

"Where is your dad this year?" a reporter asked.

"He's gonna kill me for telling," Junior said with a sly smile. "He just had a doctor's appointment to remove a piece of metal that had been in his head since 1977."

This brought big laughs. And added another thread to the tapestry that was the legend of Dale Earnhardt—the most revered driver in the half-century-plus history of stock car racing. Ironhead indeed.

Though the story was technically true (an MRI taken for his neck injury revealed the sliver of metal), the full truth was different. Earnhardt was in Daytona Beach, Florida, test driving a Corvette sports car on the road course at the Daytona International Speedway.

Father and son would be teammates for the first time as they joined the Corvette team in the most prominent road race in North America:

the Rolex 24 Hours at Daytona. The twice-around-the-clock race, held the weekend before the Winston Cup cars arrived in Daytona, would be the first-ever sports car race for either Earnhardt. For Dale Earnhardt, one thing stood above all others: winning. And he was damn sure going to be prepared for his debut in the sleek, DayGlo yellow Corvette.

Tongues were still wagging about Dale Jr.'s Daytona 500 prediction four days later when nearly 200 media members sat down in the main showroom at Dale Earnhardt Inc. (commonly known as DEI) in Mooresville, North Carolina.

The massive DEI complex was a gold-plated, red velvet–trimmed, gleaming palace of speed. Rising from the countryside along a two-lane highway outside of Mooresville, its gaudy redneck opulence was out of place in its rural surroundings, leading to its nickname: the Garage Mahal. But there was no questioning the hard work that took place within Earnhardt's expanding race business. The headquarters featured massive work areas for the three Winston Cup teams he owned, as well as an engine-building division. The corporate offices were upstairs, and a window lined with Earnhardt's seven Winston Cup championship trophies looked down on the public entrance into the gift shop and museum on the ground floor.

Each year, thousands of fans made the pilgrimage to DEI. Greeting them inside the main entrance were four large banners featuring black-and-white portraits similar to the cover of the Beatles' 1964 album, *Meet the Beatles*. The four faces, half in shadows, were those of Dale Earnhardt and the drivers he employed: Dale Jr., Steve Park, and Michael Waltrip. The newest banner featured Waltrip, a close friend of Earnhardt, who had just been hired to drive for DEI despite a record of 462 starts without a points-paying Winston Cup victory.

Behind the banners, a massive wall of glass allowed fans to see into the showroom, which was usually filled with cars, boats, and tractors from Earnhardt's personal collection. Fans scoured the gift shop, happily paying dearly for an endless array of baubles featuring Earnhardt's face, his number, his car, and/or his trademarked signature. If their timing was right, fans might even see one of the famous drivers through the glass. If they were *really* lucky, they might catch a glimpse of Earnhardt himself.

But this morning, as a featured stop on the annual Lowe's Motor Speedway Media Tour, the showroom's slick-as-ice, black-tile floor was filled with journalists, photographers, and video cameras. Because nearly all of the teams in the Winston Cup Series are located in a small radius around Charlotte, North Carolina, the tour allowed those who cover the sport to visit all of the biggest names within one well-orchestrated week. Each team tried to outdo the other, staging elaborate sponsorship unveilings or media giveaways.

Earnhardt, a notorious early-riser who openly relished being called the Intimidator, had already turned in several hours of work, but his youngest son—the third of his four children and a notorious late-sleeper—was late.

"Go get his butt over here," the Intimidator spat, with a sharp emphasis on "butt," sending me, the Budweiser-paid publicist, careening across the highway to make sure Dale Jr. was awake and dressed in time for the media conference. Junior's home, owned by his father and stepmother Teresa (Dale's third wife), was only a quarter-mile from the main gates at DEI, and easily within range of the many security cameras that dotted the complex.

With moments to spare, Junior ambled into the showroom, half asleep and looking as if he wanted to be anywhere but here. His khaki pants and beige shirt were nearly as pale as his complexion. However, when his time came to step up to the mic, he was alert and ready to go.

Almost every stop on this media tour generated the same quotes, as each driver, team owner, and crew chief expressed optimism for the coming season. *"I can't wait to get the season started in the [insert sponsor name here] [insert make and model of race car here]. I think we'll be good this season."* The mind-numbing sameness could quash any hope of excitement or spontaneity. But this stop was different because it was the first opportunity to ask Dale Earnhardt about his son's dream.

"He sleeps a lot," Dale chuckled, "so he oughta have a lot of dreams."

Asked to respond to his father's jab, Dale Jr. didn't back down.

"He probably thinks I'm an idiot," Junior quipped, "but we'll see who the idiot is in February."

While Earnhardt could joke about his son's sleep habits, there was one thing that seemed to rile the man with many nicknames.

"Don't be callin' me 'Earnhardt Senior,'" he said, his Cheshire grin making listeners unsure if this was real or feigned anger. "He's 'Junior,' I'm just Dale Earnhardt. 'Senior' makes me sound old. I've been Dale Earnhardt for a lot longer than he's been around. Just call me Dale Earnhardt . . . or just Dale."

~

Steve Crisp's phone rang just after sunrise on Saturday morning, one week before the 24 Hours at Daytona. At that hour, the call could be from only one man.

"Get over here," Earnhardt Sr. growled. Within minutes Crisp was on his way to his boss's home.

Crisp wore many hats for Earnhardt, including maintaining Earnhardt's massive car collection and wrangling Dale Jr. through two championship seasons in the NASCAR Busch Series, a proving ground for Winston Cup hopefuls. The quick-witted Crisp has an encyclopedic mind, especially when it comes to cars. But this morning, his role was slightly different: ambulance driver.

Earnhardt loved few things more than getting up with the sun and performing any number of he-man duties on his considerable swath of farmland. But while chopping wood that morning, he missed the target and sliced into a meaty hunk of his lower leg.

The Intimidator's doctor was summoned. This morning, Earnhardt had a special request for his physician, whom he referred to as "Doogie Howser" because of his youthful appearance: Earnhardt wanted to watch as the doc explained and demonstrated each step of the stitching procedure.

"I'm always huntin' out in the middle of nowhere, so I want to be able to stitch myself up if I'm hurt," he explained.

Earnhardt's hunting trips were most often taken with his close friend and team owner, Richard Childress. While Earnhardt owned his own racing business with three Winston Cup teams, he actually drove for a team owned by Childress, and had done so since 1981 (with the exception of a short stint in 1982–1983 when Earnhardt drove a Ford for team owner Bud Moore). Together, Childress and Earnhardt won six championships and the 1998 Daytona 500, and made the black No. 3 GM Goodwrench Chevrolet the most recognizable automotive icon in the hemisphere.

The two shared a similar background, coming up the ranks with a ton of desire, a lot of rough edges, and a sparse supply of dollars. Childress and Earnhardt had been competitors on the track, but became a dynamic duo after Childress gave up his driving career to become a team owner.

Beyond their brotherly bond in auto racing, they shared a deep love of the outdoors. As their success grew, the hunting trips became more epic as they traversed the globe in search of big game. For men accustomed to making a living at nearly 200 miles per hour, a normal hunting trip just wasn't much of a challenge. On one trip in New Mexico, the two were almost killed when their horses slipped on an icy mountain, nearly sending both over a cliff. Pondering their mortality over a few drinks at the campsite that evening, Childress and Earnhardt promised each other that if one of them didn't make it back from an adventure, the other would continue racing.

So it was with hunting trips in mind that Earnhardt insisted that the now nervous Doogie Howser M.D. be both healer and teacher, explaining in detail what he was doing with each stitch. Earnhardt, the man doing the lecturing in almost every other scenario, watched closely.

After the procedure, the freshly stitched champ had one request.

"I'm hungry," he said. "Let's go to Wendy's."

At the fast-food joint, Earnhardt hung out and joked with several locals who were most likely just like him: born and raised in small local towns like Mooresville or Kannapolis. At Wendy's, he wasn't the Intimidator or Ironhead or Big E—he was just Dale.

chapter 3

24 hours

Daytona Beach, Florida

Chevrolet had unveiled its plans for the 24 Hours at Daytona during an October news conference in the DEI showroom. The Corvettes on display featured decals with each driver's name and national flag along the roofline. Embarrassingly, the decals read "Earnhart," but the misspelling didn't bother the Intimidator.

Big E was less than 48 hours removed from an incredible victory at the Winston 500 at Talladega Superspeedway, the most super of all superspeedways. Earnhardt made a seemingly impossible charge in the final laps, snaking his way from 18th place to victory. It was the most spectacular of his record 10 wins at the Alabama track where more than 150,000 frenzied supporters hung on every move of his black Chevy. Earnhardt had fans everywhere, but in Alabama, no one besides Paul "Bear" Bryant could have challenged him in a vote for governor.

At the news conference, Earnhardt insisted the endurance racing effort was serious, and if he didn't believe they could race for the win, he wouldn't have even considered the invitation. He also let slip a small part of the team's strategy.

"We'll have Dale Jr. drive at night since he's always up so late," he said, drawing the expected laughs from the audience.

Dale Jr. responded with a less-than-hearty chuckle. While his public façade remained confident, the young driver, called Little E by many, was suffering pangs of uncertainty.

He had finished 14th at Talladega, a respectable finish for a rookie, and had even led for 28 laps, showing a chip-off-the-ol'-engine-block style he learned by spending nearly all of his 26 years watching his father drive lap after lap. But all of the positives were washed away by a single, stupid mistake at the end of the race.

On the next-to-last lap, Dale Jr. found himself in the inside lane, tucked behind Mike Skinner, his father's teammate. As the black No. 3 swept into the middle lane, Junior mistakenly believed it was the final lap. Instead of staying tucked in Skinner's slipstream, Dale Jr. made a banzai charge, diving onto the track apron in an attempt to take the win. Realizing the race wasn't over, he was suddenly steering for his life ("All assholes and elbows," he later described), trying to slide back onto the banking of turn one with an angry nest of cars roaring past him at 190 miles per hour. As miraculous as his father's win seemed, it was equally remarkable Junior's move hadn't caused a massive crash and taken out the entire field.

"Dad would have *killed* me if I had pushed Skinner to a win," Dale Jr. moaned to me soon after the race, trying unconvincingly to rationalize or justify his ill-advised dive.

"I thought it was the last lap, so that's why I made that move. It was a now-or-never kind of deal," he said to his crew, who were thrilled to have led so many laps and finish the race with a car that wasn't crumpled in a thousand pieces. "I saw Dad make his move and it was too late for me to help him. I can't believe I saved it. I was wild outta shape and I thought I was gonna end up upside down or something."

His confidence waning, Dale Jr. was reluctant to try sports car racing, something far out of his comfort zone. His hesitation was made more acute with the realization so many people would be watching. It had taken several years of convincing to get him to commit the time and effort to the 24 Hours, and while he was happy to be teamed with his dad for the first time, he confided, "This is a colossal way to make an ass of myself in front of the world."

From his first time in a go-kart, to his first laps in the 1979 Monte Carlo he bought for $500 with his half-brother Kerry, and all the way to the Winston Cup Series, the greatest fear Dale Jr. had was embarrassing himself or the name his father had given him. He learned at a young age to bear the expectations and demands from others, especially the crush of those who wished him to be exactly like his father. He tried his damnedest to live up to those expectations but also understood how important it was to be his own man.

Also important was the family that surrounded him.

Dale Jr.'s NASCAR crew chief—the equivalent of the head coach in football—was his uncle, Tony Eury, better known as Pops. Big E and Pops were close friends who grew up racing and carousing on local short tracks around North Carolina. They were such close friends that they married sisters. The young ladies happened to be the daughters of a legendary fabricator and mechanic named Robert Gee.

When Earnhardt started his own fledgling team to enter a few Busch Series races, his brother-in-law became his crew chief. Working part-time, Pops led Earnhardt to five consecutive victories in the season-opening Daytona Busch Series race from 1990 through 1994. When Earnhardt opted to enter his small team in the season-long Busch tour with driver Jeff Green in 1996, Pops became the full-time crew chief.

While Dale Jr. had aspired to be a driver like his dad and grandfather, Ralph Earnhardt (who had won the NASCAR Sportsman championship in 1956), his cousin, Tony Eury Jr., also followed the path of his dad and grandfather Gee. After working on race cars and doing odd jobs for Grandpa Gee in the early days of Hendrick Motorsports, Tony Jr. joined his father at Dale Earnhardt Inc. at age 18, learning the ropes as car chief (the crew member responsible for all of the mechanical aspects of the race car). Tony Jr. soon became the team's race-day strategist and a member of the over-the-wall pit crew, changing the front tires in the heat of battle.

Tony Jr. and Dale Jr. were close friends growing up, sharing a deep love for racing, but the cousins were also quick to argue or fight just as passionately. While Dale Jr. claimed the Washington Redskins as his favorite NFL team, Tony Jr. predictably chose their most heated rivals, the Dallas Cowboys, as his team.

When it came time for Dale Jr. to become a professional racer, Big E knew his stern, no-nonsense brother-in-law was the man to lead his son into battle. "Go make him a race car driver," were his instructions to Pops before the 1998 season, as Dale Jr. stepped into the Busch Series full-time, behind the wheel of DEI's No. 3 AC-Delco car.

Dale Jr. was thrilled to finally work with his uncle and cousin. At that time, he would have been happy to work with just about any full-time crew, as he had struggled on his own in the tough late-model stock car races at small tracks around the Carolinas. There he won only four feature races in more than 100 starts, but he learned many hard lessons, working on his cars himself with whatever small pittance he could earn as an oil-change man at his father's Chevrolet dealership. Driving a race car had certainly never paid the bills.

With the Eurys in charge, Dale Jr. performed far beyond his inexperience, winning 13 races and the Busch Series championship in 1998 and 1999. After conquering the junior circuit, the trio brought their efforts to Winston Cup for five races in 1999, followed by a full campaign in 2000 with the massive backing of Budweiser.

Despite their Busch Series triumphs, nothing prepared them for the early success they found in Winston Cup. Dale Jr. and the Bud team won for the first time in only their 12th Cup start, then tied an all-time NASCAR record when Dale Jr. won for the second time in his 16th start. Two weeks after that, he became the first rookie driver to start in the NASCAR Winston All-Star Race. He then went out and won the All-Star tilt, earning more than a half-million dollars with a spectacular drive from the back of the field after a pit-lane mistake and a hard brush with the wall. The team followed their All-Star conquest by starting on the pole and finishing fourth in the Coca-Cola 600.

Headlines screamed "Juniormania!" as the kid showed he had the talent to stand on his own rather than rely solely on a famous name. But the easy road to the top quickly got very bumpy.

The summer heat brought challenges the team was ill-equipped to handle. The 600 was the last top-5 finish of the year, and a 10th-place finish the following week at Dover was the team's last top-10 in the final 22 races. Fighting within the team simmered as the season ground to a halt.

"We all had ego problems," Dale Jr. later explained. "And we all kind of lost respect for each other, me and my [crew]. We just kind of let it get to our heads—the success we had the first [half] of the year. When we couldn't repeat that like we wanted to, we never really pointed fingers at each other, but we did let each other know we weren't happy. It's just not healthy."

In their first season in the major leagues, driver and team burned out. They were simply too new at the game to properly pace themselves within the extreme demands of a Cup season.

A crucial survival skill in Winston Cup racing is the ability to put bad race results behind you, something the entire team struggled to learn. A poor finish meant Dale Jr. and the Eurys fought among themselves much of the following week, which poisoned their preparation for the next race. As the bad finishes stacked up, the vicious cycle got worse.

"We need to grow up, be men and handle failure, things like that, in stride," Dale Jr. explained. "[We need to] be able to come back next week with a good, positive attitude."

Dale Jr.'s inexperience in the Cup car meant he struggled to give detailed feedback about the car's handling. Sometimes he seemed to give confusing or conflicting feedback, which meant the Eurys were unable to make much-needed adjustments. More often than not, they struggled to make the right changes during the race. One example was the August race in Michigan, where the team grabbed the pole position in qualifying but struggled mightily in the race, dropping to 32nd place, one lap behind the leaders, before the engine (mercifully) blew with a few laps remaining. The more they struggled, the more they fought.

But heading into the 2001 season, driver and team were committed to each other like never before.

"We'd rather run like shit together than run good apart from each other," Dale Jr. insisted

The 24 Hours represented a new type of racing for Dale Jr. with a strange new crew that didn't include his uncle and cousin. Doubts raging, Dale Jr. worried about learning an all-new race car and competing against the finest sports car drivers in the world.

His father saw the opportunity from a much different perspective.

Though he had won a record 34 races on the 2.5-mile tri-oval at Daytona International Speedway, Dale Earnhardt had never raced on the 3.56-mile road course. He was the all-time best on its high-banked turns, but new to the course that slithered through the vast infield. He was especially excited to race with his son, but beyond that, the race represented a glimpse of the future for the 49-year-old.

After surgery on his neck, Earnhardt was feeling better than he had in years. Entering the 2001 season, he aimed squarely at winning his eighth title. Seven championships in the bank tied him with Richard Petty for the most in NASCAR history, but what athlete wants to be tied for anything? Earnhardt was driven to set himself apart from every other driver in stock car racing history.

He had been close to title number eight in 2000, finishing second in points to first-time champion Bobby Labonte. But NASCAR had become a younger man's game, and the grind of a Winston Cup season meant Earnhardt was most likely headed toward retirement from driving full-time. Richard Childress Racing had signed him to a driving contract through the end of the 2003 season, but the future beyond that was unclear. As hard as it was to imagine Superman turning in his cape, RCR was already grooming a young, brash Californian named Kevin Harvick as the likely successor when Earnhardt stepped from his black car.

But sports car endurance racing was another thing altogether. Because the lengthy races featured a team of drivers, Earnhardt the Driver could continue for many years. Movie legend Paul Newman had driven in the 1995 24 Hours, winning his class at age 70! That gave Earnhardt a window of two decades—not three to five years.

Earnhardt's thriving business building race engines could certainly grow by providing the Chevrolet horsepower for the Corvettes at Daytona and at races around the world, including the 24 Hours of Le Mans. The French wouldn't know what hit them when the Intimidator's V-8 Chevy power rained down with a deafening American rumble.

Earnhardt saw another benefit from this new form of racing: his legacy. At the time, Mario Andretti and A. J. Foyt were the only men to win both the Daytona 500 and the 24 Hours at Daytona, and Earnhardt savored the chance to join them.

In earlier decades, drivers made their living by racing wherever and whenever they could. During the 1960s, Andretti and Foyt, along with guys like Dan Gurney and Parnelli Jones, were as adept on a dirt track in a sprint car as they were in an Indy car at Milwaukee or a Formula One car at Monaco. Their versatility prompts historians to place them at the top of the short list of greatest-ever American drivers.

Since that era, the sport has grown and evolved. Drivers can now make a very good living specializing in a single series, which prompted the end of the "have helmet, will travel" era (though drivers such as Ken Schrader and Tony Stewart do their best to keep it alive). While Earnhardt's unquestioned mastery of the stock car was revered, he understood he could complicate things for historians by adding another successful chapter to his career.

The typical NASCAR race can last four hours or more, but the Earnhardts were climbing into new territory with the 24 Hours. They were teamed with two of Chevrolet's top road-racing specialists: Englishman Andy Pilgrim and American Kelly Collins. Both were a part of the GM factory effort and tasked with helping ease the transition for the stock car boys into the much lighter and more exotic Corvette.

During test sessions in January, the Earnhardts bonded well with Pilgrim and Collins, and their hard work showed they were team players eager to learn and soak in as much knowledge as they could. Earnhardt the Elder was cautious at first. The brakes on the Corvette are designed to work at certain temperatures, and the harder you use them, the better they stop the car. But after years of babying the brakes on massive Winston Cup cars, Dale began the test session by failing to generate enough heat in the brakes, cautiously easing into the corners.

Junior approached the test from the opposite end of the aggression spectrum. He was amazed at the power and braking capabilities of the Corvette compared to his Cup car. He had jokingly called stock cars "Flintstone-mobiles" at Indy the year before, and he was finally able to experience a car that accelerated faster, braked harder, and cornered much better than those to which he was accustomed. But his aggression also meant he was inconsistent and made too many mistakes.

The Corvettes carried computer sensors that generated an immense amount of data, so Collins and Pilgrim were able to work with each driver, comparing their laps, inch by inch, with the laps of the experienced drivers. The graphs showed every steering, throttle, and braking detail, and the data helped them urge Big E to brake harder and encourage Little E to be smoother. By the end of testing, the two Es had met in the middle with similar lap times.

"These cars kick ass," Junior said after the test session. "So much easier to drive than the Cup cars."

Though slightly less apprehensive about making an ass of himself, Dale Jr. still had a lot to ponder.

A Winston Cup driver never has to worry about racing in the rain because the combination of slick tires and high speeds on an oval make it too dangerous to run with any moisture on the track. But these sports cars run no matter what Mother Nature says. Traction and visibility are crucial factors for any racer, and rain changes both immensely. Junior had heard all the jokes about being a night owl, but he had never experienced a road circuit where the headlights illuminate the track, unlike the bright spotlights that shine on an oval. There was so much more to learn in such a short time, including rehearsing the driver changes.

Then there was the issue of traffic. In a NASCAR race, even the slower cars are at a relatively similar speed, but in the 24 Hours, three categories of cars with wide-ranging speeds are on the track. The Corvette C5-R was in the middle class, known as GTS, which featured exotic, high-powered cars that—at least on the surface—looked like a Corvette, Porsche, or Viper available at your local dealership. A driver in the GTS category can easily pass the much-slower GT cars but must constantly watch the mirrors for the fastest cars, the Sports Racing Prototypes. It was a recipe for disaster for a first-timer, especially since nearly 80 cars would take the green flag.

At a prerace media session, Dale Jr. was asked how he planned to handle traffic.

"I'm not sure they know which way I'm going," he said, "because a lot of times I don't even know which way I'm going."

Big E was more serious. "I want to be competitive," he explained. "If I'm not fast, they can take me out and put someone else in. My priorities are: don't make a mistake, make all of the shifts, don't go off course or do anything to damage the car."

The addition of the NASCAR stars meant the biggest crowd in years for the 24 Hours. The Speedvision network signed on to televise the entire race nationally for the first time, and media credential requests spiked.

The practice sessions prior to the race went well, as Junior discovered the lighting was brighter than he had imagined. Driving in the darkness actually helped his concentration by eliminating many of the extraneous visual distractions on either side of the track.

After qualifying 19th, the experienced Pilgrim was the driver in the No. 3 Corvette as 79 cars took the green flag at 1 p.m. Pilgrim drove the first 90 minutes of the race in heavy traffic, then handed the Corvette over to Big E. The team's driver schedule was scrambled an hour later when rain started to fall. Earnhardt was called to the pits so the team could put rain tires on the car and the more experienced Collins in the cockpit.

Dale Jr. was scheduled to climb in the car at 5:30 p.m., but that changed when Collins spun the Corvette in the rain, then ran out of fuel and had to be pushed to the pit lane. With the team dropping positions quickly, they decided to keep Collins behind the wheel for an extra stint.

At 7:10 p.m., more than six hours after the race started, Dale Jr. strapped in for the first time and slowly crawled down a very wet pit lane. It was the first time he had raced in the rain, and his inexperience showed when he spun the Corvette soon after leaving pit lane, but was able to quickly continue. The combination of a wet track, heavy traffic, and cold tires were a rough indoctrination into road racing, but after a second harmless spin he managed to get into a solid rhythm and completed his one-hour stint.

"I didn't want to go out in the rain," he admitted after he crawled from the car. "You have to work yourself up to it!"

At 9:30 p.m., Big E was in the car when he had to make an unscheduled pit stop to replace a flat right rear tire. The team also had to replace one of the headlights Earnhardt had damaged when he made contact with another car. In the NASCAR world, Earnhardt was the guy most likely to use his front bumper to move a competitor, but the low-slung nose on the Corvette didn't compare favorably with his stock car, and a hard bump was more likely to damage his own car than his competitor's machine.

"It doesn't have much of a bumper," he said with a grin.

After the early fueling issues, the team clawed to sixth place by midnight as Junior climbed in for the second time. Less than 30 minutes later, he limped to pit lane with what he believed to be transmission issues. The team changed the transmission in slightly more than 20 minutes, but then discovered the real culprit was a broken half shaft, a key component in the rear axle assembly. It took an additional 18 minutes to change the axle, which dropped them to 15th place.

With his car intact, Junior completed the rest of his stint without any additional drama, climbing out of the car at 2:45 a.m. The team encouraged him to get some rest in his motorcoach, but with adrenaline pumping, he was unable to sleep a wink as the rain continued throughout the night.

Big E was back in the car as the sun appeared at 6 a.m. His progress behind the wheel was remarkable as he became more comfortable. Each lap seemed quicker than the one before, and the in-car cameras showed Earnhardt thoroughly enjoying his Sunday drive.

Mechanical woes hit the team again before 9 a.m., and they had to replace a broken hood. An hour later, Pilgrim limped to pit lane with another broken half shaft.

Though the overall win was out of reach, the team charged hard in the final hours to grab fourth place overall and second in the GTS class. Their teammates in the sister Corvette (with a driver lineup of Ron Fellows, Chris Kneifel, Franck Freon, and Johnny O'Connell) won the race as the entire field of faster Prototype cars crashed or broke down, giving a rare 24 Hour overall victory to a production-based vehicle.

The Earnhardts helped their team complete 642 laps, covering more than 2,285 miles. Despite the mechanical problems and the challenges of horrible weather, the team persevered to finish only two laps behind the third-place car.

Dressed in matching white Corvette driver uniforms, both Earnhardts were jubilant as they received their trophies and posed with the complete team of Corvette drivers. While they hadn't won, they had shown they could compete with the finest sports car drivers in the world.

"I wanna come back whether Dad does or not," Dale Jr. gushed, pointing toward his father, who was wearing a huge grin as if he had won. Dale Jr. was certain he would be back many more times.

chapter 4

earnhardt vs. earnhardt

Daytona Beach, Florida

Following the 24 Hours, Dale Jr. spent a brief time at home in North Carolina and then was back on a plane to Daytona on Wednesday afternoon to attend a charity event hosted by Mark Martin at the New Smyrna Speedway. Junior was quick to agree when Martin asked if he'd sign autographs to help to raise money for his son's quarter-midget racing series. Martin, a veteran driver whom Dale Jr. liked and admired, had been helpful to Junior in his first two seasons in the Busch Series. This was a small way for Junior to repay the help he had received.

When Junior arrived at the oval just south of Daytona Beach, the line for his autograph stretched across turn one of the half-mile track, along the outside wall, and all the way down the front stretch to turn four. The lines for Martin, Matt Kenseth, and 1989 Cup champion Rusty Wallace were considerably shorter, which, to Junior's way of thinking, meant the other three drivers would be able to finish and then chill out much sooner than he would.

The autograph session was loose and relaxed as the quartet of drivers laughed and joked with each other. Seeing the four drivers together, the distinction was clear: Wallace and Martin were veteran drivers with a past, while Kenseth and Junior were young drivers with a future.

All four stopped midway through the event to watch the takeoff of the space shuttle *Atlantis*, which rocketed into the evening sky from Cape Canaveral, less than 50 miles south on the Florida coast. Everyone marveled at the raw power of the rockets as they made massive vapor trails through the sky. Though it took longer than had been scheduled, Junior stayed to sign for each person in the line.

Most Cup drivers have their own charitable foundation or designated charity, and the unwritten code among drivers is, "If you help me, I'll help you."

During the offseason Junior pondered the considerable stack of charitable requests he had received. Rather than devote a fragmented slice of time and money to many different charities, he believed he could make the most positive impact by focusing on the Make-a-Wish Foundation as his official charity. In addition to fundraising, Junior committed to meet as many Make-a-Wish kids as his schedule would allow. Now he knew he could rely on Mark Martin to return the favor.

One of my duties was to coordinate Junior's calendar, making certain to dovetail the Make-a-Wish visits into his racing schedule and sponsor commitments. The schedule for a Cup driver is like a jigsaw puzzle: it takes precision and patience to make it fit together. When one piece is out of place, it impacts the other pieces around it.

Dale Jr.'s 2001 race schedule after the 24 Hours included 38 Winston Cup races in 19 states. The three days of practice, qualifying, and racing each weekend took precedence over everything else. Next, his contractual obligations to sponsors were placed into the calendar, followed by media opportunities to keep his name (and his sponsor's name) in the spotlight.

Sponsor commitments for the season included 74 days for photo and video shoots and personal appearances around the country. Sponsors are prioritized by the size of the check they're writing to the race team or driver. Anheuser-Busch, the parent company of the Budweiser brand and the sponsor writing the checks with the most zeros, got first access to the dates between races. Their contract also required Dale Jr. to attend a meet-and-greet appearance at the track before each race. Since Anheuser-Busch was the client of my company, fingerprint inc. (I was contracted to them, not to the team or to Dale Jr.), it meant they had a set of eyes and ears around Dale Jr. at all times.

After Budweiser, Junior had commitments to companies such as Chase Authentics (the company that produced T-shirts and trinkets carrying the driver's name and likeness), Coca-Cola, EA Sports, Gargoyles Sunglasses, Chevrolet, Nabisco, NASCAR Café, Outlaw (oil supplements made by parent company Pennzoil), Remington Arms, and Interact (maker of video-gaming accessories such as steering wheels). Each sponsor had their own ideas of when and where they wanted Dale Jr. to appear, which made my job similar to that of a diplomat: making sure everyone remained happy while still protecting the main priorities.

Many of the decisions were determined by geography. Although most drivers have a private jet or helicopter to get them to their destinations quicker and easier than commercial travel, smart planning meant less travel time and fewer expenses. Dale Jr. was one of the few drivers without his own plane, but his dad owned a company called Champion Air that provided a jet for Dale Sr. and a fleet of larger planes to fly the entire squadron of DEI teams to each race.

A smart schedule allows the driver to make a sponsor appearance Thursday evening in St. Louis before he is due to begin on-track action Friday morning in Kansas City, just as it makes sense to book an appearance on "The Tonight Show with Jay Leno" the day before or after a race in Phoenix or Los Angeles.

If handled poorly, the travel calendar can be a costly mess, with the driver zooming from one end of the continent to the other in what we called "Star of David" patterns, which always meant heartache and hassle from the driver and the team owner. It was my goal to prevent that from happening. If the schedule is managed well, the driver can take one day off per week. (Junior's day off meant I was free to work on my own company business and to get the calendar ready for the next week of action. For several seasons, Junior believed if he had a day off, it meant I was off as well. I finally convinced him keeping his calendar up to speed required attention seven days a week.) Since he's a night owl and likely to check his calendar at 2 a.m., we developed a private online calendar that he could view whenever and wherever he liked.

~

After Martin's charity event, Junior's next commitment was the following morning at the NASCAR Media Day. The sanctioning body created Media Day as an opportunity for the print and broadcast media to interview each driver en masse, and allow a driver to dispense with months of interview requests in a single day.

Dale Jr. had always challenged himself to give a unique answer to each question no matter how many times it had been asked. Media Day was superb practice, as the same few questions were lobbed his way throughout the session, giving him the chance to volley them back with a slightly different spin each time.

His best line was in response to a question from Ed Hinton of the *Orlando Sentinel*. Hinton, a longtime *Sports Illustrated* writer, asked about the possibility of father and son working together in the Daytona 500.

"With forty [laps] to go, that father and son crap goes out the window," Junior deadpanned. "Dad's idea of working together is him in front and me behind. I don't always agree with that."

The considerable laughs didn't mask the underlying seriousness of his reply. Despite his laid-back nature, Junior never shied away from acknowledging the considerable weight of expectations that come with being the son of a living legend. Many questions forced Dale Jr. to compare his young career with his father's considerable body of work.

"I look at his career and how he started out with a rookie [-of-the-year] title and then a championship after that," he explained. "But then he went through several years of mediocrity where he just struggled to finish well, but he was still winning races. Hopefully, I will give myself the tolerance of a few years to get it down."

One questioner asked about the possibility of his father's retirement as a driver.

"I think about that a little bit," Junior replied after a thoughtful pause. "I'd say he's got three, four, or five more years. I figure by then if I haven't figured it out, I won't ever. I'll give myself a few years to get it down and to get my program, my team, and everything worked out where we're one of the top three or four or five guys. I think the pressure will mount year after year to be there. If I can't, after that I don't know I'll ever consider myself as good as him or as good as some of these guys that I'm racing with."

Junior attended another media event that afternoon to select the starting lineup for the weekend's all-star race called the Budweiser Shootout at Daytona. The made-for-TV race began in 1979 as the Busch Clash, a fun way to recognize the previous season's top qualifiers. With Budweiser sponsoring the hottest young driver in the sport, it seemed a shame that his father, a six-time winner of the race, didn't win a pole position during the 2000 season and wasn't be eligible for the Shootout . . . until Budweiser and NASCAR chose to conveniently alter the rules, allowing past winners into the starting lineup for 2001.

Thanks to the rules change, Budweiser could trumpet a "father versus son" promotional theme. They produced thousands of posters and flyers with the bold headline EARNHARDT vs. EARNHARDT. Both men appeared on the poster wearing black leather jackets, Big E in his dark sunglasses and Cheshire cat grin while Dale Jr. tried to assume his best 26-year-old badass pose. The names of the other drivers in the field were also included, but in a type size requiring a magnifying glass.

The exhibition race was the debut NASCAR broadcast for FOX TV, a dress rehearsal before the Daytona 500. Previously a 25-lap sprint, the Shootout was extended to a 70-lap race, allowing FOX to sell more 30-second advertisements.

The 2001 season represented a huge leap for NASCAR as they debuted a new broadcast package from FOX, TNT, and NBC. Until then, television rights were sold individually by each racetrack, creating an alphabet soup of networks that televised Winston Cup races. Unless you were a diehard fan, it was nearly impossible to keep up with the week-to-week TV schedule, which leapfrogged among CBS, ESPN, TBS, ABC, and TNN.

NASCAR stepped up to negotiate for the entire series beginning in 2001, resulting in contracts that promised more than $2.8 billion over the course of eight seasons. FOX would televise the first half of each season while TNT and NBC would televise the second half. The monies from the contracts were divided among the tracks (65 percent of the proceeds), the teams (25 percent of the proceeds via increased prize money at each race), and NASCAR (the final 10 percent). Along with continuity for the fans, the contracts also meant each network would promote the races much more aggressively than before.

This was a terrific windfall for nearly everyone in the sport, and if the new deal increased the ratings for each broadcast as expected, the teams could demand higher prices when negotiating their sponsor contracts. When DEI announced Budweiser's deal with Dale Jr. in 1998, the five-year pact was worth approximately $10 million per season. Now, with more attractive national television exposure, the teams could expect to negotiate larger sponsor contracts in the future.

"Earnhardt vs. Earnhardt" was the first of many promotions Budweiser planned for the duo in 2001. The Anheuser-Busch executives in Daytona for the Shootout held a meeting in Big E's motorcoach where they unveiled plans for several humorous television commercials starring both Earnhardts. The commercials were a part of their larger marketing efforts to continue building the younger driver's image. Securing an enthusiastic reaction from father and son, Budweiser's ad agency began finalizing plans for a massive film shoot in Los Angeles in the days before the Las Vegas race, three weeks away.

Budweiser had always prodded Dale Jr. to be genuine when dealing with fans and media. They wanted him to simply be himself, thus standing apart from most other drivers who robotically rattled off a long list of sponsors in every interview. The sponsors who coach drivers to do this fail to understand how viewers tune out when a driver jumps into their rote sponsor listings. Budweiser encouraged Dale Jr. to mention their brand only when it made sense in the context of his answers.

Budweiser's sponsorship of Dale Jr. was designed on one simple concept: appeal to 21-to-35-year-olds by presenting a sincere young athlete who guys wanted to have a beer with—and who girls *really* wanted to have a beer with. It also didn't hurt that three generations of Earnhardts mirrored multiple generations of the Busch family, who had operated the American beer company for more than 120 years.

The presence of Anheuser-Busch executives in Daytona allowed me to complete the 2001 emergency plan, a multipage document with detailed instructions for responding to situations during the season. Every business should have an emergency plan in place, but especially those in motorsports. Racing is a dangerous business, and preparing for the worst is, sadly, a necessary priority. The confidential emergency plan remained with me during each event, and copies were given to appropriate personnel at Bud and DEI.

The key element of the document was a flowchart for internal communications in each company, as well as among the race team, NASCAR, and sponsors. Even more crucial, it outlined procedures for external communications with the media, listing who was an authorized spokesperson for the team and sponsor. In case of an emergency, the plan also instructed the use of landline phones only, as cell-phone frequencies can be scanned and monitored by others. Finally, the plan included family contact information and insurance details for the driver.

Because accidents can happen at any time, the emergency plan required me to be present whenever the Bud car was in action, whether at practice, qualifying, or a race. It was a responsibility I took very seriously, having experienced several driver deaths in my time working for Mercedes-Benz in the CART IndyCar Series.

During the 2000 season, the document was used only once, when I rode on the Medevac helicopter with Dale Jr. after a hard crash at Pocono. He insisted he wasn't hurt, but one of the medical workers erroneously thought he lost consciousness for a moment. In the "better safe than sorry" category, NASCAR wouldn't allow him to get into the backup car until he was checked out. The helicopter seemed like overkill, but it was the quickest way to reach the medical center in Allentown, 50 miles from the track. Dale Jr. refused to go until he had a cigarette (*"You* hit the wall that hard and tell me if you don't want a smoke!" he insisted). At the medical center he napped on a gurney in the emergency room while I worked the phone, notifying NASCAR officials and key people with Budweiser and DEI of his condition. He checked out OK, and was given clearance to get back in the car immediately.

chapter 5

the shootout

Daytona Beach, Florida

As the first practice session began, Dale Jr. brought out a new helmet. The sleek, full-face helmet was a departure from the old-school open-face numbers he had worn in previous seasons. While his red open-face helmets featured intricate, customized designs of skulls and 8-balls, the new one had an ominous Darth Vader look: a polished black finish with no design other than small white Bud decals. A dark visor completed the look, shielding his eyes in bright sunlight. The team was unanimous in its approval, deciding the helmet was, officially, Bad Ass.

Dale Jr. decided to switch to the new helmet after testing for the 24 Hour race. Because ventilation inside the Corvette was almost nonexistent, an air hose was attached to a full-face helmet, pumping fresh air directly to the driver. After getting used to that feel during the 24 Hours, Junior decided to give the combination a try in his stock car.

The Bud team blasted out of the box at Daytona with two fast cars. Their primary car, a proven chassis that had been fast at Talladega the year before, would qualify and run in the Daytona 500, while the second, a new and untested chassis, was slated to run in the Budweiser Shootout. If the new chassis survived the Shootout intact, it would become the team's backup car for the 500.

There was calm among Dale Jr. and his crew as practice began. They were older, wiser, and more focused. Everything about the previous season had been new and none of them had known what to expect. Everything had happened fast, every minute a sprint. One season later they understood that the Cup schedule is a marathon, not a sprint, and they began with a more deliberate and relaxed pace.

The practice session offered the first chance to see all the cars on the track at the same time, especially the newcomers from Dodge, who were returning to Winston Cup for the first time since the early 1980s with a huge amount of hype and capital investment from their parent company, DaimlerChrysler. Dodge had hired Ray Evernham, considered one of the greatest crew chiefs of all time during his championship-winning years with Jeff Gordon and Rick Hendrick, to mastermind their return to the sport. While Evernham had his own factory-backed team, several other prominent teams had joined Dodge to compete against Chevy, Pontiac, and Ford.

When the Intimidator walked over to check on his son after the first practice session, the first thing he saw was the full-face helmet hanging inside the car.

"Goddamn it! Get it the hell out of there," he snapped at Dale Jr., pointing to the helmet.

Even though the vast majority of racers had long ago switched to the full-face helmet, Earnhardt was a stubborn throwback with his open-face helmet and bubble-style goggles. He believed the open-face style was lighter and more comfortable, and offered better peripheral vision, which he was convinced improved his ability to avoid accidents. The open-face also gave him a more acute sense of hearing when a competitor's car was close alongside. Finally, Earnhardt worried a full-face helmet could snap forward in an impact, causing a broken sternum.

Even with his old-school helmet, a broken sternum was one of the multiple injuries Earnhardt suffered in a horrific crash at Talladega in 1996. Two weeks later, driving primarily with one hand, he won the pole position in the road-course event at Watkins Glen, New York. If Earnhardt's fans believed he was capable of almost anything behind the wheel, that qualifying effort added to the lore as he topped the field with one hand (symbolically at least) tied behind his back. He finished the 90-lap race in sixth place, most likely grimacing through each lap.

Without argument, Dale Jr. grabbed the black helmet and handed it to me. I placed the Vader unit in Junior's locker inside the team hauler and brought him one of his red open-face helmets.

It wasn't the only drama of the afternoon: teammate Steve Park spun through the infield grass on the front stretch when Mike Skinner bumped him from behind. Skinner, the inaugural champion of the NASCAR Craftsman Truck Series in 1995, was known for his aggressiveness, but to push so hard in the first practice session was over the top.

The good-looking and personable Park was one of NASCAR's young and ascending stars, starting his third season in the major leagues in the bright yellow Pennzoil-sponsored No. 1 car. He had been Earnhardt's driver of choice when DEI first moved into the Cup Series in 1998. In 2000, DEI's Cup effort expanded to two full-time teams with Dale Jr. and the Budweiser No. 8. That season, Park grabbed his first Cup win at Watkins Glen while the Bud boys won three times. With similar driving styles, the two worked well together, allowing their crews to compare notes and share setups, thus doubling the possibility of finding a fast combination each week.

Earnhardt created a third team for 2001, with sponsorship from NAPA Auto Parts and Michael Waltrip behind the wheel. Earnhardt and Waltrip had long been close friends, but Michael was mostly known for walking away from several horrific wrecks and being the younger brother of Darrell, an articulate driver with three Cup championships. Some wondered aloud if Earnhardt had lost his mind hiring the affable journeyman driver who had yet to win a Cup points race after more than 15 years of trying.

~

The second day of on-track action featured the Budweiser Pole Qualifying session for the Daytona 500. With a complex system to determine the starting lineup for the 500, only the top two positions from single-car qualifying would be locked in. Winning the pole thus allowed a team, sponsor, and manufacturer eight full days to promote their success.

In the final practice before qualifying, the Bud car was fastest for much of the morning until Ken Schrader turned a better lap by a slight margin. Not happy being second quickest, the team decided to make another test run.

As the team pushed Junior's car to pit lane, I was the only animate object in the garage.

"Are they making another run?" Big E asked as he came up behind me at the scoring monitor.

"Yeah, they're on-track now," I replied.

"Damn it! Why the *hell* are they making another run?" he asked.

"Uh . . . you're asking the wrong guy," I stammered.

"They have the fastest car out there!" Big E snapped at me. "Why the hell are they hurting that engine? They need to get it ready to qualify!"

As quick as he appeared, he stormed off in a flash.

While a race engine is built to last 500 miles or more, a qualifying engine is built to produce maximum power for only a few laps, which makes it a brittle mechanism on the edge of exploding if pushed too hard.

The team laughed when I passed along the stern message, confident they had the speed to earn the pole.

As qualifying began, Dale Jr. walked to pit lane wearing a Corvette team T-shirt with a single bold *E* on the front. (Matching shirts with a lower-case *e* commemorated Junior's 24 Hours effort.)

"E? That's for *Eury*, right?" Tony Jr. hollered when he saw the shirt. The car chief and driver laughed, punched, and wrestled with each other as if they were 10-years-olds back home in Mooresville.

Just before the Bud car rolled onto the track, Bill Elliott, driving one of the new Dodge Intrepids for Evernham's team, turned a sizzling lap time.

As Dale Jr. steered the car on his qualifying attempt, the engine felt weak, not pulling nearly as hard as it had earlier. Big E was right: they had hurt the engine by making an extra practice run. At the end of the session, Elliott's Dodge was still on top, while the No. 8 was 18th quickest, far below where they had hoped.

"It's all right," Dale Jr. said, trying to put on a happy face for the media, but his answers were short and clipped.

"The wind changed a lot, and it slows ya down," he said. "We woulda liked to have been faster, but there's nothing you can do. We just didn't back it up."

The team had only a short time to bury their disappointment before the final practice session began for the Budweiser Shootout. After several laps, the car was handling great and Pops Eury decided to bring the machine into the garage to ready it for the race. Coming off of turn two, Dale Jr. waved his right hand to the drivers behind him, indicating he was pulling to the inside lane. He turned off the engine and coasted toward the pit area.

"What the hell?" was Junior's surprised response on the radio. While coasting, the Bud car had been hit from behind by the car of Jeff Burton. It seemed out of character for Burton to have made such a mistake in practice, and he climbed out of his Roush Ford as soon as he could and headed to the Bud garage to find Dale Jr.

Burton explained he had locked his brakes trying to avoid the Bud car after being cut off by a careening Skinner, who had crossed from right to left in front of a pack of cars without using hand signals. Two sessions and two damaged DEI cars, courtesy of the same driver.

"What happened?" asked pit reporter Steve Byrnes, live on FOX Sports Network.

"I dunno. I was in front!" Junior said with a laugh as he surveyed the bent bodywork on the left rear of the Bud car. "I was already outta the way and then someone ran into me. Jeff just said he was cut off."

Junior crawled under the car to inspect the damage, which could be easily repaired before the following day's Shootout. Relieved it wasn't more serious, he headed toward his father's garage area. On the way, he spotted Burton being interviewed by the same FOX crew. Junior ran up from behind, barging in on Burton's interview in mock panic.

"Hey, Jeff! Jeff, my pop wants to see ya!" he said, causing Burton and Byrnes to laugh loudly.

When Junior found his father, he explained what Burton had told him about the incident.

"I've seen that look before," Junior told me as Big E walked away with a growl. "I wouldn't want to be Skinner right now."

A hubbub was taking place next door to the Bud garage as fans and media surrounded Elliott's car. Dale Jr. walked over, looking closely at the No. 9 car with the Dodge Ram logo on its hood. When asked what he thought of the pole-winner's car, Junior borrowed a line straight from the mouth of DEI's Steve Crisp: "I don't think I could race a car with a billy goat on the front," he laughed.

That evening at the Budweiser Shootout dinner in the Bill France Room inside the Daytona USA attraction outside of turn four, each of the Shootout drivers (except for Earnhardt, who was a no-show) found seats at the head table. To the left of the podium, no one sat next to Skinner.

After the function, Junior stuck around longer than the others, signing autographs for Budweiser's guests, including a local bartender who was barely wearing her leather pants and halter top.

I told him I was proud of him for staying longer than any other driver, and he laughed loudly.

"Damn, man!" he said. "I could see her tits. You would have stayed too!"

"No one sat by Skinner," I said.

"Once an asshole, always an asshole," he quipped.

~

Daytona and Talladega are the longest and highest-banked superspeedways on the tour, and speeds had risen consistently through the years, culminating with Elliott qualifying for the 1987 Winston 500 at Talladega with an average speed of 212.8 miles per hour. In that race, Bobby Allison had a horrifying crash on the front stretch, nearly flying through the fencing and into the grandstands. At speeds above 200 miles per hour, cars tended to become airplanes, becoming airborne if they spun sideways or backward. This presented a danger to the drivers, but much more ominously, it presented a very serious danger to spectators.

NASCAR (and their insurers) acted quickly.

To limit speeds at Daytona and Talladega, NASCAR implemented rules requiring restrictor plates on the engines to hold speeds below 200. The plates slowed the cars by restricting airflow into the engine. The result was a unique type of racing at the big tracks: the plates equalized speeds, bringing the cars closer together and causing them to run in large packs.

The plates also made drafting an essential part of the racing equation. Aerodynamically, two or more cars running together can run faster than a single car by slicing through the air more easily. Restrictor-plate races meant working with other cars in the draft. Since a single car didn't have enough horsepower to pull out and pass another car, drivers had to rely on others to help draft and push forward in the pack.

Though he claimed to despise plate racing, no one spent as much time and effort on the plate races as Earnhardt. His engine shop worked an immense number of hours perfecting the plate engines. Earnhardt had also helped create a partnership between three teams to share technical data gleaned from expensive days spent in wind tunnels across the continent. Called "RAD" (referring to the first names of the owners of Richard Childress Racing, Andy Petree Racing, and DEI), the group pooled their funds to maximize their technical understanding of how best to get lumbering behemoths to slice through the wind.

During the 2000 season, NASCAR implemented an additional adjustment designed to slow the cars even further by adding a strip of metal less than two inches high across the top of the car, just above the windshield. The upright strip, which made the cars look like taxicabs, cut a larger hole in the air, making it easier for a slower car to "suck up" to a faster car in the draft.

"I could race the UPS truck with this roof strip," Dale Jr. had explained without a smile.

Earnhardt Jr. still had some subtleties to learn, but he was a very quick study after watching his father for many years. Earnhardt Sr. had discovered a number of minute ways to utilize the draft to his advantage, winning more plate races than any other driver. Frustrated competitors marveled at his mythic ability to "see" the air, using the draft in ways no others could.

Other than an unquenchable hunger to win, what made Earnhardt so great?

While seeing the air is, of course, impossible, the greatest athletes in the world have something scientists call "field sense." Hockey great Wayne Gretzky, for example, was famous for skating not to where the puck was, but to where the puck was going to be. In basketball, great point guards possess a heightened sense of where each player is on the court at all times, even if not in their field of vision. In racing terms, Earnhardt's field sense and spatial acuity allowed him to place his car in the best possible position, even while racing in tight packs. His ability to use the air around the race cars in ways never before imagined only heightened this sense.

Earnhardt also had superb peripheral vision, a trait Dale Jr. shared. In the scientific realm, studies show many successful athletes have better than 20/20 vision, and strong peripheral vision only adds to that advantage. Better vision offers more refined hand-eye coordination, and athletes in many sports have used it to their benefit. In football, teammates joked that Gale Sayers, one of the most elusive running backs in NFL history, had such great peripheral vision he could "see his ears." Though Earnhardt could see neither air nor his ears, a keen sense of vision unquestionably contributed to his success.

A common phrase in racing is to say someone is driving "by the seat of their pants." Drivers often describe their race car as an extension of their body as they're strapped tightly into a custom-fitted seat, allowing them to feel each aspect of the car's performance (known as yaw, pitch, and roll) as it rollicks through the corners. Defense-contracting company QinetiQ conducted tests of fighter pilots who were strapped into their jets in a similar manner and found the most acute sense of these forces takes place in the body's nervous system near the coccyx (the tailbone). Thus, the "seat of the pants" description is scientifically true: the driver with the most highly tuned ass is likely to be a winner.

~

With Dale Jr.'s ass in the Shootout for the first time, the Bud team took the race very seriously. There was much to be learned before the 500, and because the race sponsor was also the largest logo on their car, it was a source of pride to do well. The 70-lap race meant the team would be able to make a pit stop in the heat of battle. They had practiced their high-speed ballet all winter, but it was impossible to replicate the pressure of fueling and changing tires in the midst of a race.

The driver would have the help of his team in the pits, and the eyes of his spotter would help him through the traffic. A NASCAR spotter is an extra set of eyes for the driver, perched atop the tallest building or grandstand with a view of the entire track. The spotter is in constant contact with the team and driver via two-way radio. Perhaps more importantly, the spotter acts as an amateur psychologist, calming the driver when necessary and giving him a pep talk when emotions wane.

Junior's spotter was Ty Norris, the general manager at DEI and the man most responsible for the day-to-day operation of Earnhardt's racing empire. Norris's calm voice on the radio would help the driver traverse close quarters and, more importantly, keep the driver in the right state of mind. It was crucial for Junior to respect Norris, as he would be placing so much trust in his judgment during the heat of battle.

The strategy for the No. 8 bunch was very simple: be aggressive. Starting from the 10th spot, it took only four laps for Dale Jr. to go three-wide in the pack, bump drafting with Jeff Gordon and then his father, using his front bumper to push both veterans to the front. As if they had choreographed it, father and son, their cars nose-to-tail, swept into first and second on lap 12.

After helping his dad into the lead, Dale Jr. took the top spot himself for the first time on lap 20.

When his father made a pit stop on lap 25, Junior was forced to look elsewhere for drafting help, finding it with Joe Gibbs Racing teammates Tony Stewart and Bobby Labonte, the latter the 2000 Winston Cup champion. With the Gibbs cars tucked behind the No. 8, the Eurys began to formulate their own pit strategy.

Because the draft is so essential, teams work together in the pits as they do on the track, coordinating when to come to pit lane so they can maximize their speed after their pit stops.

"If the 20 [Stewart] pits, we'll pit," Tony Eury Jr. told Dale Jr. as they planned to make their stop on lap 45.

But their plans went awry when Junior was separated from the Gibbs drivers in the draft. He came to the pits in tandem with the Ford of Mark Martin, and the two cars exited pit lane together, ahead of the rest of the field. But a two-car breakaway simply cannot push through the air as fast as a larger pack, and Martin and Junior had no defense for the larger, faster pack swarming from behind.

"They'll run right over us!" Earnhardt Jr. yelled. "We need to stick together!"

As the pack rushed by, Junior was able to pull out of line quickly, "grab" the slipstream of Dale Jarrett's car, and manage to keep his red car in fifth place.

After several frantic moves to get back in front of Jarrett and Martin, Junior swung three-wide to pull behind his father. With Junior pushing his dad's No. 3 as if they were glued together, Big E and Little E clawed their way back into first and second.

As the laps wound down, Budweiser executives could barely contain themselves as their poster roared to life. Earnhardt vs. Earnhardt was playing out as the duo led the field with five laps remaining. With Stewart joining the push, the three drivers pulled away slightly from the rest of the field.

Though his tires were a few laps fresher than those of the other two, Junior's car wasn't handling as well. He tried several times to make a move in the high line but his car simply wasn't as quick unless he was hugging the inside line around the speedway.

"Look out high in [turns] three and four," Norris reminded him.

With four laps to go, Dale Jr. led, but he was stuck in the lower line, driving a car that would be unable to block an attempt to pass him on the outside.

"They're trying every lap," Norris explained as Stewart and Big E poked out of Junior's draft to test the waters in the second groove. "Nice patience buddy . . . way to go."

While Junior's car was happy only on the bottom, his father's car was the opposite, and Earnhardt saw his moment when Stewart and Junior made slight contact with three laps to go. In an instant, Big E pulled to the high side, grabbing the lead in a three-wide move around the youngsters. Stewart managed to slide behind the black No. 3 car, while Junior was by himself on the inside, helpless to stop them from streaming past.

With two laps remaining, and left all alone in the low lane, Junior had to force his way back into the draft in seventh place while Stewart and Big E raced side by side for the lead. On the final lap, Junior was able to gain a position while Stewart and Earnhardt battled in an exciting duel to the finish. At the finish, Stewart managed to edge ahead of Earnhardt to win his first Budweiser Shootout.

Even without a victory, Junior and the team were thrilled—they had led three times for nine laps and had shown the speed to run at the front of the field. As Junior pulled onto pit lane and climbed from the car, he was surrounded by a happy crew with high fives all around. They had shown they could run with the best, and fading to sixth at the finish wasn't enough to lessen their optimism looking forward to the Daytona 500.

"Are you disappointed you didn't win?" FOX Sports pit reporter Jeanne Zelasko asked.

"Yeah, but it ain't nothing a cold Budweiser won't fix!" Junior quipped.

Acclimated to Cup races of 400 or 500 miles, the short 175-mile race left Junior with an excess of energy and adrenaline as he helped push the Bud car back to the garage area.

"We have a great backup car," Junior gushed, referring to the Shootout car that would now go back into the team's hauler, waiting there in case they damaged their 500 car.

"Tony [Stewart] is one of the guys that really worked with me," he explained. "I really couldn't make a move there at the end. We were good down low, but I just couldn't go high to block them.

"How 'bout that? Dad and I worked together a lot. That was fun," he beamed. "But he kinda hung me out there at the end. I just couldn't run where he wanted me to. It was scary there with three wide. I'm just glad we didn't wreck."

"We're gonna go out and celebrate tonight," he commanded the entire crew. "It was a good run. But, hey guys, we didn't win, so everyone is on a three-Bud limit tonight!"

chapter 6

the finish will be different

Daytona Beach, Florida

With the Shootout (and three-beer limit) behind them, the Budweiser team turned their focus toward the Daytona 500. A week of practice and a qualifying race allowed them ample time to fine-tune their race car, and Monday's practice session started well until the car began to react strangely.

"If I'm pushed [in the draft], I haul ass," Junior told the crew. "But if they go past me, it'll slow down."

After a few more laps, he radioed again, in faux panic.

"Not haulin' ass!" he yelled. "*Not* haulin' ass!"

Junior pulled into the garage and the team crawled across the Bud car like ants, looking for the source of the problem. They discovered the brake fluid level was too high, which was closing the left front brake calipers slightly. With the fluid level corrected, Junior returned to the track.

"Haulin' ass!" he laughed. "Haulin' ass!"

Junior's evening included his annual trek across the street to the Volusia Mall for the national radio broadcast of "Fast Talk with Benny Parsons" on the Performance Racing Network. Inside the mall, several hundred chairs were filled by early afternoon as the diehards grabbed a good view of the star-filled show hosted by Parsons, the beloved former NASCAR champion turned broadcaster.

Dale Jr. was pleasantly surprised as we arrived backstage to find several gorgeous women from Jamaica Air, a sponsor of the radio show. The airline was promoting their annual December race-themed trip, and Junior had been one of their star attractions for several years.

"Damn, she is fine," he whispered to me before he went on stage, nodding in the direction of one of the Jamaican girls. "Can you imagine the shit storm if I walked down pit lane with her?"

After introducing Dale Jr., Benny asked about his dream of winning the 500, which gave Junior another chance to insist how vivid and realistic it seemed. Following the Shootout, his confidence level was soaring, and the dream come true seemed more of a possibility than ever.

Parsons pressed him to predict who his toughest competition might be in the 500.

"That 22 car looks like the fastest one out there," Junior answered, referring to the Dodge of Ward Burton and echoing a sentiment he had expressed earlier in the day. "They haven't shown us what they can do, and that car looks really solid."

The comment was an example of a tendency among racers to refer to rivals not by name but by number. Saying "the 20 car" instead of "Tony Stewart" tends to depersonalize a rival. It's easier to race hard against "the 17" than against Matt Kenseth, Junior's good friend.

Junior hoped his rivals would be cursing the back bumper of "the 8" for the entire season.

~

Earnhardt Jr. woke up Tuesday morning with a bad case of the flu that had been making its way through the garage area. "I get sick twice a year," he said as he walked miserably to the car for a brief practice session. "Once when the weather changes in the spring, and again in the fall."

Dehydrated and weak, he was helped out of the car after the session. He headed directly to his motorcoach for a few hours of sleep. He had canceled a video shoot with FOX Sports that afternoon, but insisted on keeping his evening commitment with the syndicated TV program "The George Michael Sports Machine." Michael, based in Washington, D.C., always enjoyed interviewing Dale Jr., relating stories of the hometown Redskins, Junior's favorite team.

The interview proceeded smoothly in Daytona's victory lane until Tony Stewart snuck up from behind and doused Junior with a frigid sports drink. Off-camera, the two joked and laughed that they might have to battle one another for victory in the 500.

~

Junior was still feeling rough Wednesday morning and asked if he could skip the FOX shoot, which had been rescheduled for that afternoon. The FOX production crew had taken over a hangar at the nearby airport, creating a massive TV studio where they could shoot each driver in a variety of artistic settings. These shoots would become the footage used on broadcasts throughout the season, as artistic "bumpers" in and out of commercial breaks, and during feature stories.

I called to ask if Junior could reschedule a second time, knowing it wasn't really an option. The television crew was tearing down the makeshift studio later that day, and the producers insisted it was essential that Junior be included in that day's shooting. Despite my repeated urgings, Junior held tight to his refusal.

Thirty minutes later, the door of the motorcoach flew open.

"Damn it, get up!" Big E insisted. "Get up and go do the FOX shoot. This is important. Get your ass up and get over there."

Within 15 minutes, we were on our way to the hangar.

~

Junior felt much better Thursday as he prepared for his 125-mile qualifying race. The Gatorade Twin 125s, which determined the starting grid for Sunday's 500, split the field into two equal lineups for races of 50 laps each. With the front row of the field locked in based on the previous Sunday's qualifying, Junior stood to earn a starting spot as high as fourth in the 500 if he were to win.

In the first 125-miler, Sterling Marlin won in his silver Dodge. Big E finished third, which was unusual because he had won a record 12 Daytona qualifying races in total, with a stunning feat of 10 consecutive wins from 1990 to 1999. Earnhardt had led the race on the final restart, but Marlin passed him on the last lap.

"I was a sitting duck," he said. "And they were all hunters."

Junior started ninth in the second 125, taking the green flag from the inside of row five and driving DEI chassis No. 004.

"Only one way to go," Junior said, promising to be aggressive as the field rolled toward the green flag. "If I crash it, we got a helluva backup car in the truck."

The aggression had to wait, as a major bottleneck at the front of the field caused Junior to drop to 20th by the end of the first lap.

"No worries here, we'll be all right," Junior assured the crew as he began drafting with Kenny Schrader in the M&M's machine. Schrader had been fast all week, and the two drivers worked together all the way to the front. Schrader led lap eight, then they swapped spots as Dale Jr. led lap nine.

After dropping back a few positions, the duo was joined by a third car when Stewart pulled behind Junior. The trio ran nose-to-tail, climbing forward with ease.

"The 20 car says he's happy where he is," explained Ty Norris from the spotter's stand.

At the halfway point of the race, Junior led a line of six cars that slipped away single-file from the rest of the field. Stewart and Schrader were right behind.

With less than 20 laps remaining, Schrader made a move to the inside of Junior to take the lead.

But after a few laps in the high lane, Stewart could not stay on the bumper of the Bud car.

"The 20 says he can't go high," Norris said. "He needs to stay low."

Junior and Stewart quickly ducked into a small gap behind Schrader on the inside lane, holding steady until a yellow flag flew on lap 35.

Under yellow, a bumbling pit stop of more than 20 seconds dropped the Bud boys from third place to 10th. Pops was livid.

"C'mon, guys!" he yelled, red-faced. "That's fucking terrible! We can't win this thing if you guys can't get it together!"

"Sorry about that mess," Norris interjected, trying to calm everyone down. "We know we got us a wheelman. This'll be fun!"

"Hell yeah!" Junior, the wheelman, replied. "I don't care who it is in front of us. We're gonna make a badass run."

With 10 laps remaining, the action was much more aggressive as everyone fought to position themselves for the win. By lap 43, Junior had moved up four positions to sixth, but an ambitious move on the outside sent him backward to ninth when no one followed him in the draft.

Junior jumped back in line, making contact with the rear bumper of Mike Skinner's car on the backstretch. With the Bud car pushing Skinner, the two angled toward the front with five laps to go.

With two laps to go, the duo got shuffled back in heavy traffic and Norris preached patience, reminding Junior, "Think about the big picture. Don't tear up your stuff. Protect the bottom. Stay on the bottom."

Junior urged Norris to pass a message to Skinner's spotter as he dropped to sixth place.

"Get over and tell Skinner not to do anything dumb," he shouted, "coz I'm happy runnin' second."

As the white flag came out, Dale Jr. was third, but with a big push from Jeff Burton, he somehow managed to slingshot to the inside of Skinner's car, pushing Skinner to the high lane. So much for being happy running second.

With Burton pushing hard, Junior edged into the lead on the backstretch as the field scattered for the final two corners.

"Good push inside," Norris said. "Big push with ya! Burton is pushing you. You've got the help. Skinner is looking high. He's outside . . . he's outside."

The two Chevrolets rolled through turns three and four with Junior in the low lane, Skinner to his outside.

As they rocketed off of turn four, Skinner pulled extremely close, side-drafting in the slipstream of Junior's car, inching his machine door to door with the Bud car.

The cars rolled under the checkered flag in unison, and a split second of uncertainty ended as soon as NASCAR's electronic scoring showed Skinner crossed four-thousandths (0.004) of a second in front of Junior for the closest finish in the history of Daytona qualifying races. The race featured 11 lead changes among nine drivers, both records for a 125-miler.

While Skinner pulled his car to victory lane, Junior and the team displayed no disappointment. They knew the big money would be paid on Sunday, and they had again shown their team, car, and driver were capable of competing for the win.

The media surrounded Junior on pit lane. "Tell us about the last lap," someone asked.

"We got some help from Jeff Burton," he said. "He stuck with me. Even if it was only for a lap, it helps a lot."

"Did you think you'd won?"

"I didn't think I won," Junior answered quickly, full of adrenaline after the short race. "If you're within half a car length, you can get a draft alongside. The only other place for me to go was the apron. He was a little behind me off of turn four and he had a pocket of air beside me. I saw the way he got a run, so I was pretty sure he beat me. We weren't looking good with two laps to go. I was in jeopardy, but Jeff Burton stuck with me. I was glad to be in the middle of it at the end there. It was crazy!

"Maybe I should have just turned right and went into the side of him to slow him down," he said with a laugh. "But it's only the 125s. We wouldn't want to take such a big risk."

"I think we're looking good," Junior said when asked about his thoughts for the 500. "We'll be good. I hope it's like today: real exciting, real intense. I've been talking trash and talking about the dream . . . so I promise you that finish today would be different if it was the 500."

Full of excitement, driver and team headed to the hauler to debrief and develop their strategies for the 500. Once inside, Junior emphatically repeated his promise to the Eurys: "I'm tellin' you right now, that finish will be different in the 500."

chapter 7

the man

Daytona Beach, Florida

As the garage area closed following Thursday's qualifying races, Dale Jr. headed toward the Daytona Beach Marina where ESPN had stationed their crews for the week. Because of the huge bushels of dollars from the new broadcast contracts, NASCAR made the incredibly short-sighted decision to not allow ESPN cameras on the property during any of the Winston Cup events. Even more bizarre, ESPN's daily racing show, "RPM 2Night," was only allowed to show still photos of the races. Despite this, ESPN crews worked double-time during the season to secure driver interviews anywhere they could, often staking out the airport where the drivers boarded their private jets following each race. For Speedweeks, the name given to the three weeks of events leading up to the Daytona 500, ESPN found a scenic spot along the water and relied on the drivers to venture several miles from the track for interviews.

The rest of the No. 8 team headed farther up the beach to where Budweiser hosted a large dinner and banquet at the Adams Mark Hotel. Usually the driver gets the perks and the fawning attention, but this evening was a chance to recognize and thank the guys who busted their asses to make the Bud car go fast.

Host Michael Waltrip got laughs from the gathering as, one by one, he introduced the crew members seated at the head table. After the program, the Budweiser guests filed across the front of the room, getting autographs from each of the grateful crew members as they relaxed with cold Buds, smoking cigars and basking in the attention.

After his ESPN interview, Dale Jr. headed back to the track where he and Stewart met for more than an hour, discussing their qualifying race and possible scenarios for the 500. The discussion paused when Junior turned to the Comedy Central network to see his half-hour interview (taped in Los Angeles the previous November) on the talk show "Turn Ben Stein On." Junior was happy to be the first driver to make an appearance on the network. The droll Stein ("Bueller . . . Bueller . . .") marveled at the danger Junior accepted every day, then challenged the driver to a radio-controlled car race before insisting they both perform 20 pushups as the credits rolled.

~

Friday was quiet for the team, with only one practice session. Fully recovered from the flu, Junior spent much of the day relaxing, reading the huge NASCAR cover story in *USA Today* with a large photo of his father on the front page.

That afternoon, a few of us gathered around the TV outside of Junior's motorcoach to watch the International Race of Champions (IROC) race.

The IROC series was conceived to put the best drivers from different racing disciplines around the world into 12 equally prepared cars, showing their prowess on road courses as well as ovals. Theoretically, the champion could then be called the greatest driver in the world. However, as IROC evolved during the 1990s, all of the races eventually took place on NASCAR ovals, so the field was now mostly Winston Cup drivers with a few others added as sacrificial lambs.

Dale Jr. had driven in the IROC series in 1999 and 2000, representing his championships in the Busch Series. In 1999, he had a remarkable race at Michigan, battling his father to a side-by-side finish similar to the one the day before with Skinner. He lost that race by seven-thousandths (0.007) of a second, but was exhilarated to have raced so close and so hard with his father. Then, in 2000, after a thrilling opening race where the pair again dueled for the win at Daytona (Dad won that one as well), Dale Jr. found himself driving less-than-equal cars, twice dropping out with engine problems. It so frustrated and embarrassed him that he declined IROC's invitation in 2001.

Dale Sr. excelled in the series, winning the IROC championship four times. He was the defending series champ when the 2001 season-opener at Daytona began. It was the usual superspeedway race with close drafting and many lead changes. As the field headed toward turn one with two laps remaining and Earnhardt in the lead, journeyman IndyCar driver Eddie Cheever made an aggressive move, pushing Earnhardt's machine off the track and into the infield grass at an incredible rate of speed.

Most drivers would have spun through the grass, sliding out of control as their car left the asphalt. But as his car hit the grass, Earnhardt somehow held it in a four-wheel drift as if he were back on one of the rugged dirt tracks of his North Carolina upbringing. He eventually slid back onto the banking of turn one—in seventh place!

Those of us watching in the infield were stunned at the car control he had displayed.

"He is *the* man," I said reverently.

"Hell yeah," Junior answered.

Dale Jarrett won the race, and as the cars slowed, Earnhardt sped toward Cheever. Just off turn two, Earnhardt hooked the rear bumper of Cheever's silver Camaro, spinning him off the track as he gave Cheever the finger.

As the cars came to a stop, everyone waited to see if Earnhardt would track down Cheever, and if so, what kind of rumble would break out. As the Intimidator stormed out of his car, Cheever stood his ground. Earnhardt approached quickly and in one swinging motion . . . put his arm around Cheever's neck for a few private words.

Almost immediately, both drivers were laughing and the tension dispersed.

"I told him we were even now," is about all Earnhardt would tell the media after the race. Cheever refused to give specifics about their embrace because, as the open-wheel driver put it, "there are too many ladies present."

For all of his on-track bluster and roughhousing, for all of his devilish glee at being called the Intimidator, this was prime evidence that Earnhardt was not a man who used his fists. Though he was known as someone who would spin out a good friend or family member to win a race, fistfights had been left at the short tracks where he learned his craft. In the last decade of his Cup career, Earnhardt's most violent post-race exchange took place in 1995 when Rusty Wallace threw a water bottle at him after an incident at Bristol. After a number of run-ins, Darrell Waltrip described his frustration at Earnhardt by saying, "Somehow Dale could convince you that the wreck was your own fault, even when you knew it wasn't!"

With the IROC drama concluded, it was time for Dale Jr. to hop into his brand-new white Chevy Tahoe and drive to a large concert stage outside of turn four for a live national radio show on the Motor Racing Network. As we approached, the security staff opened a side gate and Junior quickly drove into the backstage area.

The crowd recognized him as soon as he climbed from the Tahoe, and they surged forward when he was introduced. Cars on International Speedway Boulevard crept slowly past the stage, passengers craning to see Junior's face projected on a large video screen. After several queries, the radio hosts turned the questioning over to the crowd, which resulted in confusion and chaos.

First to the microphone was an older gentleman, who had a tough time formulating a question.

"Your grandpa was the most awesome, the greatest," he drawled.

"Thanks," Junior replied.

"He would show up at the track and he was always the coolest one there," the gentleman continued.

Not sure how to answer, Junior chuckled while the radio hosts looked for the next questioner in the crowd.

A female audience member asked, "Dale Jr., will you take your shirt off?" The request resulted in hoots, hollers, and wolf whistles.

Junior politely declined and was soon done with the interview.

Because our arrival had drawn considerable attention, many fans circled to the gate where we had to exit. It took several minutes for the security guards to back the crowd away so the gate could open wide enough for the truck to exit. While the adulation and attention is flattering, at times it can be fraught with the very real danger of people being hurt or trampled. This was one of those times.

As Junior slowly pulled toward the gate, the crowd pushed forward, then began yelling and screaming when it became clear there was no way he could stop and sign autographs for everyone. A few pounded the windows and the sides of the small SUV. Others shouted and jeered.

"Fuck the King," Junior muttered as we crawled inch-by-inch through the crowd.

"What?" I ask incredulously.

"The King ruined it for all of us," he laughed, though I'm not certain if he was half-joking or half-serious. "It's great that we sign so many autographs, but since Richard Petty would sign for anybody and everybody back in the old days, the fans still expect every one of us to stop everything and sign whenever they want something. Damn. There would be a riot if I stopped. The King ruined it!"

No thanks to the King, we finally reached the security of the tunnel that burrows under turn four. Emerging unscathed, Dale Jr. headed to the motorcoach lot because he wanted to read the feature story about him that had just been placed online at Playboy.com. It was an online-only interview, not in the magazine itself, but it was a small step in the right direction to reach *Playboy* readers, who represent the 21-to-35-year-old, affluent male demographic that NASCAR and Budweiser covet.

The interview, as could be expected, was more open about sex and other subjects rarely mentioned among the motorsports media. Junior laughed aloud at his own revealing responses. He was in rare form as he dished dirt about Goodyear tires, commented on how to deal with pit lizards (i.e., guys and girls who hang around the tracks, hoping to be near a driver), lamented his troubles trying to find a serious girlfriend, named his favorite Playmate (Renée Tenison, 1990 Playmate of the Year), and talked about inhaling forbidden weed before he became a professional driver.

"Damn, man," he asked. "You think we'll get our ass kicked for this?"

"No way," I assured him, though I wasn't certain the exceedingly conservative NASCAR would be thrilled about his openness. "Budweiser will love it."

~

The day before the biggest race of the year included a final practice session for the Cup cars. Most teams run only a few laps on Saturday, not wanting to damage their car. Dale Jr., with approval from Pops and Tony Jr., had other ideas. With Stewart pushing him, the two worked on steering their cars in tandem, drafting through traffic. Hooked together, nose-to-tail, the two cars improved their lap times in the session by almost three-tenths of a second.

After the session, Junior seemed quieter than usual. Something was bothering him. Finally, he spoke up.

"The race engine just doesn't seem to have the same power, the same oomph," he said to Jeff Clark, the team's engine tuner. The team had installed a new engine after Thursday's 125-mile race.

"We tried a few new things with the other engines," Clark responded, "but they only had to run hard for 150 to 175 miles. This one has to go a full 500 miles so it's slightly detuned. I promise you, you'll have enough to run 'em down."

Seemingly convinced, Junior huddled with the Eurys for some prerace discussions, then headed to his motorcoach for a quiet night with his Sony PlayStation 2.

Budweiser's Tim Schuler, the man responsible for bringing me aboard with Anheuser-Busch, stopped by to see the team, and we walked through the garage as twilight began to fall over the speedway. We spotted Ken Schrader, a native of the St. Louis area and one of the most likable guys on Earth.

Budweiser had sponsored Schrader for several years when he drove the No. 25 car for Rick Hendrick. Even though his car was now painted bright yellow and had decals of M&M's candies on it, there were frequent references to Schrader's "lifetime personal service agreement" with Budweiser. At first I thought these references were inside jokes, but Schrader is one of Budweiser's biggest fans—and the feeling is mutual.

Schrader was having a great Speedweeks—his Pontiac was at the top of the speed charts for much of the week. He was clearly excited about his chances in the 500, and we leaned against a stack of tires to listen to some of his hilarious stories.

The tales eventually turned to Earnhardt, as Schrader explained how much Big E had helped him when he was trying to make his way in Winston Cup after a career on Midwestern dirt tracks. It was typical of Earnhardt, whose gruff public persona hid a soft spot that prompted him to help many racers who struggled on their way up the ladder.

"He has a heart," Schrader chuckled, "it just doesn't beat on the racetrack."

Schrader told about a time the two were driving on a two-lane highway in the middle of nowhere and sped past a strange vehicle beside the road with a "For Sale" sign on the windshield.

"Turn around," Earnhardt told Schrader. "Let's check that out!"

The vehicle was a strange concoction that could operate as a car or a boat. Dale and the owner agreed on a price and Earnhardt convinced Schrader to split the purchase with him, taking co-ownership of the amphibious oddity. Problem was, Earnhardt didn't have any money on him, so Schrader paid the full amount. After hauling the monstrosity back to Mooresville several days later, Schrader was stuck with the useless machine when Earnhardt "forgot" making any promise of joint ownership.

We were near tears laughing at the stories when we heard a ruckus on pit lane. It was Earnhardt and former football great Terry Bradshaw, now a part of the NFL football coverage on FOX. Bradshaw was the grand marshal for the 500 and would wave the green flag to start the race the following day. Big E had just taken a Busch beer contest winner for a lap in the pace car and had offered to do the same for Bradshaw, who was wearing a driver's uniform and carrying a crash helmet. The two climbed in. A few seconds passed, then the window rolled down and Earnhardt's big hand threw Bradshaw's helmet out of the car as the tires squealed and smoked down pit lane. The helmet spun to a rest as they sped into turn one.

Earnhardt ran it hard and fast, taking the car within inches of the outside wall. After several laps, he dove onto pit lane, where, to the joy of a few of us watching (and the FOX cameras), he slammed the emergency brake, sending the car into a spin and coming to a perfect stop—facing the opposite direction.

Suddenly, Earnhardt was out of the car, yelling for Bradshaw to jump out as fast as possible and climb on top of the car with him to celebrate as if they have won the race. Under the lights at Daytona International Speedway, two of America's most popular and successful athletes were yelping and screaming like children on the trunk lid of the car. Then they jumped to the ground arm-in-arm, laughing hysterically.

chapter 8

the morning

Daytona Beach, Florida

It's difficult to overstate the optimism and excitement that dawned on Sunday morning, February 18, 2001. This was the day of the 43rd annual Daytona 500.

The entire NASCAR community begins looking forward to the 500 as soon as the checkered flag falls on the final race of the previous season. Most Cup races are two- or three-day affairs, but as the season-opening race, the 500 is the dramatic climax of weeks of preliminary events at Daytona International Speedway. By 2001, it had surpassed the Indianapolis 500 as the most-watched American motorsports event, and it offered the largest purse of any Winston Cup race. The winner would receive a check of more than $1.3 million; the total purse exceeded $11 million for the first time. Even the last-place finisher would take home more than $111,000.

The new TV contract meant billions of dollars would be pumped into the sport over the next few seasons. FOX had promoted the race for months, especially during their NFL playoff coverage throughout January. Larger TV ratings promised to bring more new fans than ever before, which meant more sponsors for the teams, more ticket sales, and more advertisers on the broadcasts. Each aspect fed the others, making the future look as bright as the sun that shone through a blue, cloudless sky that February morning.

The TV contracts were also NASCAR's best tool to legitimately take its place as the fourth major American sport, and to be universally recognized as something more than a niche, regional pastime. It had taken more than 50 years, but NASCAR was on the launch pad that morning, and everyone could feel the excitement.

To humanize a sport that relied so heavily on machines, FOX focused much of its coverage that day on Dale Earnhardt. The larger-than-life icon with a blue-collar work ethic embodied the American Dream. From ramshackle tracks to shiny boardrooms, Earnhardt was a man many Americans aspired to emulate—he had done it all without losing an ounce of his Everyman appeal.

Earnhardt's son also presented an interesting tale, striving to become his own man, hoping to be defined by his actions rather than his name. He represented a younger, hipper, and, most importantly, more affluent audience. The American Dream? Nothing seemed as red, white, and blue as the dream which told Junior he was going to win the Great American Race.

Almost nothing is routine about Speedweeks, but that morning it was important to follow the race-day routine we had developed the year before.

The contract between Dale Jr. and Budweiser included a meet-and-greet before each Cup race. Sometimes it was a massive affair, with Junior taking questions on a stage in front of hundreds of Budweiser guests. Other times it was a more intimate setting in a luxury suite with 20 to 30 VIPs. No matter the forum, it was always scheduled 60 minutes prior to the mandatory NASCAR drivers' meeting. Most Sundays, Dale Jr. slept as late as possible, rolling out of bed without a moment to spare.

The job of waking him usually fell to his motorcoach driver, Shane Mueller, but it wasn't uncommon for me to draw the dreaded duty if it was crucial that he be on time to meet high-ranking Budweiser executives or guests.

Junior usually slept in the spacious bedroom at the back of his million-dollar-plus luxury motorcoach. Sometimes, after a particularly strenuous night of video gaming or movie watching, he fell asleep on one of the long, dark couches in the front section of the coach. He never tired of chuckling when I crept from the bright sunlight into the darkened coach and knocked on the bedroom door—only to be startled out of my skin when he awoke on the couch behind me.

When Junior was ready to go, the logistics fell to Joe Glynn, who managed the at-track program for Bud. Glynn's duties ranged from managing the Budweiser Pole Award ceremonies to babysitting executives and orchestrating appearances by the Budweiser Clydesdales, an especially massive undertaking. Driving one of several golf carts painted to look like the No. 8 car, Glynn transported Dale Jr. in the smoothest manner possible. That meant scouting the location prior to race day and devising the best route—even if it meant getting creative and occasionally slipping a security guard a hat or autograph card (or, ahem, a six-pack) in order to get through gates that were otherwise locked or blocked.

Usually we could slide Junior into the suites or hospitality village on race morning quick and stealth-like without too much hassle. Once the fans learned he was inside the suite or tent area, however, the crush was on. Fans congregated in droves between the exit and the golf cart, hoping to catch an autograph. We usually relied upon security or law-enforcement officers to help get Junior back to his bus in one piece.

Because Dale Jr. had been in town for several weeks and had already made a number of Bud-related appearances in Daytona Beach, the meeting that morning was with a small, calm group and we were able to slip in and out without much drama, other than a security guard briefly stopping Dale Jr. because he didn't have a credential or hard-card (a NASCAR season pass). Once he realized who he had stopped, the guard sheepishly allowed us to enter.

Up next was the drivers' meeting.

Before his first 500 in 2000, Dale Jr. wore a sharp new suede jacket to the meeting, only to have it ruined when the crush of autograph seekers left it streaked with black, indelible ink from their outstretched Sharpies. Lesson learned—he never again wore anything other than sponsor apparel to the meetings.

At Daytona, the meeting took place in the garage area. For the 500, it's always a crowded, lengthy affair because every celebrity and sponsor executive is introduced to a smattering of polite applause before NASCAR officials outline the rules and details about the day's race. The thousands not lucky enough to be allowed inside the meeting hover outside the garage.

Before Speedweeks 2001, a large, modern medical center had been built adjacent to the motorcoach lot. The new building meant the dingy old infield care center was now mostly empty. This provided a perfect opportunity for us to drive through a small gate there and sneak into the meeting undetected. The slick entrance seemed another example of everything falling into place this week for Junior.

Everything in NASCAR is a competition, and seating for the prerace meeting is no different. Most of the time, Dale saved a seat for Junior, allowing him to sit in the front row alongside the champions—veteran drivers such as Rusty Wallace and Dale Jarrett. Rookies and newcomers sit in the back while the big guns take the front, unless your dad is the alpha male.

Following the meeting, there was the usual rush to exit, but Big E and Junior hung back. Dale wrapped his arm around his son's neck, pulling him close with his trademark move. Even though Dale was not a large man, it was as if he could completely envelope anyone by slinging his arm around their neck to impart his wisdom, whether you wanted it or not.

This was their first conversation of the day, and the two talked quietly, forehead-to-forehead. As they walked slowly, the mass of people seemed to dissipate. It was clear the two Earnhardts were in a private moment and not available to sign autographs. Without a glance, the two drivers ignored a hapless radio reporter trying to get an interview and walked arm-in-arm through the teeming garage area.

Dale Jr. had always idolized his father, and he relished the fact they were closer than ever before. For 26 years, he had struggled for his father's attention, affection, and approval. He was thrilled to finally have all three.

As a young boy, whether watching on television or playing with his toy cars while listening to the race on the radio, Junior's imagination put him in his dad's car for every lap. Following his father's races made him feel closer to the man who was physically and emotionally distant. While his dad and stepmom traveled the country, Dale Jr. and his sister Kelley were at home with the nanny. The hope for a closer bond with his father seemed an almost impossible wish to the youngster.

Dale Jr. struggled as an aimless teenager, floundering until being sent to a military boarding school for two years. As much as his father (a man who dropped out of school after the eighth grade) emphasized education, it hurt Junior deeply when his dad didn't attend his high school graduation.

Dale Jr. spent years racing the local late-model stock car circuit with no help—financial or otherwise—from his father. He finally began to receive more of his father's attention when he became a full-time professional racer in 1998. Even then, it wasn't always easy.

The first time father and son raced each other was an exhibition event that year at the Twin Ring Motegi racetrack in Japan. (NASCAR staged exhibition races there in an attempt to lure Japanese sponsorship dollars to the sport.) With the backing of Coca-Cola, Dale Jr. entered the race in an old DEI chassis and he was in ecstasy during the opening practice session. After years of constantly dreaming about racing with his dad, he was now on the track with the Intimidator.

During the race, Dale Jr. made a dramatic pass on his father, which was followed by a rough Intimidator-style love tap as Dad lifted the rear of Junior's car off the pavement. As the race neared an end, Tony Jr. and several others in Dale Jr.'s crew somehow managed to sneak a fresh set of tires from the pit area of the No. 3. After a late pit stop, the fresh tires helped Junior finish sixth to Big E's eighth. Rather than laugh at the situation, the Intimidator responded by throwing one of his driving shoes at Dale Jr.

As Dale Jr. moved from the Busch Series to Winston Cup, their relationship became closer. His father seemed to mellow (somewhat) after his Daytona 500 win, and Dale Jr. achieved a level of skill and success that made him feel as if he had finally made his father proud. Each victory Dale Jr. notched was meaningful, not because of the riches or fame, but because he could see such joy in his father's face.

Junior's father was his boss, landlord, and team owner, a man whose hard-earned millions (and a savvy third wife) had built Dale Earnhardt Inc. after years of monomaniacally pursuing victories. Dale Jr. so completely trusted his father on business matters that he had been driving for DEI since 1998 on barely more than a handshake. Junior's inexperience and disinterest in things as basic as paying his utility bills led to a free-and-easy existence. He had breezed through life without wondering whether the glass was half-full or half-empty, asking only if the beer was cold.

Yet, in a world where fewer than 50 drivers make a living as a Cup driver, Dale Jr. had made it to the top with a combination of perseverance, raw talent, and a famous name. He and his father were part of the very small fraternity, confidants at last. Only a few people understood the rush of relying completely on each of your senses while racing 42 other men at nearly 200 miles per hour, or how it felt to crash at that speed then bravely climb back into the car the very next week to try again. Fewer still knew the thrill of winning in the Cup Series. Yet, even among this tiny fraternity, it was difficult to share with your competitors and rivals. While some drivers were helpful, most were unlikely to confide in a young, inexperienced driver. Even though his father was slow to share his own secrets, Junior trusted his dad completely to guide his career in the right direction and provide him with a successful path for the future.

After a lifetime of trying, Dale Jr. and his father had finally landed on common ground, and they walked together as peers into the drivers' motorcoach lot.

"We're gonna work together to win this thing," Big E insisted before angling to his bus (predictably parked in the best locale, closest to the garage area). "You've got the fastest car out there, so take care of it. But we need to work together to get it done."

Although he had been cool and calm for weeks, Junior exuded nervous energy as he changed into his red-and-black driver's uniform. An hour before driver introductions, Junior grabbed a quick lunch. Someone from NASCAR had indicated that actress Neve Campbell, a sultry brunette, would be at the track and wanted to meet Dale Jr. The minutes ticked away with no sign of Campbell.

His lunch finished, Junior fired up his laptop and began playing the *NASCAR 4* computer game. To make things interesting, he offered $100 to Shane or me if we could drive a single lap around the digital Daytona without spinning or crashing. The catch? Junior would prepare the game settings to be as close to reality as possible, including fresh, cold tires that simply do not want to grip the pavement.

Shane slowly crept toward turn one before he slid off the track. To Junior's delight, I began by immediately spinning into the wall on pit lane. Several more tries for each of us proved futile.

"I tell ya, that's what it's really like on new tires. It's like ice," Junior laughed as he shooed the amateurs away from the laptop. "That's real as hell. It's just like that!"

With Junior at the wheel, the game looked effortless as he ripped off fast, clean laps. He was focused and ready.

Meanwhile, his father was lounging outside his motorcoach, feet propped up. Already wearing his uniform, Big E looked relaxed, as if he were preparing to watch the race from his easy chair. During the FOX prerace show, Matt Yocum stopped by for a quick interview.

"I think it's gonna be exciting. Exciting racing," Earnhardt told Yocum as he broke out into a huge mustached grin. "You're gonna see somethin' you probably haven't ever seen on FOX."

When driver introductions were near, we took advantage of our secret side entrance to the garage area, and before the fans realized who it was, we were already on pit lane. Protected from the masses by the pit wall and a long line of uniformed officers, Dale Jr. quietly walked toward a large, portable stage on pit lane.

With one arm already wrapped around wife Teresa, Big E wrapped the other around Junior as soon as he arrived. The three talked quietly before each driver was introduced to the crowd of more than 160,000.

When his name was called, Junior waved to the crowd as he walked across the stage, then strode in a determined line toward his race car. The red machine had been stationed silently on pit lane in its grid position for several hours. Dale Jr. would start sixth, on the outside of the third row.

Junior looked calm and collected, but a nervous twitch of his foot indicated otherwise as he leaned against his car, quietly talking to the crew while the prerace hoopla continued around him.

In the FOX booth, Darrell Waltrip was in the midst of the first major broadcast of his new life. The three-time champion had retired as a driver at the end of 2000 and was beginning his new career as a TV analyst. Waltrip's wife Stevie was on the grid, looking for Earnhardt. A deeply religious woman, she had developed a strong relationship with Dale, and for several seasons had given him a Bible verse before each race. She handed Dale a card quoting the 10th verse from the 18th chapter of Proverbs: "The name of the Lord is a strong tower; the righteous run to it and are safe."

On the way to his black No. 3 car, Dale stopped to talk with Kyle Petty, who had qualified 28th. Petty was racing the No. 45 car in honor of his son Adam, who had been killed in a practice crash the year before at Loudon, New Hampshire. The two shared a heartfelt father-to-father chat and an embrace before Dale walked to the red No. 8 car.

Dale wrapped his arms around Dale Jr. and Teresa for a few moments.

"You've got a car that can win," Dad told him. "Just take care of it. Be careful out there."

chapter 9

the 500

Daytona Beach, Florida

In the final moments before the race began, the energy and tension in the air was supercharged. Each driver and every team member held hope this day would be theirs. History. Fame. Fortune.

For the competitors, the seemingly endless prerace pageantry can be almost painful—they feel like young children on Christmas morning, waiting until it's time to burst forth and open their presents. The obligatory prayer and the singing of the national anthem (by generic boy band O-Town) only prolonged the delicious agony.

Everyone tried to seem cool and composed, but signs of tension were everywhere. Fingers and toes tapped in double time. Some laughed nervously. Fingernails were chewed, lips were bit. Nerves jangled like tightly wound guitar strings.

Amid the clamor, two drivers with the same name prepared to climb into their cars.

Earnhardt gave Teresa a kiss, while Junior knelt down to strap heat shields onto each shoe. The odd contraptions prevent a driver's heels from being burned by the severe heat of the exhaust under the car. Inside the cockpit, air temperatures can reach 140 degrees Fahrenheit. The floorboard is even hotter.

With the steering wheel removed, Junior threw his right leg up and over the door, then did the same with his left, sliding through the window and into the custom seat constructed specifically for him. With the help of crew member Brian Cram, Junior attached the five belts into a metal latch near his navel: one from over each shoulder, lap belts from each side of his torso, and a crotch belt, which prevents a driver from sliding downward out of the seat in a hard, front-end collision.

He handed his Budweiser cap and sunglasses to Cram before he slung old-school bubble goggles onto his face, then pulled his helmet into place. He slid fire-resistant gloves up to his wrists before reattaching the steering wheel, clicking it into place with a quick-release connection.

Inside the cockpit, Junior made final adjustments. The silence seemed to suck all the oxygen from the air.

Finally, James Kelly, the CEO of UPS (one of NASCAR's newest major sponsors), was introduced.

"Gentlemen," he intoned, "Start . . . Your . . . Engines!"

The rumbling growl of 43 monstrous V-8 engines roared to life, joined in harmony by a mighty burst of noise from 160,000 full-throated spectators. Sitting along pit lane in perfect two-by-two symmetry, the garish explosion of color on each car gleamed under the bright sun. Months of preparation and anticipation were nearly over as engines revved like angry dogs begging to be unleashed.

Row-by-row, drivers clanked their gearshift levers into first gear and rolled away from the grid.

During the slow crawl of the pace laps, the team and driver synchronized the RPMs needed to stay within the speed limit on pit lane, but there was very little chatter on the radio channel—Dale Jr. and team members were alone with their thoughts.

As the clock rolled into the afternoon, the wind picked up, whipping the flags that lined the track more briskly than at any time during the week. Combined with slightly cooler temperatures, the wind concerned the Eurys. With the horsepower-sapping restrictor plates, choosing the correct gear ratios can be critical. The Eurys made their gearing decision based on a wind blowing behind the cars on the long back straight. As the field of 43 rolled slowly out of turn four, they hoped they had made the right move.

"Here we go," Earnhardt Jr. said as Terry Bradshaw waved the green flag. It was 200 laps and 500 miles to the finish.

Any worries the Eurys might have had about the car were quickly pushed aside as Dale Jr. took only four laps to launch into the lead. But restrictor-plate racing means the lead changes hands frequently, and just as Dale Jr. predicted, Ward Burton in the No. 22 Cat-sponsored car and the similar Dodge of Sterling Marlin seemed to be the class of the field in the early laps.

If the ovation from the crowd was loud when Junior led on lap 4, it was deafening on lap 27, when Big E took the lead with Dale Jr. second. This was what the fans paid to see as the Man in Black held the first position for the next 10 circuits.

The first yellow flag of the day came out on lap 49 for a minor crash involving Jeff Purvis. After pit stops, Junior restarted in 11th place but easily moved forward, taking the lead four laps later. The No. 8 car was handling well, especially in traffic.

In the Bud pit area, the team had a celebrity crew member. MTV VJ and Los Angeles nightclub impresario Riki Rachtman was having the time of his life, wearing an official Bud team shirt and pulling a pit cart of empty gas cans to the Union 76 pumps to be refilled after each pit stop.

As the race rolled past the 125-mile mark, I settled into my race responsibilities. During each race, I worked closely with the pit reporters from the TV and radio networks, feeding them team details and storylines for the live broadcasts. I kept detailed notes of each team decision and radio discussion, timed each pit stop (the team called it "stop to drop"—I would start the stopwatch the moment the car stopped in the pit box, then stop the timer as soon as the jackman dropped the car to the ground), and managed the video machine that recorded each stop. One never knows what moment in the race will be the turning point, so accurate, in-depth notes are crucial for post-race reports and analyses.

The middle stages of a long race can sometimes be less than sparkling, as most teams and drivers settle into a rhythm of preservation, protecting their cars in order to have the best chance of racing hard near the finish. Even when the action seems calm, restrictor-plate racing causes the field to bunch closely in large packs, running two and three wide within inches of the car or cars alongside. It's exciting for the drivers and the fans, but a small mistake— such as one car clipping another at the wrong angle or a driver trying to squeeze into a hole that's simply too small—sets the cars hurtling into each other and the wall. These huge chain-reaction crashes became known as The Big Ones, and nearly every Daytona and Talladega race featured at least one such calamity.

Because of The Big One, some teams opt for a very conservative strategy, staying on the lead lap while hanging far enough back for much of the race to avoid being swept into the carnage of a large crash. For Dale Jr. and the Bud team, the conservative strategy was never an option, They believed strongly the best way to avoid an accident is to be in front of it when it happens.

Ward Burton led for nearly 20 laps with Junior cruising easily in the top five. However, on lap 79 Earnhardt Jr. was shuffled into the high groove, losing all drafting help from behind. As the only car in the outside line, he dropped to 19th within a few seconds.

Mired in the middle of the pack, Junior's urgency to get back to the front of the field was apparent in his demeanor on the radio.

"Don't be quiet when I'm in the middle of this shit," Junior yelled at his spotter Ty Norris. "Keep talking!"

Despite his urgent tone, Junior made his way through the traffic with several cautious moves, placing his car immediately behind his father's as the black No. 3 car slammed hard into the side of the white, unsponsored car of rookie driver Kurt Busch. The contact caused minor cosmetic damage to both cars, and we laughed loudly in the Bud pit area when the video replay showed an angry Earnhardt giving Busch a middle-finger salute.

During their second pit stop, the team made several adjustments, and the Budweiser car suddenly came alive like a red rocket. Junior maneuvered through traffic, artfully moving from 12th to the lead by lap 112, with drafting help from his DEI teammate, Steve Park. Tony Stewart's orange car also made its way through the gaggle to draft with Dale Jr.

With 70 laps remaining, Junior had a line of friendly cars behind him: Stewart, Park, and, for the first time, his new teammate, Michael Waltrip. The quartet took to the high line, streaking past Big E, but the white car of Busch moved to block, impeding their forward progress. With a full head of steam, Junior and his drafting mates were in no mood to slow down as Junior stuffed the nose of his car under Busch's rear bumper in an aggressive move intended to push Busch forward or convince him to move out of the way.

This was not the first time Junior and Busch had run nose-to-tail. They had a run-in at the Rockingham race at the end of the 2000 season when Junior crashed after contact from Busch. Many laps later, an angry Earnhardt Jr. returned to the track in his damaged race car, menacingly stalking Busch lap after lap until NASCAR, Norris, and Eury convinced him to back off.

Tony Jr. feared a repeat of the Rockingham conflict, and didn't want to see his race car damaged for no good reason. It was much too early for so much aggression.

"Just be patient," Tony Jr. urged his cousin on the radio. "Be patient with that kid in front."

Busch eventually slid to the inside line, likely out of self-preservation, and Dale Jr. found himself with an unexpected dancing partner: the No. 40 car of Sterling Marlin. Together, the two pushed to the front, where they traded the lead with Ward Burton for several laps. It had been a calm race so far, but the intensity of the drafting was picking up as the drivers began to position themselves for the final 50 laps.

The Bud car and the rest of the leaders soon began making pit stops, with most of them coming to pit lane on lap 153. If the race remained under green flag conditions, this would be the final pit stop. With the pressure on, the pit crew performed brilliantly, filling the car with nearly 22 gallons of fuel and replacing four tires in 14.82 seconds. As Junior returned to the track, he slotted behind his father, pushing him into second place.

The yellow flag came out for the second time when Busch spun into the infield grass on lap 157. After more than 100 laps at top speed without a break, it was a perfect time for everyone to catch their breath before a frantic, final push to the finish.

Since they had stopped only a few laps earlier, the Bud team decided not to make another stop.

"We're staying out," Tony Jr. said.

"Yes, we are staying out," echoed Eury Sr. on the radio.

"OK, if you guys are staying out, I'll stay out with ya," joked Dale Jr.

Under the yellow, Marlin held the lead, followed by Dale Jr, Big E, and Park.

Norris, spotting from the rooftop of the main tower at Daytona, took advantage of the slow pace to speak with the other spotters, trying to develop a strategy for the final laps.

"The 3 and the 1 car want to work together with you," Norris told Junior, echoing the theme the Intimidator had been preaching for days.

"I'm willing to work with them, if they'll work with me," answered a slightly skeptical Dale Jr., who had been shuffled out of contention by his father in the final laps of the Bud Shootout the week before. "We may not have the speed to lead or pull them along."

"Just do the same thing you've been doing all day," Norris replied.

Though Junior had led three times, and had easily run among the leaders, he had only been able to stay in first place for one lap at a time. While his car worked very well in the draft, it was simply not as good in clean air.

"I just can't keep it up there," Dale Jr. said. "We're fast and we're running good. I'm just afraid we'll get into the lead and then drop back to fifteenth."

Junior encouraged the team, pleased with how well the race had gone so far.

"We got a good car here boys," he said. "We didn't lead [this race] at all last year, so we're better off this time."

As the field began to gain speed for the green flag, the leader Marlin slowed dramatically with a flat tire. Just that quickly, the red Bud car was in the lead, followed by his dad and Park. With their help, Junior was finally able to lead for more than a lap, holding the top spot for five circuits until he was passed by a streaking blue car.

"Where did *he* come from?" Junior laughed as Michael Waltrip took the lead in the blue NAPA-sponsored car.

Two laps later, Park's yellow Pennzoil car passed Waltrip, and the three DEI cars began an intra-team squabble for the top spot, followed closely by their team owner.

With 30 laps remaining, the intensity level ratcheted still higher as many of the drivers who had chosen a conservative strategy began to creep toward the front, making their moves to win the Daytona 500. Tension grew as champions such as Jeff Gordon, Dale Jarrett, and Bobby Labonte began to show their hands.

For the second time, Stewart put the nose of his car behind Junior's bumper. Because both were still relatively new on the circuit, many veterans had been hesitant to work with them. Though they weren't teammates, they could count on each other as the laps counted down.

On lap 171, Tony Eury Jr. pumped his fist as the orange and red cars screamed past on the front stretch, nose-to-tail in second and third place.

Two laps later, Waltrip and Earnhardt Jr. had pulled away slightly from Stewart as they rounded onto the backstretch. Then, as quickly as he had arrived, Stewart disappeared.

The Big One began when Ward Burton and Robby Gordon made contact, sending Burton's car into the right rear of Stewart's Pontiac and launching the orange No. 20 car into the backstretch wall. After sliding backward, Stewart was launched into a sickening series of tumbles, flips, and violent gyrations. Several cars slid completely under Stewart's machine as it flew through the air. Others could not miss him, including his teammate Labonte, whose car erupted in flames as Stewart's mangled wreck landed on his hood. At 200 miles per hour, the crash happened so quickly the track was completely blocked. More than 20 cars were involved in the carnage, including Park, Jeff Gordon, and Jarrett.

Somehow, the Intimidator, running behind Ricky Rudd, avoided the crash by steering quickly to the inside lane, narrowly missing Burton's spinning car.

The cars came to a rest, strewn in every direction like a brightly colored salvage yard. Everyone held their breath to see if anyone, especially Stewart, had been injured in the horrific chain reaction.

"I hope Tony gets out of that," Dale Jr. said as he slowed down for the caution flag. Junior saw Stewart go airborne in his mirror, but now he was able to see a replay on the giant video boards in the Daytona infield.

"That was a rough ride," Dale Jr. said quietly. "Let me know when he's out of the car."

After a long pause he continued.

"Guys, we were fortunate to be outta that one," he said, describing the crash scene as he slowly rolled down the backstretch.

"What a mess," he uttered as crept slowly through the debris, followed by his father and trying to avoid the thousands of bits and pieces, any one of which could easily slice into one of his Goodyear tires.

"Let me know how Tony is," he reminded his crew. "We should be thankful we weren't in that. Let's remember that tonight. We should be very thankful. We were so lucky to miss that crash."

Once past the debris, the Intimidator pulled alongside his son's car and gave him a big thumbs-up, as if to say, "We made it through." Though his car was unscathed, Big E expressed his concern to his car owner.

"Richard, if they don't do something about these cars," Earnhardt radioed to Childress, "they're gonna end up killin' somebody."

"We need to get four tires," yelled Tony Jr., taking no chance of suffering a flat tire like Marlin on the previous restart. The flat had knocked Marlin out of the lead and left him almost a full lap behind, but his misfortune also allowed him to avoid the crash.

"I'm coming in as soon as I see the flag [signaling the pits are open]," Dale Jr. said. "There's shit *everywhere*. They oughta stop us."

On lap 175, NASCAR implemented the red flag, which stopped the race so crews could clean the debris from the track. The stage was set for a 25-lap battle to the finish.

The remaining cars, less than half the number that started the race, rolled to a stop on the apron approaching turn one. Waltrip was the leader, followed by Dale Jr. The black No. 3 stopped beside them at the front of the line.

Sitting amid the eerie silence, Junior radioed the crew.

"Looks like we're gonna have a shot at this thing," he said, calculating that many of his toughest competitors, such as Burton and Stewart, had been taken out by the crash.

"I thought this race would be a lot more fun," he said soberly after a few minutes. "There's been a lot of backing off and half-throttle shit. It's so hard to be patient."

Realizing the time for "half-throttle shit" was over, Junior was pondering what he needed to do to win the Daytona 500 when word came that Stewart had been transported to the hospital for a precautionary check up, having most likely suffered a concussion and minor shoulder injury.

Dale Jr. was relieved to hear the news. Now he could focus fully on the final laps.

"Guys, we got us a great car here," he said.

The chance for Dale Jr. to win in only his second Daytona 500 starkly contrasted the struggles his father had encountered there in his first 19 starts. Each year it seemed fate denied the elder Earnhardt the victory he most coveted. Each year, his frustration increased.

For 19 seasons, Dale Earnhardt won more races on the Daytona track than any other driver, yet his massive list of achievements did not include a victory in the biggest race, in which he suffered every kind of defeat. Crashes. Running out of fuel. Engine failures. In 1990, he led the race until the third turn of the last lap, when a flat tire ended his bid. He finished second four times, with 10 top finishes.

Scientists use the terms "counterfactual thinking" and "pain of nearness" to explain how Olympic bronze-medal winners are happier about their experience than silver-medal winners. It seems counterintuitive, but a typical silver medalist suffers frustration and regret because of how close they came to a gold medal, while a bronze medalist is more likely to be grateful to receive any medal instead of finishing fourth. Earnhardt gained no satisfaction finishing anywhere other than the top of the podium. It was a gold medal or nothing, and so many close calls only increased his pain of nearness.

No incident better exemplified Earnhardt's efforts than the end of the 1997 race, when he was involved in a crash that sent his car tumbling upside down on the backstretch with 12 laps remaining. He had been running second, in perfect position to make a late charge. Sitting in the back of the ambulance, Earnhardt noticed the car still had four wheels attached, so he leapt from the ambulance and crawled back into the car. He refired the mangled machine and, to the delight of his fans, drove it back to the pits where his crew taped a trunk lid and spoiler to the back of the car, allowing him to return to the race. He finished 31st, five laps behind the winner Jeff Gordon.

The following year, in his 20th start, Earnhardt finally earned his gold medal in the Daytona 500. As a sign of respect, crew members from nearly every team lined pit lane to give Earnhardt a high five. Since that win, Earnhardt had seemed more content, especially now that his legacy, his business, and his son were doing so well.

Sixteen minutes and 25 seconds after the red flag brought action to a halt, NASCAR restarted the race under yellow flag conditions and the pits were opened.

As Dale Jr. approached the pit box, Tony Jr. gave one last command.

"Let's go, boys," he urged. "We've won 'em like this before!"

The crew responded and sent Dale Jr. back out as the leader of the race with a stop of 14.63 seconds. They now led the biggest stock car race in the world with 21 laps to go. Only nine cars remained on the lead lap.

Norris became cheerleader as much as spotter. "We got us a great wheelman here," he said. "The blend line is your restart point. I'm not gonna say anything. You're the leader. The start is up to you."

At the green flag, the sprint to the finish was on. Ricky Rudd slid inside of Dale Jr. in turn two, but the black No. 3 pushed Junior on the backstretch, sending him back into the lead. Could this finish match the 1988 Daytona 500, when father Bobby and son Davey Allison finished first and second?

Junior hugged the yellow line that marked the inside of the 2.5-mile track. As the race wore on, the outside line of cars was able to pull even with the leader, but struggled to complete the pass on the high side of the banking.

On lap 181, Dale Jr. made a young driver's mistake by actually running *too* fast. On a track where the draft is so strong, a lead of more than several car lengths allows the cars behind to gain much more momentum and then use that momentum to slingshot past. Suddenly, Junior was alone, helpless to stop the field from flying past. The mistake dropped Dale Jr. to sixth place as Marlin, a two-time 500 winner, grabbed the lead on lap 182.

"All right Ty," Tony Jr. scolded Norris after the fact. "Don't let him get too far ahead!"

Seconds later, Junior made an aggressive move, going through the middle of the pack, pushing his father and Waltrip to the front. The Man in Black led lap 183, then Waltrip led the following circuit.

With 16 to go, Junior was thinking ahead.

"I need a lap count," he shouted. "Gimme a lap count as we get close!"

With 15 to go, the tall, thin scoreboards at Daytona International Speedway read 15-40-8-3-55-7 from top to bottom: Waltrip, Marlin, Dale Jr., Earnhardt, Bobby Hamilton, and Mike Wallace.

With 14 laps remaining, Marlin made a move to grab the lead from Waltrip on the outside, opening enough daylight for Junior to pounce into second place with his father immediately behind him in the inside lane.

"Ten to go," Norris said calmly. "Ten to go."

As the laps counted off, the field jockeyed for position, but the three cars out front remained in single-file: two DEI cars and DE himself.

"Seven to go."

"Six to go. Six."

The tension was almost too much to bear. The Bud crew watched the cars go by the start/finish line (the only part of the massive speedway we could see) then immediately turned to watch the rest of each lap on the huge video screen behind the pit box.

Waltrip held the lead as his older brother nervously called the race for the millions watching from home.

"Protect the bottom," said Norris.

"Protect that bottom," Tony Jr. repeated.

The field roared down the backstretch like a slithering snake, following every move Waltrip made.

With four to go, the top six cars raced in single file as they began passing lapped cars that had been wounded in the big crash. Earnhardt made a great save through the tri-oval area when Marlin made contact while trying to get to the inside lane. With a flick of his wrists, Earnhardt straightened the car after it made a wicked wiggle.

"Protect the bottom. The 3 car is with you," said Norris.

With two to go, Waltrip and Dale Jr. pulled away slightly.

With five miles of pavement before the checkered flag, Kenny Schrader showed the speed of his machine, moving up in the outside line while Rusty Wallace also surged forward.

For more than 10 laps, Junior had run inch-by-inch in the tire tracks of his teammate, but as they took the white flag and headed into turn one for the final time, Junior took a slightly higher line than Waltrip, "breathing" the engine by getting some fresh air on the nose of the car in order to gain momentum coming out of turn two. At the same time, he was careful not to run high enough to open the low line for the others bearing down on them.

As they sped down the backstretch, Waltrip and Junior were single file while Big E was in the middle of a frantic battle for third. Schrader on the outside then Marlin on the inside both briefly edged ahead of Earnhardt.

"I have no help!" Junior yelled at the end of the backstretch, as he and Waltrip were now far ahead of the pack. With no one on his bumper to help him draft, Junior knew his opportunity to win was slipping away.

"I have no help!" he screamed again.

"Just you and the 15 . . . just you and the 15," said Norris as the two cars streamed through turn four. Without drafting help, Junior had no hope of passing for the win.

Behind them, Big E somehow regained third place in turn three, barreling ahead of Schrader and Marlin. The cars bounced through the bumps in turn three, inches apart. Earnhardt made a slight move to protect the inside line, but bobbled slightly, causing Marlin to make contact. The black No. 3 nosed slightly down onto the apron, then careened hard to the right, shooting up the turn-four banking, collecting Schrader's car. The two machines slammed nose-first into the outside wall.

Seconds later, Michael Waltrip crossed the line to win the Daytona 500, his first Winston Cup victory in his 463rd start. Close behind was Dale Jr.

"You guys should be proud, this is a good car," Junior radioed to his crew as he slowed down going into turn one on the cool-down lap. He had finished second by a margin of 0.124 seconds.

"I'm proud of Michael," Junior said. "I was really just hanging on there. I had no help. I just couldn't get a run at him there. Hey, we finished second in the Daytona 500!"

chapter 10

after the crash

Daytona Beach, Florida

At 4:25 p.m., the late afternoon winter sun cast a harsh glare on Earnhardt's black car as it slid down the banking and came to a stop in the grass, still enmeshed with Schrader's car. Schrader climbed out and walked toward Earnhardt's crumpled car. He reached to take down the window net, and began gesturing for emergency crews to hurry to the aid of his friend.

Junior had seen the wreck briefly in his rearview mirror as he streaked to the finish line, and his excitement about a good finish was tempered when he rounded the final turn. Staring into the glare, he saw the ambulances and emergency vehicles surrounding his father's car. A veil of smoke from the wrecked cars wafted into the surreal golden light. It looked, he explained later, like a scene from a movie. For a split second, he started to pull over to go see his father. Deciding it would only concern the fans, he rolled past slowly onto pit lane.

As a top-5 finisher, Dale Jr. was required to stop on pit lane to speak with the media. I ran to the car with a towel and bottle of water, looking forward to celebrating a second-place finish with him.

"How's my daddy?" he asked as I leaned in the window of the car.

"I have no idea. I haven't heard anything," I replied.

As Junior unbuckled, reporter Marty Snider approached.

"How's my daddy?" Junior asked as he climbed from the car.

Snider had no answer, so Junior turned to a nearby NASCAR official.

"How is he? What are they saying?" he asked.

The official told him there hadn't been any word on the radio.

"Let's go see Dad in the care center," Junior said. After a few steps, he began jogging down pit lane with me following. Dale Jr. was concerned about his father, but he was also excited to share the joy of his good finish. As we neared the gas pumps, Junior spotted a couple of his father's Goodwrench crew members.

Again, no answers.

Several reporters followed, with the sole purpose of interviewing the second-place finisher. Winston Kelley, a pit-lane reporter from the Motor Racing Network, the radio network carrying the race live around the world, tried to get a quick word, but Junior began jogging toward the garage area, which was a beehive of post-race activity.

Winding between crews, cars, and pit gear, Junior headed toward the old infield care center. As we approached, he realized the old building was no longer in use and the gate was closed. Dale Jr. turned 180 degrees and was met by the followers. Kelley, still live on the air, asked a quick question, and Junior answered as we ran, this time toward the back of the garage area where the new care center was located.

"Look for someone who can take us there," he said, as we spotted someone on a Joe Gibbs Racing golf cart.

"Take me to the care center," Junior insisted as we hopped on. The cart took us out of the garage area, curved around several barricades, and stopped outside the front door of the medical center.

Inside, Junior's gaze met Schrader's for a fleeting moment. At that moment, he sensed something was seriously wrong. Dale Jr. was told his father had been taken directly to Halifax Medical Center, less than two miles from the track.

Outside the rear doors, an area usually reserved for ambulances, a large SUV pulled up, and Junior climbed in with Teresa; J. R. Rhodes, Big E's longtime media rep; and Jimbo Biggs, Big E's motorcoach driver. They pulled away for the short trip to the hospital.

A large group of media gathered at the barricades, swarming Schrader to record his brief, cryptic comment as he exited the care center.

"I'm very happy for him [Waltrip]. I just wish he could enjoy it more because his boss," Schrader paused for a second, "is not there to help him."

Meanwhile, Waltrip was celebrating his first victory. He told the television audience he "owes it all to Dale Jr., who stuck with me. I couldn't have done it without his help." After waiting so long for a win, Waltrip and crew celebrated in style, spraying Budweiser and Gatorade wildly into the air, soaking the car, the trophy, and each other.

Ty Norris, DEI's general manager, joined the celebration but wondered why no one named Earnhardt had come to congratulate Waltrip for the momentous victory. Norris became concerned when he was asked to accept the Owner's Trophy for the victory. A few minutes later, a stunned Schrader walked into victory lane, embraced Waltrip, and told him it didn't look good for Dale.

At the hospital, Teresa Earnhardt and Richard Childress were joined by NASCAR executives and team and family members such as Danny Earnhardt, Dale's younger brother and a crew member on the Bud team. Waiting for word from the doctors, Dale Jr. pondered how seriously his father had been injured. He hadn't imagined the worst-case scenario. Superman was invincible, right?

"We did the best we could," were the haunting words uttered by an emergency room doctor.

At 5:17 p.m., Dale Earnhardt was pronounced dead.

we've lost
dale earnhardt

Daytona Beach, Florida

"**I**just fucking exploded. I was hysterical," Dale Jr. told *Rolling Stone* magazine, describing his immediate reaction upon hearing his father was dead. One observer described it as a guttural wail that seemed to echo for minutes inside the somber hallways of the hospital.

After his primal outburst, Junior tried to make sure Teresa and the others were being cared for, but he wasn't interested in sticking around the hospital. He didn't want to look at his father, didn't want his last memory to be of a cold, clinical emergency room. The only thing he wanted was a cigarette. Maybe an entire pack of cigarettes.

A dazed Junior left the hospital with his uncle Danny and headed back to the track where he changed out of his uniform before meeting with the glassy-eyed DEI executive staff of Norris, Steve Hmiel, and head engine-builder Richie Gilmore. They decided to meet with Teresa early the following morning to determine how Dale Earnhardt Inc. should proceed.

Dale Beaver, the young pastor who had been a valuable confidant to Junior since the year before, waited outside the motorcoach until he was signaled to enter.

"I couldn't cry," Dale Jr. said in the same *Rolling Stone* article. "I just wouldn't for some reason."

~

Entirely unaware of the seriousness of the situation, I had wandered into the Benny Kahn Media Center, a small, dank box of a building that was always filled beyond capacity for the Daytona 500. I began writing my post-race media report when a staffer from Daytona's communications department asked me to come to a small office no bigger than a closet adjacent to the main room.

With the door closed behind me, Julie Giese, one of the track's media representatives, said quietly, "He's gone."

"What?" I said, not able to comprehend what she had uttered.

"Dale's dead," she said.

I sat down, trying to catch the breath that had been slammed from me.

The only thing I could do was retrieve the emergency plan. The clinical step-by-step guide seemed to be the only thing keeping my mind and heart from exploding. I was given a small corner of the office to call Anheuser-Busch executives with the sad, confidential details. Walking back into the media center, I had to keep the horrible secret for nearly 90 minutes.

"My heart is hurting right now," Waltrip said in his post-race news conference. "I'd rather be any place right this moment than here."

While offering no news or updates on Earnhardt's condition, NASCAR had taken the extraordinary step of closing the garage to only essential personnel, just one sign of the gravity of the situation. Tony Eury walked through the garage with a torrent of tears streaming down his face. Tony Jr. and the other crew members hugged and cried in full view of the small media center.

NASCAR staff began quietly informing the media of an official announcement at 7 p.m. Some in the room were already in tears.

As the hour arrived, Mike Helton, NASCAR's president and one of Earnhardt's closest friends, stepped to the small podium overloaded with microphones.

"This is undoubtedly one of the toughest announcements I've ever had to make," he said with haunted and empty eyes. "But after the accident in turn four at the end of the Daytona 500, we've lost Dale Earnhardt."

~

If it's difficult to overstate the level of optimism prior to the 500, it is almost impossible to describe the immediate impact of Earnhardt's death. Millions of fans mourned the loss with a sorrow that seemed to know no bounds. Dale Jr. understood their pain—there was no bigger fan of Dale Earnhardt than his namesake.

As Dale Jr. flew home to North Carolina, leaving his father and his carefree life behind him, innumerable levels of loss and pain pressed against his chest. How could he go on?

He had lost his father, but he had also lost his mentor, his confidant, the man who provided the road map for his future. Junior had lost his team owner, his landlord, and the man who meant more to him than almost anyone could fathom.

Junior's sole motivation inside the race car was to please his father. He had lived to see his dad's smile, and now that smile was gone forever. What could possibly motivate him to continue?

All the sorrow in the world seemed to be in his heart, but what scared and worried Dale Jr. far more than anything that night was the fear of the unknown. Was he expected to walk into DEI the following morning and take charge? With his father gone, he was the only Dale Earnhardt that remained. Would the more than 200 employees expect him to take over? Would they expect him to immediately become the leader and sharp businessman his dad had become? Would Teresa have any interest in running the business, and, if not, did that place the entire operation on his 26-year-old shoulders?

Junior's dream of winning the Daytona 500 in his second try hadn't come true. The reality had become his worst nightmare.

chapter 12

dark days

Mooresville, North Carolina

News of Earnhardt's death rocketed across the globe as the lead story on every network and 24-hour cable-news outlet. A number of drivers had lost their lives in a NASCAR stock car, but none had been so prominent or died in such a dramatic moment. This was far beyond a sports story. It was front-page news.

Hundreds had already made the pilgrimage to Dale Earnhardt Inc. Sunday evening by the time Dale Jr. returned home from Daytona. The low-lying fence that lined the highway in front of DEI had become a wailing wall of grief.

By sunrise Monday morning, more than a dozen satellite trucks lined Coddle Creek Highway, beaming pictures of weeping fans who had gathered in the chilly February air outside the gates of DEI. Security had always been in place at the complex, and it was heightened as the crowds continued to grow. Fans traveled hundreds of miles to share their grief and stand in front of the palace of speed. Traffic along the highway slowed to a trickle as cars crawled past or simply parked beside the road.

The roadside was covered in an endless array of heartfelt, homemade signs, banners, and flowers. Many of the mourners brought their most prized Earnhardt souvenirs and clothing, leaving them atop the spires on the wrought-iron fence. In the South, Earnhardt's death resonated like no other since Elvis Presley passed away in 1977. DEI had become Earnhardt's Graceland.

Inside its walls, the DEI complex was quiet and somber as early-morning meetings were held to determine the short-term fate of the race teams. As Teresa asserted her intent to lead the company forward, Junior's worries persisted. Would he be forced to become a businessman in addition to a driver? Despite his pangs of uncertainty, the only logical choice for a company full of lifelong racers was to continue preparations to race the next weekend in Rockingham, North Carolina.

Typically, the morning after a Daytona 500 is a hungover blur of celebratory appearances for the race winner. The winning car is placed inside the Daytona USA museum, where it will sit for the next year, and the winning driver is interviewed in person and across the land via satellite. Michael Waltrip was unable to enjoy his greatest achievement. Instead, he bravely answered questions about the death of his close friend. In the midst of his own pain, Junior called Waltrip Monday morning as a sign of support and friendship.

If Junior took small solace in anything, it was in knowing his dad had lost his own father at nearly the same age. In 1973, Ralph Earnhardt died at the age of 45, suffering a heart attack in his garage while working on a race car. Dale was only 23 when his father passed, putting even more pressure on him to support his family, which by that time included an ex-wife and son Kerry in addition to his second wife, Brenda, and a newborn daughter, Kelley. Dale Jr. was born the following year. (Some old-timers insist Junior's driving style is more similar to his grandfather than to his father's bull-in-a-china-shop approach.)

In the ornate DEI dining area known as the Trophy Room, a television was tuned to a news network, showing what seemed to be an endless loop of the crash and giving Earnhardt's considerable obituary. Dale Jr. tried to hide his emotions with a somber demeanor, but he was clearly pained to see his father's photo with the caption "1951–2001" below it. The cold, hard numbers seemed to hurt him to the core, as if confirming that his father's death wasn't just a nightmare, but very real.

Everyone in the building seemed in shock. For me, each conversation seemed to take place in a strange fog, like listening to an AM radio station that's not quite tuned in. But I wanted to be there with Dale Jr. and the others, doing whatever I could.

Teresa instructed all DEI employees not to speak with the media; no one in the entire Earnhardt family offered a public comment or interview. Every fax machine at DEI and at my office ran out of paper as media outlets continued their constant barrage of calls, emails, and faxes, making their pitch to interview anyone whose last name was Earnhardt. Meanwhile, torrents of quotes and tributes spilled in, both from within the sport and from politicians, celebrities, and other athletes.

"NASCAR has lost its greatest driver ever, and I personally have lost a great friend," was the brief quote from NASCAR's chairman Bill France Jr., the son of NASCAR's founder. The two had become close during Earnhardt's many championships. As the unofficial spokesman for the drivers, Big E frequently called France to lobby his point of view.

France Jr. had been fighting a fierce battle with cancer, so it was a surprise in February 2000 when he appeared at the track, unannounced and sitting in a small grandstand in the corner of victory lane after Earnhardt won the IROC race. Earnhardt stopped the entire post-race celebration to run up the bleachers and sit with his friend.

By Monday evening, the scale of the tragedy's impact became more apparent inside the DEI complex. While we could see the masses in front of the building, word soon came of candlelight vigils and memorial services across the land. At racetracks from Las Vegas to Atlanta and Kansas City, and from Daytona Beach to Virginia and Northern California, thousands of mourners showed up to share their loss. Funeral homes began offering books of condolences to sign, promising to send the books to the Earnhardt family.

Staff from Winston's Sports Marketing Enterprises had arrived at DEI the morning after the crash to help in any way they could. Teresa opposed their suggestion of a public memorial service, preferring a private, family-only ceremony. Tuesday morning, Teresa relented to their persistence, agreeing to a Thursday afternoon memorial service for the NASCAR community.

For the first time, I was able to sit down with Dale Jr. privately and explain that his Budweiser commitments and media bookings had been canceled or put on hold. They would proceed only when he was ready. We had been working for some time on a book about his rookie season (which would become *Driver No. 8*), and it too would be shelved for as long as he liked.

"Maybe we should do the book as a tribute to Dad," he suggested. "All about my last year with him."

With Teresa's gag order regarding interviews, my role became a tough one. Inundated with requests for interviews with Dale Jr., I was quick to turn them down. However, the media abhors a vacuum, and I was worried that an extended period of silence from the family would lead to unfounded speculation and rumors. I ventured outside several times that afternoon and throughout the week, speaking with reporters and producers from each major network as well as CNN and ESPN. Though I was not authorized to speak on the record about the family, I worked hard to correct misconceptions and provide off-the-record guidance and deep background material, protecting the family as best I could.

The requests also came from a wider array of outlets, many that wouldn't have given a glance at NASCAR in the past. The *New York Times* and ABC's "Nightline" with Ted Koppel devoted significant space and airtime to the story, focusing on NASCAR safety efforts and the nationwide outpouring of grief.

Amid the media flurry, strange stories began to appear, primarily online. There were all kinds of quirky conspiracy theories and numerological coincidences involving the number three. Many fans even reported seeing a "3" in the clouds. We also received disturbing word that a small number of angry zealots were blaming Sterling Marlin for the crash, as his car had been the first to make contact with Earnhardt. Dale Jr. was angered when he heard rumors of death threats toward Marlin.

Bootleg merchandise began to appear as T-shirts and bumper stickers suddenly sprouted, seemingly out of nowhere. The licensing staff at DEI began an aggressive fight, enlisting a series of law-enforcement agencies to prevent the creation and sale of unauthorized merchandise. Despite these efforts, the unlicensed merchandise persisted for many months.

Among the many expressions of sympathy, Dale Jr. was touched most deeply by the words of people he admired and people he felt were more of his generation than his father's.

One of those was Dave Grohl, leader of the band Foo Fighters and drummer for Nirvana, a band that had been very influential during Junior's teen years. Prior to the 2001 season, Gibson Guitars released a limited edition Dale Jr. model Les Paul guitar. Designed by racing artist Sam Bass, it featured Junior's signature and Bud racing graphics. Junior, who was given a handful of the guitars, sent one to Grohl. Two nights after the crash, Grohl played the guitar during an MTV concert at the House of Blues in West Hollywood, California.

"Dale Earnhardt Jr. is a huge rock and roll fan," Grohl said from the stage. "He has a great love of music and he sent me this guitar a week ago. It's one of the coolest guitars I've ever had in my life. In honor of his father, I thought I'd play it tonight to let everybody know it meant something to me."

The following night at the Grammy Awards, U2 guitarist The Edge wore a No. 3 jersey. Grohl spoke about the Dale Jr. guitar after Foo Fighters won the award for Best Rock Album. "I plan on using it just to let him know we're rocking it for him," Grohl told the Associated Press.

Junior was also surprised to hear from other celebrities, including Kid Rock and Jay Leno.

The DEI staff began collecting the hundreds of items left alongside the fence each night, only to see new signs, flowers, and memorials fill the space within hours each morning.

Four generations of Earnhardts gathered Wednesday morning for a small, private funeral at St. Mark's Lutheran Church in Mooresville. (To prevent it from being defaced or damaged by well-meaning devotees, the location of Earnhardt's grave remains closely held among the family.)

Later that day, Dale Jr. and DEI technical director Steve Hmiel went to see Earnhardt's car, hoping to better understand what had happened inside the cockpit. Surveying the wreckage, Dale Jr. noticed his father's Goodwrench hat resting at the base of the gearshift lever. Big E had always kept a hat inside his car, allowing him to climb out of the car with a cap perfectly in place. Dale Jr. would later place the white hat inside his pickup truck, where it served as a constant and comforting reminder of his father.

To the naked eye, Earnhardt's crash hadn't looked nearly as destructive as Tony Stewart's tumble on the backstretch, which is precisely why it was such a deadly blow. In Stewart's case, the parts and pieces that his car shed were visually frightening, but they dissipated the violent energy of the crash, making it safer for the driver. Dale Earnhardt had no such benefit because the severe, head-on angle of impact with the turn-four wall brought his car to an immediate and sudden stop.

Earnhardt died of a basilar skull fracture, a horrific injury where the lower skull separates from the spinal cord due to a severe impact or whiplash-type rebound. In such an impact, a driver's torso is restrained by the five-point seatbelt harness, but the head has no such protection, causing it to whip forward violently.

Sadly, it was not an unusual injury. In fact, it had been the cause of death for three other NASCAR drivers in the previous nine months.

Adam Petty, the young and personable fourth-generation driver with an electric smile, lost his life when the throttle stuck on his Busch Series car in turn three at New Hampshire Motor Speedway in May 2000. Kenny Irwin died in the same manner at nearly the exact same location when his No. 42 Winston Cup car slammed into the wall less than two months later. Tony Roper died in a Craftsman Truck Series crash when his vehicle hit the wall head-on at Texas Motor Speedway in October 2000.

To help prevent such injuries, sports car racer Jim Downing worked closely with Dr. Robert Hubbard, a biomechanical engineer at Michigan State University with an extensive background in automobile safety, to develop the HANS (Head and Neck Support) device. Made of light but strong carbon fiber, the HANS device fits like a collar around a driver's neck and shoulders. The collar is strapped under the shoulder belts and connects to the side of the helmet with two tethers. In the case of a head-on impact, the HANS, which weighs less than two pounds, keeps the head and neck anchored with the torso, preventing the driver's head from being flung so far forward.

Despite impressive test results and use by drivers in other racing series, most NASCAR drivers, including Earnhardt, expressed scorn for the device. In 2000, Brett Bodine became the first NASCAR driver to wear the HANS, subjecting him to criticism from other drivers. The day following Earnhardt's death, Downing and Hubbard reportedly received numerous calls from Cup drivers now anxious to add the device to their safety gear.

Thursday morning, the day of the NASCAR memorial, was a tough one for Dale Jr. In fleeting moments of sorrow, he pondered giving up racing completely. But those were only momentary impulses. He knew his father had provided him with a great race team and a great opportunity that he would be foolish to squander. He was still bothered deeply by seeing his father's image with the dates listed below, but he tried to focus on the dash between the numerals: what his dad had meant to him and the world during the 49 years he was alive.

While they had initially resisted, Teresa and Dale Jr. understood a public memorial was something Dale's fans deserved to see.

"Teresa said something one day that really struck me; I'll never forget it," Dale Jr. said years later to Marty Smith of ESPN. "She said we can't be selfish and be sad because we're missing that person. Her point was, it's selfish for us to miss that person in our lives, as if they belong to us solely.

"There's a lot of people obviously sad and mourning, and we should be happy he was a part of our lives. . . I was like, man, you're right, that is so life. I should be thankful I was a part of his life. I shouldn't be selfishly mourning the fact that he's not a part of mine anymore. I thought that was a good way to look at it."

For the memorial service all of the employees wore matching black DEI shirts and boarded a fleet of buses in front of the complex for the ride to the Calvary Church, south of Charlotte. I was honored to be invited to ride along, sitting at the back of the final bus and listening to Steve Crisp and Andy Pilgrim tell Earnhardt stories.

In the days since the accident, many Big E stories had been told, often repeating a similar theme. Despite his Intimidator image, Earnhardt was quietly charitable to a large number of racers and many others in the community. "Don't tell nobody," he would tell them, as if word of his generosity would undermine his rough-and-tumble image. Now that he had passed, many of the stories came to the fore: tales of farmers who received his support when weather damaged their crops or of a small church whose parking lot was paved courtesy of Earnhardt.

For many years, Earnhardt also had a close relationship with local law-enforcement agencies, often hiring retired officers for his security staff. As the buses pulled onto the highway, North Carolina state troopers stopped traffic at each intersection, saluting crisply as each bus passed.

The memorial was the first time together for many in the NASCAR community since leaving Daytona. The turnout of drivers, officials, and team owners represented a nearly complete roster. Though President George W. Bush was unable to attend, he released a statement and sent White House aide Joe Allbaugh to represent him at the memorial. "I am saddened by the untimely loss of this American legend, and want to express my deepest sympathy to his family, friends and fans," the statement read. "Dale was an American icon who made great contributions to his sport. Dale's legacy will live on for millions of Americans."

Country-and-western duo Kix Brooks and Ronnie Dunn, who were friends with Earnhardt (he appeared in their "Honky Tonk Truth" music video), also attended the service.

With seating for nearly 6,000, more than half of the cavernous nondenominational church was filled. Hundreds of fans who weren't able to get in stood outside in the freezing rain.

The ceremony was televised live by the FOX Sports Network under strict limitations. The Earnhardt family maintained all rights to the broadcast, which would never be shown again. In addition, news organizations were not permitted to use footage from the ceremony.

Teresa was brought into the church on the arm of a state trooper, followed by Taylor, her 12-year-old daughter and Dale's youngest child, as well as Kerry, Dale Jr. and Kelley.

Randy Owen, lead singer of the band Alabama, performed several acoustic numbers before Dale Beaver, the pastor from Motor Racing Outreach, gave a brief sermon, encouraging everyone to celebrate Earnhardt's life by sharing their favorite Big E stories.

The ceremony, which lasted slightly more than 20 minutes, concluded with a heartbreaking moment as Teresa came to the podium but was only able to muster, "Thank you, thank you," in a barely audible whisper.

chapter 13

you ok, junior?

Rockingham, North Carolina

The forecast seemed fitting: the North Carolina Speedway would be blanketed with dreariness, as rain and cold were expected through the weekend.

Drivers arriving at the private motorcoach lot inside turn one couldn't help but notice parking spot No. 3 had been left vacant except for a few small flower arrangements. Each had to pass the empty spot whenever they entered or exited, a small reminder of who and what had been lost.

When the Winston Cup garage area opened Friday morning, a lot of attention was focused on the Goodwrench team's hauler as the crew rolled out a completely new paint scheme. The car was primarily white with black numerals. The No. 3 was gone (except for a small decal on the driver's door), replaced by the No. 29.

Before practice began, a large tent outside turn four was packed beyond capacity with the largest media turnout in NASCAR history. NASCAR had called the news conference to announce its initial findings in the accident. After the presentation, Richard Childress was scheduled to introduce Kevin Harvick as the driver stepping into Earnhardt's team. Following Harvick, Dale Jr. would speak with the media for the first time since the crash, joined at the head table by teammates Park and Waltrip.

Mike Helton and Gary Nelson, NASCAR's Winston Cup Series director, began the news conference by announcing their preliminary findings. Helton said their investigation found Earnhardt's seatbelt, made by Simpson Performance Products, had failed in the crash. The failure, combined with the angle of impact, caused Earnhardt to hit the steering wheel with his face and chest. Earnhardt's injuries included eight broken ribs on the left side of his body, most likely caused by impact with the steering wheel.

"We don't know how, we don't know why, and we don't know when," Helton insisted when asked for more details about the broken belt. Nelson said no one could recall a previous example of a failed lap belt in the 52-year history of NASCAR.

Childress insisted the belts were a brand-new item on the car at Daytona, and NASCAR's explanation only increased speculation in the garage about what might have happened. Many in the garage came to the defense of Simpson's products. No matter what had happened to Earnhardt's belts, every team checked and rechecked the installations in all of their cars.

"Dale Earnhardt and I talked about what would happen if I was in Africa and got run over by an elephant, or fell off of a mountain, or if something happened to him in whatever manner, what we would want and what we would want to do," Childress began. "And it is to go on. Both of us are racers, and Dale Earnhardt was a racer. We made a pledge to each other that we would go on . . . .. That's what we're going to do, and we're going to do what Dale would want us to do and that's race this week. I mean it's tough. The toughest thing we'll do when that green flag falls is to start that race without Dale Earnhardt."

Sunday's Winston Cup race would be the first since September 1979 that didn't include Dale Earnhardt, a string of 648 races.

Childress introduced Kevin Harvick as the driver of the No. 29. He was careful not to say Harvick was "replacing" Earnhardt.

"Dale Earnhardt was probably the best race car driver there ever is going to be in NASCAR and nobody will ever replace him," Harvick said in his opening comments. "I think we all know that. I would hope that you guys [the media] don't expect me to replace him, because nobody ever will."

When the floor opened for questions, Harvick was asked if he intended to wear a HANS device. Harvick explained he would wear the Hutchens Device, a series of straps that wrapped around the driver's torso and attached to the helmet in a similar location as the HANS. It was designed by Bobby Hutchens, an employee at Richard Childress Racing for nearly 20 years.

After Harvick and Childress left the stage, Dale Jr. sat down, joined by his teammates. His discordant outfit included a bright-orange sweater and a red North Carolina Tarheels cap turned backward. The drivers had chosen not to take questions after their statements.

Junior spoke slowly and somberly without notes. Earlier in the day, he declined when I offered to help him with his remarks.

"I'm just going to speak from my heart," he said as we waited nervously outside the tent.

"First off, I want to thank all the fans and the entire NASCAR family and everybody involved for the respect they've shown us for the past several days," Dale Jr. said. "It's been a difficult time for the family, and for the Dale Earnhardt Incorporated family. They've treated us to the best of their ability, and have done a real good job of giving us our space and allowing us to take a deep breath and to put everything in perspective. I really don't know what else to say. I might be able to take some other questions some other time.

"My main focus right now is to try to maintain what my father had in mind for Dale Earnhardt Inc. to the best of my ability, with the help of these two fellows next to me and the rest of the family at DEI. We're going to try our best to maintain and carry on with the racing program.

"I do want to say that any notion or any idea or any blame placed upon anyone, whether it be Sterling Marlin or anybody else for that matter, it's ridiculous. It's pretty incredible some of the things that I've heard or been told about. But one of the things this teaches you about is how selfish you are about things like this. I mean, I miss my father and I've cried for him, but out of my own selfish pity is the reason for those emotions. And I'm just trying to maintain a good focus for the future and that he's in a place that we all want to be and that's really all I have to say."

~

Being at the track felt good for many, including Dale Jr. Being in the race car provided a sense of purpose he hadn't been able to find in the preceding days.

In qualifying, Junior tried too hard, overdriving into each of the corners. He qualified 25th, while Jeff Gordon wore a black Earnhardt hat after winning the pole.

After the session, Kyle Petty came to the Bud hauler where he found Dale Jr. in the lounge. With the door closed, the two men talked for more than an hour. The discussion proved to be a great comfort to Junior, lifting some of his worries. Dale Jr. felt as if he had the entire weight of the sport and Dale Earnhardt Inc. on his shoulders. At age 26, he felt incapable of handling all of those responsibilities. Petty, who had lost his son in a crash only months before, urged Junior to focus instead on his job as a driver, and to trust others to run the company and the sport. If Dale Jr. did his job behind the wheel, the rest would fall into place.

After the on-track activities ended, Dale Jr. and a few of his friends went to his motorcoach, where they were building radio-controlled cars. These weren't toy cars, but expensive and highly detailed machines with gas-powered engines. There were hundreds of parts to put together and a variety of bodies to paint and cover with decals. For the next few months, this would become his obsession as Dale Jr. constructed at least one car each week. The intricate, detailed process allowed him to focus on something other than his loss.

After the flurry of the past week, Saturday seemed quiet. The Winston Cup cars had a single practice session between rain showers, allowing Junior to spend much of the day with his friends.

Reporters who had never been near a NASCAR race returned to the track after the news conference the day before, and I found myself pulled in many directions, eventually meeting privately with two writers from *People* magazine. I provided them as much background as I could without undermining the privacy the family demanded.

After the Busch Series race concluded, I found some solitude walking down pit lane, away from the crush of questions, inquiries, and requests, when my phone rang. A longtime friend from my hometown was calling to tell me a woman I had dated for several years had inoperable brain cancer and was given only a short time to live. After struggling to keep a level head for Dale Jr., I could barely fathom this news.

Sunday seemed to be the hardest day for the Eurys, as if the prospect of a race without their close friend, boss, uncle, and brother-in-law hadn't really sunk in until that morning. Always ones to wear their emotions on their sleeves, it was clear the loss of Dale was nearly as significant to them as it was to Dale Jr. Everyone tried to keep a brave face, but it was a quiet morning inside the Bud garage.

Dale Jr. was slightly late to the drivers' meeting after finding an ambulance parked behind the No. 8 hauler. A crew member's wife had a diabetic seizure and was quickly stabilized, but it seemed like drama and heartache were following Dale Jr. wherever he went.

After the meeting, Junior walked to the Goodwrench hauler to see the guys from his father's crew. He had known some of them since his earliest days at the track, and this was the first time he was able to speak with them and make sure they were doing all right before the race.

With rain seeming inevitable, NASCAR notified the drivers they would hold the driver introductions as scheduled, even if the race was delayed. Soon after, a light rain began to fall and Junior chose not to change into his uniform, instead grabbing a Budweiser jacket and hat on his way to the front stretch.

When we arrived backstage, each driver was wearing a black "3" hat with bold red swirl designs. Though he had been given one of the hats, Dale Jr. insisted on wearing his Bud hat in a conscious effort to show he was prepared to stand on his own.

He had qualified one position ahead of Sterling Marlin, which gave him an opportunity to make another strong statement. As Marlin was introduced, Junior climbed the stairs with him, walking across the stage arm-in-arm as a show of support and to quell any thoughts that Marlin was to blame for his father's crash. As he walked onto the small stage, the cheer from the crowd was loud but respectful. Junior waved, acknowledging the cheers, but his somber expression didn't change.

As Ingrid Bergman, the actress most famous for her role in *Casablanca*, once said, "It is not whether you really cry. It's whether the audience thinks you are crying." In the same way, Junior's translucent complexion, stiff jaw, and stoic demeanor seemed a perfect blank screen on which others could project their own emotions. Some saw sorrow and sadness; others saw strength and determination.

The race was delayed more than 90 minutes as the track dried. For most of the delay, Dale Jr. perched on the outside wall of pit lane, sharing stories and even a couple of laughs while sitting alongside Waltrip and Park. As the start neared, Dale Jr. walked to his car on the grid. There, he was visited by a number of competitors and friends, all of whom offered a prayer or kind word. Stevie Waltrip came by, handing Junior a Bible verse just as she had done for his father.

As the pace laps began, the DEI and RCR crews waved "3" banners and pennants while fans did the same. Many waved homemade signs in tribute.

After an unbearably sad week, it was finally time to get back to racing.

Led by the pole-sitter Gordon and Park, the field streamed quickly into turns one and two and then down the backstretch. Going into turn three, several cars ahead of Dale Jr. slowed, causing him to get on the brakes. Ron Hornaday couldn't slow in time, getting into the rear of the Bud car and lifting its rear wheels off the pavement. Junior bounced off the No. 27 car of Kenny Wallace, slid to the left before the car overcorrected, and whipped nose-first into the wall at nearly the same angle as his father's crash.

How could this be happening again?

"You OK, Junior?" a shocked Norris asked, as it seemed the entire world held its collective breath.

"Yeah," Junior replied despondently.

Junior climbed out as safety crews reached the car. Standing high on the fluid-covered 25-degree banking, Junior gingerly walked down the track with a slight limp and climbed into an ambulance for his mandatory trip to the medical center.

Unlike his dad's crash, the slower speed and a less severe angle of impact meant Junior's car hit the wall and then ground along the barrier, dissipating energy for a few hundred feet. The front end of the Bud car had been flattened, but the impact hadn't hurt the driver.

Heart in my throat, I ran to the medical center as Junior received his brief once-over from the doctor. A few moments later, he emerged, walking without a limp and with a strange expression somewhere between a wry grin and a bewildered grimace. Inside the fenced compound, I assured him he could take a golf cart directly to his motorcoach if he chose not to speak to the media.

"Nah, I'll do it," he answered as he waved over Matt Yocum, the FOX pit reporter.

"It got bottled up there getting into three," he explained, "and somebody got into the back of me and I couldn't keep it under control once that happened. I just got into the wall a little too hard. I think I killed the car.

"We're doing all right. I want to tell everybody back home we're feeling OK. I was just ready to get back to racing. I guess we'll have to wait until Vegas."

"It looked like you were limping?" Yocum asked.

"Yeah, the track was slick," Junior answered. "The lap belt was a little tight and I'm just a little bruised up. We'll be OK."

We walked toward the golf cart.

"Do you want to go to your bus?" I asked.

"No, I want to go see my guys," he replied.

The garage area seemed more crowded than the grandstands as camera crews crowded around the crippled No. 8 machine. With NASCAR's help, we managed to move them back far enough so Dale Jr. and the crew could talk privately.

"I'm sorry," Dale Jr. said.

The Eurys and the rest of the crew assured him the important thing was he wasn't hurt.

"The priority was to be there, be on the track," Dale Jr. explained several weeks later on a media conference call. "Just to get on the track and turn some laps. We didn't have that chance. The guys in the pits were dying to make a pit stop. Working was better than standing around with our hands in our pockets."

As the crew began scrounging through the bent and broken race car, the rains came, stopping the race on the 52nd lap. Under the red flag, NASCAR rules prevented the Bud team from working on the car, so Dale Jr. and the guys walked to the hauler, where they stood in dazed disbelief.

"Who hit me?" Junior asked.

"We're not sure. We think it was Hornaday," someone explained.

"Well, at least I'll have a job in six weeks," Junior said with a streak of black humor, referring to Hornaday's A. J. Foyt–owned team, which had a history of frequent driver changes.

With the race stopped, it looked as if every credentialed media person had gathered behind the rear gate of the hauler, waiting for a comment or quote from Dale Jr.

"I can't go out there," Dale Jr. said quietly, and we decided to implement a procedure we called the Martinsville Diversion.

It was a trick his father taught him, and we first used it at the half-mile Martinsville oval, where the tiny garage area meant fans stood shoulder-to-shoulder at the back of the hauler. This made it almost impossible for the crew to do their job, fighting through rows of autograph seekers to fetch tires or fuel.

The plan was simple: Junior would stand inside the hauler's side door, which opened into a space no more than three feet wide between the massive haulers. When he gave the signal, I would exit from the back door, waving my arms and yelling nonsense at the crowd like, "Clear the way so Junior can come through!"

With all of the attention focused on my gyrations, Junior would slip out the side door, walk to the front of the truck, and then angle back to the race car by slipping between adjacent haulers. By the time anyone realized what had happened, he was climbing into the car.

In this case, the goal was simply to get him out of the garage and back to his motorcoach unimpeded. Upon my noisy exit, he slipped out the side unnoticed and was quickly gone.

The rain continued through the afternoon, and NASCAR announced the Dura Lube 400 would continue the following morning, starting with lap 53. Because of the extensive damage, the Bud team packed for the trip back to Mooresville. The race would go on without them.

While their teammates and competitors restarted the race under bright Monday skies, the Bud team was at the shop, watching the action on TV or listening on the radio. Their misery was helped somewhat by a spectacular finish as Steve Park slid his DEI No. 1 car in front of reigning Cup champion Bobby Labonte in the final laps, taking a second consecutive victory for Dale Earnhardt Inc.

After he crossed the line, Park slowed and grabbed his Earnhardt hat, holding it as high as he could as he made a slow crawl in the reverse direction, waving at the fans along the front stretch. In victory lane, an emotional Park did a Dale Jr.–style dive into the arms of his crew. In a teary-eyed interview he thanked Earnhardt for teaching him how to drive at the tough Rockingham oval.

chapter 14

teresa's plea

Las Vegas, Nevada

One tradition at DEI was to raise a checkered flag on one of the three towering poles in front of the complex after every race victory. For eight days, the flags had remained at half-staff, but after Park's win, DEI employees gathered the following morning for an emotional ceremony, returning to the tradition of raising a checkered flag high above the main entrance. It was a simple but powerful sign of their dedication to each other and of carrying on without their leader.

After his long discussion with Kyle Petty, Dale Jr. seemed to have less weight on his shoulders, but he still worked hard to assert his new place within the company. Unlike his previous slumbering ways, he awoke early each morning and asked himself how his father would handle the day. To show support for the DEI employees, he spent a lot more time at the race shop. He hoped his constant presence was a sign of his commitment to the more than 200 employees, but it also comforted him as he began to develop a closer connection with his own No. 8 team and with employees working for the other teams.

With the Rockingham race delayed by a day, a busy week was made busier as the teams scrambled to prepare the machines for the race at Las Vegas. Crews worked late into the night, loading the cars into their transporters midweek so the haulers could make the long trek west.

The crowds outside DEI continued, but the numbers had lessened compared to the week before. One thing that didn't abate was the flood of media requests and calls for interviews. My email, fax, and phone were inundated, and the DEI offices were deluged even more. Each day of silence from the family intensified the fight to see who could secure the first interview.

Daily requests came from all of the network news departments, but were especially frequent from the morning shows. In their cutthroat competition for ratings, they seemed to focus on the Earnhardts in a laser-like manner. When the initial calls from producers didn't receive the answer they hoped for, several of the shows had their star anchors call, offering to speak directly with Teresa or Dale Jr.

The Las Vegas trip provided a small escape from sorrow for many in the NASCAR family when Kevin Harvick and DeLana Linville, the daughter of a lifelong racer, were married Wednesday evening in a small ceremony at the Rio hotel, followed by a reception at the Stardust. The wedding was planned long before the crash, and the ceremony and reception provided the first smiles in nearly two weeks for many in the Richard Childress camp. Spending time with friends away from the shop and the track, it was the first chance many of us had to relax and enjoy ourselves since Daytona.

Dale Jr. chose to spend time at home rather than attend the wedding, arriving at the track Thursday evening with the rest of the DEI crew. When practice rolled around the following morning, the crowds were respectful, and a few fans politely asked for autographs as we walked into the garage area.

When the time came to qualify, Dale Jr. and I walked from the driver's motorcoach lot, located inside turn one. Slipping through a small gate, we climbed the inside wall and began walking up pit lane toward the car.

After a few yards, Dale Jr. made a stutter-step as if someone or something had hit him hard across the chest.

He pointed to the massive "3" floral arrangement near the grandstands in turn four. Many of us saw it during the first practice session, but Dale Jr. had missed it while focusing solely on the racing line through turn four. It was a rare example of Dale Jr. being caught off-guard, and it showed how difficult it was to be reminded of his father's death wherever he went, especially when he didn't expect it.

A tightlipped Dale Jr. made it through his qualifying lap, but a poor-handling car meant starting Sunday's race from the 32nd position.

The mood was grim following qualifying, but during Saturday's final practice the car began to respond. Compared to the rest of the field, the

No. 8 was strong on long runs. The year before at Las Vegas, they had the quickest car and led 41 laps before finishing 10th when heavy rains cut the race short. The practice session led them to believe they had regained the speed advantage they had shown in 2000.

Whispers started to buzz through the garage Saturday afternoon, hinting that Teresa Earnhardt would break her public silence and fly from North Carolina to make some sort of announcement. J. R. Rhodes, who had been Big E's bodyguard and PR rep, confirmed she was going to make an announcement Sunday morning, but refused to offer what it might be.

"This is huge," he said. "This is something everyone will want to get behind."

I spent much of Sunday morning on the phone with execs from Anheuser-Busch, who were also in the dark as to the subject of her appearance. We speculated it was an announcement of a charitable program in Dale's name, and A-B would certainly be expected to make a sizable donation. The mystery continued until Teresa stepped into the media center in the speedway's infield at 10 a.m. With Dale Jr. sitting beside her, she read a five-page statement.

After a brief introduction, she explained, "The trauma we have suffered has only grown since that tragic day two weeks ago. I have not even had time to unpack Dale's suitcases from Daytona . . . because we've been caught up in an unexpected whirlwind as a result of efforts to gain access to the autopsy photographs of Dale."

On the morning of the Daytona 500, the *Orlando Sentinel*, with their lead motorsports writer Ed Hinton, had published a lengthy story as part of an investigative series detailing trends in auto racing deaths, especially deaths caused by basal skull fractures. The story examined the safety efforts (or lack thereof) by NASCAR to address the issue. In the days after Earnhardt's death, the newspaper requested access to the autopsy photos as a part of their investigations.

Fearing the photos would make their way to the Internet, Teresa petitioned a Florida court to keep the photos confidential. She received a temporary injunction to ban the release of any photos by the Volusia County medical examiner's office. Now she was expanding her efforts to prevent media outlets from gaining any access to the photos.

"The deceased have a right to their dignity," she explained, "and loved ones have a right to be free from exploitation. Allowing access to these photos will only cause more distress and emotional harm. I'm sure every family in America can understand this."

As a call to action, she urged fans to contact Florida Governor Jeb Bush and representatives in the Florida Senate and House of Representatives, and ask them to "protect the privacy of citizens by preventing the publication of autopsy photos . . .. Finally, we encourage you to let the *Orlando Sentinel* know how you feel about this unfortunate situation."

She departed without taking questions and immediately left Las Vegas.

The newspaper sent out a news release shortly after, expressing sympathy for Teresa but also detailing the request to "have a national expert review these photographs to determine whether the physical evidence is consistent with NASCAR's explanation of Dale Earnhardt's death. We want our expert to examine the failed seatbelt theory."

The *Sentinel* insisted the request was in the interest of the public good in order to "contribute to the national debate on how race car driving can be made safer."

Though he did not comment publicly, Dale Jr. confided privately, "I'm one hundred percent behind Teresa on this. I want people to remember my daddy as he was when he was alive, not lying dead on a table."

After the news conference, a quiet Dale Jr. put on his driver's uniform and tried to focus on the 267 laps of racing he would soon face.

Starting so far back, Dale Jr. began the race cautiously, but made his way to 23rd place before the first yellow flag.

"I can drive a lot harder than that," he assured the crew. "Everybody's being real cautious."

"We're better twenty-five laps and further into the run," Tony Jr. reminded him.

"Yeah, they were coming to me," Dale Jr. replied.

Running in the top 10, the team chose not to pit with many of the leaders during a caution period on lap 96. By choosing a different pit strategy, Dale Jr. was able to take the lead by lap 159, but fell back to 15th when a yellow flag trapped him behind most of the cars on the lead lap.

With fresh rubber and a fast car, Dale Jr. clawed forward once again, only to fall out of the top 10 when a slow pit stop dropped him to 15th place again.

"We're doin' what we can to give this one away!" yelled an angry Eury Sr.

"I missed one," explained Tony Jr., who missed tightening one of the five lug nuts while changing the right front tire. "I had to go back and get one."

With less than 100 laps remaining, Dale Jr. needed to make a push forward for the third time.

"I tell ya, this car is fun to drive," Junior said as he made a three-wide pass around lapped cars. The long green-flag run was the best thing the team could have ordered, and Tony Jr. decided to roll the dice for the victory.

"We're the best car on long runs," Tony Jr. explained. "Let's come in and just get two tires. We'll get out in front and beat 'em all."

With 33 laps to go, Dale Jr. pulled into the pit stall to change the two right-side tires. Jackman Jeff Clark dropped the car to the ground at 8.21 seconds and Junior roiled the rear tires as he gunned the throttle.

Unfortunately, as Junior pulled away, the catch can remained stuck in the back of the car. The can, which is inserted into a tube at the back of the car to catch overflowing fuel, had gotten away from David Lippard, one of Junior's crew members since their championship Busch Series days.

The can fell off the car, tumbling helplessly down pit lane, but the foul had been committed. Any equipment attached to the car as it pulls outside of the pit box is a violation.

The NASCAR official stationed in the Bud pit stall gave the signal the team was required to make a stop-and-go penalty. Though the car would be stopped for only a moment, the time lost crawling at the pit-lane speed limit ended any hope of victory. As Dale Jr. left pit lane, the leaders sped past, putting him one lap behind in 24th place.

Jeff Gordon won the race, ending DEI's two-race win streak and earning his team a million-dollar bonus from Winston's "No Bull 5" promotion. In the final laps, Dale Jr. was able to regain one position, finishing 23rd.

The driver tried to rally a crestfallen crew.

"We need to hold our heads high," he said. "Even though the finish wasn't good, it was great to go out there and run so well. We really learned a lot and we'll be much better this year on the flat tracks. It's a shame about the pit deal, but other than that, we were good."

The crew hurried to pack everything into the hauler, then raced to the airport for the flight home on the team planes. They arrived in North Carolina early the next morning, and most of them went directly to the shop to begin preparing for the next race in Atlanta.

chapter 15

bittersweet

Hampton, Georgia

Though we had canceled or declined all interview requests since the accident, Dale Jr. insisted on keeping one commitment we had booked prior to the season.

MTV's "Cribs" was the hot new program, providing glimpses into the glitzy homes of the wealthiest musicians and athletes. Using connections we had made during the making of an MTV documentary called "True Life: I'm a Race Car Driver" the year before, I was able to secure a spot for Dale Jr. in a special "Car Edition" of "Cribs."

Dale Jr. wanted to be on the show because it was something he and his close friends (a crew he called "The Dirty Mo Posse," utilizing their slang term for Mooresville) could share and enjoy. His posse was composed of longtime friends who, most importantly, didn't give a damn whether he finished 1st or 41st. "Cribs" was something he was doing for himself and them—not for his sponsors and not for NASCAR.

The house was meticulously cleaned and organized, and Dale Jr. chose several photos of his father to frame and display. Most prominently he chose a photo from Harold Hinson, official photographer for the team and Budweiser, showing him and his father grinning widely in the victory lane celebration at the Winston All-Star Race.

"I never put 'em up before," he told the video crew about the photographs. "But now it means a lot to me."

Though it looked quaint from the outside, the house contained a few surprises, notably the basement. Known as "Club E," Junior's basement featured a well-stocked bar, a dance floor, and a massive sound and lighting system. That day, it also included four ATVs lined up on the dance floor. Club E gave him a place to relax with friends and not have to worry about drinking and driving, something he took very seriously (especially given his major sponsor).

Before the shoot, we spent several days brainstorming ideas to make the segment more memorable. Junior vetoed the idea of stocking his fridge with nothing but Budweiser, but did like my idea of showing off his personal vehicles, then having the garage door open slowly to reveal his Winston Cup car parked inside.

"All the rock stars with their blingin' Bentleys, they can't feel this," he said as he climbed in the race car, fired it up and drove off. It was memorable, it was cool, and it was something no other celebrity had done.

Junior's mood was darker several days later after he had qualified at Atlanta Motor Speedway. The car had been very fast in the practice session, but the stopwatch told a different story after qualifying—Junior was only 17th best.

"It pushed like a truck," was the only thing he told the Eurys as he walked from pit lane to his motorcoach. He had agreed to do a favor for Motor Racing Outreach pastor Dale Beaver, who asked if Junior would answer a couple of questions for a feature story being prepared about him for the syndicated religious show, Pat Robertson's "700 Club."

Beaver's easygoing manner had been a good fit for the laidback Dale Jr., and as a show of support, Junior was quick to say yes.

"He's the first preacher I've been around that's even close to my age," Junior explained to me. "He's the first one I could identify with, and who identified with me."

We had been assured the questions would be brief, and only about Beaver's comforting influence, not about Junior's father or his death.

A reporter named Scott Ross met us at the motorcoach. His appearance was a throwback to the early days of Elvis. Sporting a tall, greasy pompadour, Ross insisted everyone join together for a prayer before he opened the interview with a question about Beaver then quickly veered in another direction, asking for details of Junior's religious beliefs following his father's death.

I should have stopped the interview immediately at that point. They had careened off the path they had agreed to follow. Junior handled the question well, but I stood by quietly horrified, hoping the next question would return to the topic of Dale Beaver. Junior tried valiantly to answer deeply personal questions Ross had no right to ask. My inaction would haunt me.

After what seemed like an hour, but was actually more likely three to four minutes, I finally grew enough of a spine to stop the proceedings when it was clear Ross had no intention of asking about the pastor. While Ross led another prayer, his producer stepped outside to grab a large backpack. When she unzipped the bag, it wasn't filled with videotapes or camera gear, but an assortment of Dale Jr. diecast cars, hats, and other merchandise for Junior to autograph.

Dale Jr. politely signed, and they were gone.

Junior handled it well, but I had failed in my role of protecting him from such emotional intrusions from the media. My only comfort was the knowledge that Dale Beaver would receive the recognition he deserved for the tough job of being a friend and spiritual advisor for most of the garage area.

On race morning, before his church services, Beaver's face went ashen when I told him about the interview. He apologized profusely to Dale Jr., who seemed less disturbed by the incident than the rest of us. He was more focused and concerned about the race that afternoon.

"Tighten everything down, it's gonna be a long day," were Junior's words of encouragement to the crew on the pace laps, reminding them how many opportunities they would have to adjust the car during the 325-lap race.

Junior loved the high speed and the adrenaline rush that came with it at Atlanta Motor Speedway. He also loved the track's wide corners, which allowed a driver to move the car around to find the groove that worked best.

As the race started, Junior sliced through the field and into the top 10. No one passed him until lap 28 when Matt Kenseth rocketed around using the highest groove, inches from the wall. The higher line meant a farther distance around the track, but it allowed a car to slingshot off the corner at a higher rate of speed.

When the yellow flag fell on lap 84 after Steve Park's DEI engine exploded, the cars on the lead lap came to the pits. Just in front of the Bud pit was Sterling Marlin's Coors Light team, and the rival beer crew conveniently left one of their tires sitting near the outside of their pit box, blocking Junior's exit. After backing up to steer around the tire, Junior returned to action in 15th place.

A beet-red Eury Sr. growled loudly at the Coors team, threatening all sorts of colorful and painful punishment should they repeat their stray tire stunt. Meanwhile, Steve Wolfe, the rear tire changer for the Bud team was clutching his left hand in pain. During the stop "Wolfie" sliced his ring finger wide open, and my attention switched from taking notes to searching for the nearest paramedic. A medical cart took Wolfe to the infield care center where he received three stitches.

With Park's car out of the race, Mike Atwell came over from the No. 1 crew to take over the rear tire changing duties. Chad Walter, Atwell's rear tire carrier, also came over to help the Bud team.

Despite the setback in the pits, Dale Jr. easily raced forward again, reaching third place before Robby Gordon's spin in the No. 4 Kodak car brought out a yellow flag, prompting Junior to make several "driver comfort" suggestions.

"When we stop, throw four or five rags in here," he said. "This seat's hard and flat. Damn, it's hurtin' my ass!"

As the safety crews entered the track to tend to Gordon's spin, one of their trucks parked in front of the NASCAR official whose job was to wave a flag to indicate when pit lane was open.

As the cars made their second lap under caution, Dale Jr. was unable to see the flag.

"Is pit lane closed?" he screamed. "Is pit lane open or closed?"

Without a definitive reply from the team, Junior followed the cars in front of him as they rolled down pit lane. Soon after, NASCAR informed the teams pit lane was not open, and six were penalized. The penalty sent Dale Jr. to the back of the longest line for the restart. After two excursions through the field, Junior would have to do it a third time.

"These things get better over time, but damn, they sure do vibrate," he explained, referring to four fresh Goodyear tires. "These tires just won't get a hold. They're too damn hard. Shakin' my damn teeth out."

On lap 205, Junior made contact with Ricky Rudd on the backstretch.

"I'm getting aggravated!" Junior yelled, not indicating the cause. "Are we saving our best shit for last?"

"I got a good set [of tires] back here," Tony Jr. answered with a chuckle.

"I didn't mean to hit the 28," Junior said, apologetically. "I tried to help him on the straight but I didn't expect him to back off."

The only car running similar lap times was Junior's buddy, Matt Kenseth. With Kenseth in the high lane, Junior pulled to the bottom and the two ran side by side for nearly 10 laps before Dale Jr. pulled ahead slightly, closing on the leader, Dale Jarrett. But with 52 laps remaining, Kenseth's engine expired in a massive plume of smoke, sending him hard into the turn-one wall. Despite a scary fire that enveloped the car, Kenseth climbed out uninjured.

As the race neared an end, each pit stop became more important than the one before, and the crew responded with their best stop of the day. At the restart, Junior ran fourth, trailing Jarrett, Jerry Nadeau, and Harvick. But, the adjustments didn't agree with the race car.

"Too damn tight! Too damn tight!" Junior repeated. But the Bud team caught a break when another yellow flag came out, allowing them to pit again.

"All right, we're gonna free it up," Tony Jr. said.

"Get it like it was before this," Dale Jr. insisted.

"I'll do my best to drive hard," Junior said as he restarted sixth. "We've at least gotta get into the top three."

With 10 to go, Junior's car and tires started to respond as he moved to the high line on the track. With six to go, he pushed Jarrett's car down the backstretch, then swung to his inside. With Kevin Harvick in the low line, they battled for the lead, racing three wide into turn three.

"Yeah, baby!" the Bud crew members yelled as they watched their car fighting for the win. But running three wide slowed the trio just enough to allow Nadeau and Jeff Gordon into the fight.

With five to go, Harvick, Jarrett, and Nadeau crossed the start/finish line three wide, with Gordon and Dale Jr. immediately behind. It looked like a formation more commonly seen with a precision military jet team like the Blue Angels or Thunderbirds.

With four to go, Junior avoided making contact with Jarrett in turn four while sweeping past Tony Stewart, whose car had been damaged in an earlier crash and was shedding parts like a toddler throwing a tantrum.

"C'mon, Junior!" the crew screamed, hoping the heartbreak and tumult of the last three weeks would subside with a win.

Going into turn one, the Bud car suddenly slowed.

"FLAT TIRE!" Junior yelled. "Right front! Flat right front!"

The team grabbed two tires and climbed the pit wall.

With three laps remaining, the heartbroken driver was silent as the crew pushed him away from the emergency stop. Debris from Stewart's car had sliced into the right front tire.

"Just go as hard as you can," Tony Jr. commanded, but, just as the week before, they were one lap behind with no time to make it up.

The race for the victory had come down to two drivers: one was a newlywed making only his third Cup start while the other had three Winston Cup titles already under his belt. Harvick led Gordon at the white flag, but the driver of the No. 24 pulled his Chevy right onto Harvick's bumper along the backstretch.

Though it was painted white with the No. 29 on the doors and roof, everyone knew Harvick's car had been black with the No. 3, and he took Earnhardt's car on a high line into turn three, opening the bottom lane for Gordon. As they came off turn four, Gordon moved up slightly to go around a slower car, which gave Harvick enough momentum to get to the line first, winning by six-thousandths (0.006) of a second.

In the Goodwrench pits, an explosion of emotions overcame the men who had worked for Earnhardt for many years.as they cried and yelled and hugged each other in a huge huddle. After his cool-down lap, Harvick spun the car 180 degrees then drove backward down the front stretch, holding three fingers aloft to the crowd.

As Harvick pulled toward victory lane, guys from other pit crews came out to salute him, much as they had done when Earnhardt won the Daytona 500 in 1998.

It was an emotional, cathartic victory for many, but the team in the Bud uniforms felt more bitter than sweet. They were happy for the Goodwrench team—many of them were close friends—but they were pained at how close they had come to grabbing a victory themselves. It was mostly quiet as Junior pulled the car to the back of the team's hauler.

With disappointment in his eyes, Dale Jr. answered questions from reporters as the crowd continued to roar for Harvick.

"You know, I don't complain a lot, but I have to today," Junior said haltingly when asked about the flat tire. "This isn't Martinsville, this is a track where we're going two hundred miles per hour and there are guys out there cruising around at fifty miles per hour. The debris from the 20 car came off right in front of me. He was just ridin' around out there and I don't know what all was fallin' offa that thing. I had nowhere to go. It slammed into my car and the tire went flat. We've got a big hole in the front of the car. It's a shame because my guys have worked so hard to come out here to try to get a win or a top-five finish and then something like this really hurts for them.

"That may be the hardest I've ever driven. We were great for about ten or fifteen laps with new tires, almost Texas-like," he said, referring to his first career win. "I could do anything. For those few laps, we could drive past people. Anyone. But then it would become harder to pass cars after the tires went away. We had a pretty damn fast car today."

He was asked about Harvick's win.

"I know Kevin pretty well and he's doing a great job," he said. "The competitor in me is a little jealous, but I'm really happy for Richard [Childress] and especially that team because I know how much my father meant to those guys. And it really makes me feel good to go home tonight knowing those guys have something to celebrate."

When would it be time for him to celebrate?

chapter 16

tribute

Darlington, South Carolina

After the Daytona crash, Budweiser executives scrapped plans for the major commercial shoot, but approached Dale Jr. to see if he had any ideas for a commercial as a tribute to his father. Dale Jr. wanted the script to represent his father well, but also wanted a positive message urging the fans to continue enjoying NASCAR.

The script and storyboard soon appeared, based on a column Dale Jr. had written as part of his monthly contribution to NASCAR.com and *Winston Cup Scene* magazine. Titled "I Know a Man," the column was a bold and intense view of a heroic father through his son's eyes. He had written it in October and read it aloud to his father.

Junior recounted the meeting several months later, describing how his father had told him, "I always knew you loved me, but now I understand how much."

"That's too good to put online," he told Junior. "Save it for a book."

Junior was proud of what he had written, and was too impatient to wait for a book. He submitted it as his monthly contribution, and it was reprinted widely after his father's crash. (It was also included in full in *Driver No. 8*, released in 2002.)

To shoot the commercial called "Tribute," Budweiser's ad agency booked the Rockingham track a few days after the Las Vegas race. Junior asked permission from Teresa to use his father's helicopter to shuttle us to and from the track. Taking off from the helipad at DEI, we made the short but choppy hop to Rockingham on a cold and windy morning.

"My dad was tough," Dale Jr.'s narration began, with shots of him standing alone on the track, helmet in hand.

Ominous and ever-changing clouds swirled behind each panoramic shot, a pitch-perfect backdrop for the mood of the somber 30-second spot. However, the weather was less than ideal for Dale Jr.

In the heat of Daytona, he had shown me his new Simpson driver's uniform, bragging about its ability to "breathe," providing improved comfort in the confines of a sweltering race car. But now that same attribute meant he had no protection from the brisk Atlantic winds, which howled straight through him. After an hour of wrapping him in blankets between each take, a crew member was dispatched to the nearest Walmart for several pairs of long underwear.

"Nothing ever got in his way," the voiceover continued. "He pushed everything to the limit."

It was haunting to watch the on-set monitors, where the resemblance between Dale Jr. and his father was evident in the close-up shots of his tight-jawed face and eyes.

"I know he'd want us to push on," the narration concluded, followed by Dale Jr. hitting the ignition switch of his race car and speeding away while "His inspiration lives on." was spelled-out across the blackened screen.

Luckily, the final low-angle shot of Dale Jr. speeding away was captured perfectly on the first take, as the transmission of the Budweiser racer failed with a loud *thunk* a few feet after exiting the frame.

During the Darlington race broadcast on FOX, "Tribute" aired as the first commercial following the start of the race, as it would for several races thereafter before being retired, never to be aired again.

The egg-shaped track at Darlington is an historic NASCAR locale that has hosted races since 1950. The track retains many of the elements that defined it in its early days: a surface that hungrily chews up tires and a narrow groove near the wall at each end of the speedway. To run the fastest lap, drivers must put their car within inches of the wall. Since that's nearly impossible to do for 400 or 500 miles, most drivers earn what they call a "Darlington Stripe" by making contact with the wall at the exit of each turn.

Junior was particularly open about his dislike for the track, even though he had led laps and finished 11th in the Southern 500 in the fall of 2000. He always seemed to be in a bad mood on Darlington race weekends, but his mood changed Friday evening when Teresa called to say she had reached an agreement in her lawsuit with the *Orlando Sentinel*. Junior was pleased to hear an independent expert would be the only one to view and analyze his father's autopsy photos.

Before the race, Junior donned a gaudy leather jacket with a huge rendering of his father's face on the back, along with the years of his seven championships. The crowd cheered for him and the oversized jacket as he was introduced.

Starting 16th in the 293-lap race, Dale Jr. moved to 11th place in the first six laps. But, in his aggression, he had worn out his tires and began struggling with a loose race car. To save what was left of his tires, Junior slowed his pace, staying inside the top 15 until lap 45, when he slammed the wall coming off turn two. Junior was able to drive away from the contact, but a yellow flag came out after the Bud car scrubbed the wall.

The damage didn't look severe at first, but when the team inspected the car on pit lane, they discovered a bent lower A-frame, a key component in the front suspension.

Unable to replace the part, the team began a series of 13 pit stops, making adjustments and changes each time to help the car turn. But the changes were like a Band-Aid on a broken arm, and Junior's goal for the remaining laps was simply to stay out of the way of the race leaders and try not to crash the car again. Each time the caution flag fell, Junior concocted a new analogy to describe the car.

"It's like trying to steer a buckin' bronco," he told the crew.

"It's like hopping on one leg against world-class sprinters," was another example.

"I'm like a boat in a rough ocean," Junior said as the race neared an end, describing his race car—and perhaps his life.

A major crash with less than 10 laps to go brought out a red flag, stopping the race and prolonging the team's misery. The crash took out multiple cars, but with so few laps remaining, Junior wasn't able to make up enough distance to pass those knocked out of the race.

"I don't know what happened. It just wouldn't turn," he told the team during the red flag, describing his meeting with the wall. "It was sliding like glass. The front tires locked up and I hit the wall. We had a good car at the start . . . maybe too good. I might have pushed too hard and hurt the tires."

In a seven-lap shootout to the finish, Dale Jarrett took the victory (and the lead in the point standings), holding off Steve Park by slightly more than half a second at the finish. The forlorn Bud bunch finished 34th, eight laps behind the winner. After starting the season with a second-place finish, they had now fallen to 22nd in the point standings.

At least the trip home was a short one.

chapter 17

when ya gonna drive the 3?

Bristol, Tennessee

*700 Club EXCLUSIVE! Dale Earnhardt Jr. Interview Reveals
How the Death of His Father Has Changed Him Completely!*

This was the headline across the top of the news release as the "700 Club" compounded the folly of their ill-gotten interview in Atlanta. The document trumpeted falsifications claiming Dale Jr. had chosen to speak only with Pat Robertson's "700 Club" because of how his life had been changed by Jesus.

When fabricated items appeared in trashy publications found in the check-out lines of grocery stores, our response was to ignore them. Most rational humans understand the tall tales in the sleazy rags are untrue. Refuting them only served to publicize the story.

But this scenario was more hurtful because they had secured the interview under false pretenses and then took advantage of the immense, pent-up demand for an interview with Dale Jr. We decided to quickly issue our own news release, exposing the sham before it aired and misled viewers. Junior also wanted to reiterate his respect and friendship for Dale Beaver.

The response to our news release was immediate, and my email inbox was flooded with vitriol.

"You are obviously a liar, atheist, and heathen," was a common theme among the emails (some more hateful than others), while another claimed "Satan is present on any racing website that complains about someone as great as Pat Robertson." The most bizarre was a message-board post claiming "this entire episode is part of a larger plot by Budweiser against Evangelical Christians."

While I tried to resist watching a tape of the show, I had to see how they portrayed Dale Jr. and Beaver. The smarmy chatter between Scott Ross and the co-hosts made me want to throw a heavy object through the TV screen, as they introduced the segment by intimating a link between the No. 3 on Earnhardt's race car and the Holy Trinity. In the feature itself, creative editing twisted Junior's answers, and there was only a single, passing reference to Dale Beaver.

I chose not to share the tape with Junior, and we never discussed it again. He had more important things to worry about at the rough-and-tumble Bristol Motor Speedway.

Since his dad's crash, fans had been tentative about swarming Dale Jr. in the garage area, but at Bristol more people than ever seemed fevered to get his autograph as the race weekend began, as if those who missed out on Big E's signature were more determined than ever to grab his son's scrawl as soon as possible.

Because of the small infield at the half-mile oval, the crowds made it difficult for Dale Jr. to move around, and a walk from the pit box to the team's hauler became a slow-moving procession. We also started to see copies of a photo someone had bootlegged of the No. 8 car parked alongside the No. 3 and Waltrip's No. 15 during the red flag at Daytona, only a short time before Earnhardt's accident. There seemed to be a large number of people at Bristol with multiple copies of the photo, trying to get as many signed as they could, most likely destined to appear soon after on eBay. Once we realized the situation, Junior did his best to avoid signing additional copies of the photo, while I tried to steer the photos away from him amid the crowds.

Others approached with pictures of his father or his father's race car, asking Dale Jr. to sign. Each time it happened, it was as if someone was ripping the bandages from an emotional wound that had yet to heal. It was hard enough losing his dad, but it was made harder by hundreds of reminders each day.

"When ya gonna drive the 3?" they would ask over and over again, as if it would ease the grief they were feeling. "When are you gonna drive your daddy's car?"

Though he handled the queries well, the constant repetition finally wore him down.

"I understand they wanna share something with me, but what am I supposed to do with these things?" Junior asked when we reached the solitude of the hauler. "I mean, I can't be an asshole and not sign daddy's things, but I *hate* it."

The constant requests to drive with his father's colors or number were best described by a term from Greek mythology: *chimera*, something that is hoped or wished for, but is ultimately illusory or impossible to achieve.

With Teresa sequestered away with an endless array of lawsuits, every request was heaped on Junior's shoulders. While I did my best as gatekeeper, it was nearly impossible to keep him from the barrage of people clamoring for his time and attention. From the autograph seekers to mayors offering the key to their town, it seemed nonstop. I admired his strength in dealing with the requests, but one thing bothered him the most: he bristled when he was expected to accept posthumous honors or awards on his father's behalf.

"If Teresa wants to do it," he said, "she can do it. But I'm not."

Dale Jr. had been protective of personal memories of his father, but he spent considerable time that week composing his first NASCAR.com/ *Winston Cup Scene* column since the accident. He began writing the monthly columns at midseason the year before, and his very personal writings were a hit from the start.

The new column, composed over several late nights, was called "Memories of Dad." In it, Junior described his favorite moments with his father, including his first venture into waterskiing at age six. Rather than using a boat, his father conceived a crude and cruel procedure: tying a ski rope to the hitch of a pickup truck on the boat ramp. This redneck concoction dragged the minuscule Dale Jr. toward shore, forcing him to try to pull up onto the gigantic skis before he reached the pavement. After six attempts, Junior was still struggling and was repeatedly dragged across the paving, leaving him with what he termed a "strawberry" on his backside. While I saw it as a cruel story, Junior used the anecdote to describe a young boy's pleasure at merely spending time with a father who was away from home so frequently.

His father had also taught him some hard lessons about the best way to get around the Bristol track. Junior felt he had a lot to prove to his team after he crashed during both 500-lap Bristol races in 2000, including once being taken out in a collision started by his father.

Because the groove was only slightly larger than one car width, a fast car was often forced to push a slower car out of the way. The fans loved the rough action, but it could be very detrimental to a race car. While speedway cars are sleek and designed to slice through the air, the cars at Bristol and other short tracks have beefy, fortified bumpers and expanded grille openings to allow large gulps of air to cool the engine, brakes, and driver. Aerodynamics play almost no role at Bristol, but using the front bumper too often as a battering ram can bend or close the grille, which means trouble on a hot, sunny afternoon.

After a ninth-place qualifying run, Tony Jr. had a small wager for Dale Jr.

"I'll bet you knock the grille outta this thing in ten laps," he joked.

At most of the bigger racetracks, the public-address system is rarely heard in pit lane. But in the close confines of the Bristol track, with its massive, bowl-shaped grandstands, the PA could be heard loudly as Dale Jr. strapped himself into the car. Rather than the typical "Gentleman, start your engines" call, the track began a lengthy tribute to his father.

Helmet on, seatbelts pulled tight, Dale Jr. slumped forward slightly as the color drained from his face.

"It totally takes you out of that [aggressive] mindset and puts you thinking about that," he explained later. "When they're done, they sing the national anthem and move on. Then they start the engines and you're sitting in the car, totally unprepared for what you're getting ready to do. It takes forty laps for your brain to catch up. It's just instincts until the head catches up."

With his mind distracted, Junior wasn't as aggressive as usual, though he reminded Tony Jr. the grille was still intact as he passed lap 10. Hanging steady for the first 60 laps, the car's handling began to deteriorate as the tires lost grip and he dropped through the standings like a stone. By lap 149, he had dropped to 30th place, but caught a lucky break when a yellow flag allowed him to stay on the lead lap.

With the team making adjustments to the car and his head back in the game, Dale Jr. climbed to 22nd place when he received a pit-lane speeding penalty on lap 249, undoing the progress he had made. Slowly losing ground, he dropped one lap behind on lap 317.

"That was like an old silent movie," he yelled over the roar of the cars inside the bowl, "where the hero is hanging from the cliff by his fingertips, slipping away one inch at a time."

After losing the lap, a more determined Dale Jr. found a rhythm, and regained the lead lap by passing the race leader John Andretti.

"Hell yeah!" Junior screamed when the yellow flag flew shortly after. "I've never gotten a lap back like that in my whole career! I drove like hell to keep up with the 43 [Andretti]. We were movin' up!"

Soon after the restart, Junior was caught in a Bristol-style short-track accident. As the No. 17 of Matt Kenseth slid sideways, the cars behind began to brake hard, causing an accordion effect and sweeping a number of cars into the crash, including the No. 8.

"Sorry, guys," Dale Jr. said. "They were wreckin' in front of me. I just got hit and spun. Somebody got me in the right rear."

Dale Jr. limped the mangled car to the garage area, where the crew descended to repair the damage. Eury Sr. crawled under the nose of the car, welding suspension pieces back together.

"I guess it's my fault," Junior explained. "I saw the 17 sideways and I thought there was gonna be a helluva wreck. I checked up and they ran over me."

With bent bodywork removed and the suspension loosely aligned, Dale Jr. returned to the track on lap 425. Though they were in 33rd position, every spot they gained meant a few more points, and the team desperately needed points after their troubles since Daytona.

The Bud car was a mangled mess, forcing Dale Jr. to fight the car as the front suspension scraped the track under braking into each corner.

"I hope they're welded good, 'coz they're hitting the ground," Junior said.

"I don't know. I didn't have my glasses on," replied Pops, giving the team a much-needed laugh.

"S'alright. I trust ya," Junior replied.

With the Bud car crippled, the race for the win was sparkling as Elliott Sadler, driving the Wood Brothers No. 21 car, grabbed his first career Winston Cup win by less than half a second. It was the first win in eight years for the Wood Brothers, one of NASCAR's most historic teams, and Sadler had done it by holding off Andretti in Richard Petty's equally historic No. 43 car.

The great finish was overshadowed somewhat when, on the cool-down lap, an angry Tony Stewart spun out Jeff Gordon on the narrow and crowded pit lane. The two had tangled on the final lap of the race and Gordon sent Stewart's car spinning in turn four. For intentionally hitting Gordon on pit lane, Stewart was fined $10,000 and placed on probation by NASCAR until August 29.

Dale Jr. finished 31st, 44 laps behind Sadler, and was now 26th in points after six races. Despite a rough outing, the team and driver could look ahead with optimism to Texas Motor Speedway, where they had dominated one year ago.

chapter 18

being who i am

Fort Worth, Texas

"At first, when you think of someone you lost, you're sad. But then comes a time when you remember them, and you think good memories," Dale Jr. explained to Bill Campbell of the *Dallas Morning News* in an interview before the race at Texas Motor Speedway.

The week leading up to the race, where Dale Jr. was the defending winner, marked the first tentative steps toward a sense of normality in a post–Big E world.

For his first full interview since the crash, Dale Jr. decided he wanted to sit down with Darrell Waltrip for a discussion that would air on the FOX prerace show. Waltrip had been supportive of Junior long before the crash, often calling him "Junebug," the nickname his father had given him. Dale Jr. also believed Waltrip, as a former driver, would have a deeper understanding of his situation. Tuesday afternoon, the two sat down in Junior's living room for nearly an hour.

Asked if his father was the greatest driver ever, Junior initially hedged his answer, mentioning Jeff Gordon, Waltrip, and David Pearson as other candidates, before finally committing to an answer.

"[Dad] was always able to get more out of the race car, and there were very few race car drivers that were able to do that," he said. "A lot of guys could drive it one hundred percent all the time, but he always got a little bit more. I'm his son, so I'm gonna be particular about it, but he was probably the best."

Waltrip asked if Junior felt the pressure of living up to what his dad had accomplished.

"Well, I've always had," he said, stammering a bit before continuing. "You know people have always asked me that, and maybe it's more relevant now than ever before. I don't feel a whole lotta pressure to equal his success or anything like that, or try to be personally what he was, or be a reminder to people. That's an awful lot to ask somebody and it's really unhealthy, and so I've got my own things goin' on, my own interests. We all change throughout the years, and there's a great possibility that as I get older, I'll be more like him."

"That's a scary thought," Waltrip laughed.

"Well, not really," Junior replied. "I've asked some people that were real close to him about it, about how he was when he was twenty-six . . . so I feel pretty comfortable with what I'm doing now. I don't wanna try to be like that too soon or too quickly. Plus, a lot of things that bother me or worry me are my performance level on the racetrack . . . . You can sit here and say the stock answers about a good year or bad luck, but when it comes down to it, we gotta get up front if I'm gonna be a race car driver and do this the rest of my life. I gotta win some races.

"I do a lot of things I never did before, and I only do 'em because I know he'd want me to do 'em."

Junior's cat, Buddy Love, provided comic relief during the interview. Deciding he liked the warmth of the bright TV lights, he climbed between the two racers, then took a prominent spot on a small table behind them.

"How do you keep going?" Waltrip asked.

"You just try to maintain. I've put pictures on my wall of me and him, and just always remember what we did together and where he came from. And how he dealt with his father's death, basically about the same age, ya know. I just try to . . . ya know . . . get on with it."

"Do you believe your dad is in heaven?" Waltrip asked.

"I'm pretty sure. I'm sure of it, actually," Junior said, correcting himself immediately. "He was pretty adamant about living right and bein' right. . . . It's easy for me to say this and a lotta people won't take it seriously, comin' from his son, but he was *fascinating*. He was a *special* person, ya know what I'm sayin'? There were just things he could think of or do, and his level of common sense was just so far beyond a lot of people that I know. And I just believe he was so, so way above average in a lot of areas and that's why I feel pretty positive that he's in heaven. Because I don't think God would pass something like that up, ya know?"

For six weeks, Budweiser had canceled all appearances and meet-and-greets they previously scheduled for Dale Jr., but as time passed, Junior decided he was ready to book them again.

The first was a trip to St. Paul, where Dale Jr. appeared at the sold-out arena of the Minnesota Wild. He was anxious to see what kind of reaction he would get at a non-NASCAR sporting event, and seemed pleased as he was introduced to the crowd wearing a No. 8 Wild jersey. With a small smile, he waved to acknowledge the loud cheer before he led the Wild's pregame command of, "Let's play hockey!"

He was in good spirits in the Budweiser suite, where he signed autographs and spoke with the guests. Knowing we were headed to Texas the following morning, several explained their hard feelings toward Dallas—their previous NHL franchise, the beloved North Stars, had departed Minnesota in 1993 to become the Dallas Stars. Though they were fiercely proud of their new team, the sting of the Stars still remained.

The final segment of Junior's appearance placed him on the backseat of the Bud Light Zamboni for a ride on the ice between periods. He expected to be driven for a single lap, allowing him to wave to the fans, but once on the ice, the Zamboni made its usual rounds, polishing the entire rink in a series of circles and leaving Junior sitting self-consciously on the back.

"Did I look like an asshole just sitting there?" he asked me as he hopped off the massive machine. Asshole or not, it was a fun appearance and Junior seemed comforted by the sincere kindness of everyone at the arena.

As the long day came to an end, he learned that Governor Jeb Bush had signed the new Florida law making all autopsy photos private unless a judge approved their release. It had been a good week so far, and he was excited to head to Texas.

Growing up in the shadow of a legend, Junior always felt awkward as a teenager when people asked for his autograph. He knew they were asking because of who his father was, not because of who he was. It was another piece of the complex puzzle of becoming his own man rather than merely someone with the same name as the Intimidator. He also struggled to comprehend more recent autograph seekers who approached him after a poor finish or a crash. After a rough performance, he believed himself unworthy of their request.

I tried to convince him his fans liked him for more than just that day's effort, but the argument fell on deaf ears until I used an example of his favorite athlete, Art Monk, the NFL Hall of Fame receiver for the Washington Redskins.

"Would you be honored to meet Art Monk after a game, even if he had dropped one or two passes that day?" I asked.

"Hell yeah." he replied.

"Well, that's what it's like for fans who want your autograph," I reasoned.

In the same vein, he was uneasy with the outpouring of fan support during his rookie season, feeling as if they were cheering his name, not him. He didn't believe he had achieved enough at tracks like Darlington to warrant such adulation there.

Texas was another story entirely. Junior felt deserving of the raucous cheers at the track where he earned his first career win in the Busch Series in 1998 and his maiden Cup win in 2000.

"I like Texas, and they like me," he said more than once. In his short career, it was the only track where he had achieved far more than his father, who never won a race at the 1.5-mile D-shaped oval.

A surprisingly large Friday crowd rose to cheer Dale Jr. as he headed to the green flag on his qualifying attempt. Their cheers echoed across the massive complex as if their collective energy could push the car to a faster lap.

On his first lap, Dale Jr. crossed the line in 28.643 seconds. It was good, but second best to Dale Jarrett. As he came across the line on his second lap, the crowd erupted when the top spot on the scoring pylons blinked and an "8" appeared. It was a rocket of a lap at 28.23 seconds, an average speed of 190.678 miles per hour. Junior and team were ecstatic, but they were only the sixth car to qualify, which meant there were a lot of fast cars yet to take to the track.

One fashion statement Junior made as a rookie was wearing his baseball-style caps backward. Since his dad's wreck, he had worn them in a normal fashion, until now. Wearing his white Minnesota Wild hat backward, Dale Jr. walked back to his motorcoach, nervously watching the timing and scoring screen as each car failed to match his lap. When the final car crossed the line, it was official. He had earned his third career Bud Pole Award. Before leaving the bus, Junior took off his Budweiser shirt.

"We'll fuck with 'em by wearing the Minnesota jersey," he laughed, pulling on the jersey as we leaped out of the bus.

After weeks of stress and heartache, it was the first time Junior seemed to be genuinely happy as he hugged and high-fived Tony Jr. and the rest of the crew. Posing for photos in victory lane, Tony Jr. already knew what the pole winner received, and he convinced Dale Jr. the new Toro lawn tractor and trailer would look much better on his land.

"It's yours," Dale Jr. said happily.

After the required photos and handshakes, we walked to the media center for the pole winner's news conference. It would be the first time he had faced a full room of reporters since Daytona, and, buoyed by the pole, he was prepared.

"It felt really good to have that much support," he explained when asked if he could see the fans cheering his lap. "It was like a high-speed wave going down the front stretch."

He was asked about his motivation to race since the crash.

"The way I look at racing, the way I feel about racing," he said, pausing to search for the right words. "The way I feel about going to the track on the weekends, the way I prepare myself for each race is totally different than before. Some of the aspects about racing that were huge to me a year ago don't really matter no more.

"I raced for a combined three years and the majority of my enjoyment was how proud my father got, and to see him happy after a win and things like that. That's not there no more, so I guess I'm doing it kind of like everyone else is. I'm out there trying to make a living."

His effort to give detailed answers was nothing new, but now it seemed an outlet for him to crystallize thoughts and emotions he had yet to discuss otherwise.

"I think it'll be a long time before I ever feel like I felt before all that happened. I try to deal with it the best I can. I think about him all the time, and it seems like there's good days and bad days. Just when you think you're beginning to feel better about it, you'll hit a bump in the road and you'll spend two or three days where you can't think of nothing else. I don't know how long that will be, but it's not such a bad thing because I like to think about him often."

Was he concerned the sport would struggle without the Intimidator? And did he feel pressure to live up to his dad's legacy?

"I'm having a good time being who I am. I always have. Dad wasn't going to drive forever and NASCAR would have found themselves in this situation down the road. I don't think it's a situation where we need to show much concern for who's going to fill the shoes, who's going to be the next Dale Earnhardt or what not. I mean, there'll be a guy that comes along, whether it's me or somebody we haven't met yet. There'll be a guy that comes along that dazzles the crowd."

Have you matured since the accident?

"I always felt I had a little brat in me somewhere, and I think that's all gone," he said.

When will you wear a HANS device?

"I'm not gonna be too quick to start strappin' on all kinds of gizmos and what not," he said. "I've been running for several years and have been using the equipment I feel is necessary."

Dale Jr. also resumed his Make-a-Wish meetings, and he went to the media center Saturday afternoon to meet a young girl named Cheyenne. Decked out in a red jacket to match Junior's uniform, the frail and shy girl gave him a lingering hug that seemed to do as much for him as it did for her and her family. No matter how hectic things are at the racetrack, spending time with brave children fighting terminal illnesses always brought a sense of calm and added perspective for Dale Jr.

"Maybe she brought me some luck," he told Winston Kelley of FOX Sports Network after the meeting. "It's always a lot of fun just to see them smile."

Kelley made a point of apologizing for chasing after Junior following the Daytona race.

"Aw, man, no problem," Junior assured him. "You were just doing your job."

Sunday morning, the setup crew taped small medals to the Bud pit box. A fan had brought the small charms: angels with a "3" painted on each. With finishes of 15th or worse since Daytona, they were looking for anything to reverse their fortunes.

When the green flag flew for the Harrah's 500, Dale Jr. launched into the lead, looking every bit as dominant as he had at the previous year's performance. He held the top spot until Jarrett took over on lap 22. After the first pit stops of the day, Dale Jr. retook the lead, stretching his advantage to 2.6 seconds by lap 50.

The race developed into a three-car battle after lap 100, when Jarrett and Dale Jr. were joined by Steve Park. The Pennzoil team had completed a

Goodyear tire test at the track in January, and using the knowledge gained from the test, Park's car seemed to get better as the race continued.

"Hey, guys, the fan doesn't work," Dale Jr. said, as he became aware of the heat while under the caution flag on lap 188. "I need some air in here."

"It was working this morning," answered Brian Cram, the man responsible for the systems inside the cockpit.

"That ain't good enough, man," Junior said, teasing Cram while still making his point. "I wasn't in here this morning, I'm in here *now* and I need it to work!"

By lap 200, Dale Jr. had opened a lead of more than three seconds.

"Yeah, man! This is real easy," he told the team. "This is nice. This is fun, ain't it boys? Woooo! *Rocketing* down the straightaway!"

Various pit strategies jumbled the field after the next yellow flag, and Dale Jr. restarted in eighth place, but wasted little time climbing back up the charts. With a car that drove so easily, the driver's attention even turned to sponsor decals as he passed Jeff Gordon.

"Hey, guys, did y'all know that Jeff has a new associate sponsor?" he laughed.

"Good job, man," Ty Norris answered. "Now he can look at the sponsors on your rear bumper for awhile."

With 100 laps to go, it remained a battle between Jarrett, Park, and Junior, though the No. 8 car struggled for the first time to keep up with the others.

"This set of tires ain't that good," Dale Jr. said. "I don't like it! I'm losing the feel a little bit. What the hell is going on?"

When there was no response, the driver became agitated.

"Y'all hear me? Lemme know if you're listenin'," he hollered. "Ya know what I'm saying?"

"I have no idea," Tony Jr. replied, earning a round of laughs from the crew. "We're using up a set [of tires] here. We've saved the best for the end."

When a yellow flag came out on lap 265 for a Todd Bodine crash, the team made a quick stop and began furiously checking their fuel calculations.

"Save all the gas you can here," crew chief Eury told Dale Jr. "Don't use that accelerator pedal unless you have to."

"Are you *kidding* me? Jeez," was the disgusted reply.

"We're still figuring, but we think you can make it," Pops said. "The 1 [Park] and the 88 [Jarrett] will need to stop again."

"If I go out there and bust my ass just trying to save fuel," Junior shot back, "I'm tellin' ya it ain't gonna be driver error."

"We just figured it," Pops said after another lap behind the pace car. "You'll have .87 of a gallon left as you get the checkered flag."

Several of the 17 cars on the lead lap came back in to top off their fuel tanks before the green flag. Dale Jr. restarted third, after a pep talk from his cousin.

"Remember, this is Texas," Tony Jr. insisted. "You'll run out after you win this thing. Go for it. You got enough. We can make it. I'm a gambler so I don't wanna go back. I think there'll be another yellow."

Three laps after the restart, the massive Texas crowd came to their feet as the Bud car shot past Jarrett to retake the lead, but the yellow came out a lap later for a crash in turn two.

"How are those tires?" Tony Jr. asked.

"Good," the driver said.

"I think we can make it," Tony Jr. reiterated, but his driver still seemed unconvinced.

"OK," Dale Jr. said.

"Listen to me," Pops said as he jumped into the conversation.

"Every day," Dale Jr. shot back.

"We can make it," Pops said.

In the background, Dale Jr. heard the voice of Kevin Pennell, better known as "Two Beer." Pennell was also figuring the fuel mileage.

"I hear Two Beer," Dale Jr. said. "Sounds like he has a different opinion."

"Point eight nine left now," Two Beer replied. "Keep wreckin'! Caution laps save us a lot of fuel."

"We got a set of tires on the wall, if we need them," Tony Jr. said.

"Keep 'em ready. We might need 'em," Dale Jr. replied.

The green flag on lap 284 meant 50 laps remained, and it took Dale Jr. only four laps to pull away by more than a second.

"It's as good as it's been all day!" Dale Jr. said on lap 290.

Pulling away easily, Dale Jr. instructed Norris about what he needed in the final 25 laps.

"I'm gonna depend on you, Ty," Junior said. "I need a [lap] count every five laps."

As soon as the words were out of his mouth, there was another crash in turn two.

Junior was now vulnerable no matter what the team chose to do. If he stayed on-track, the cars behind would come in for at least two or more likely four fresh tires, making them faster after the restart. If the Bud team came to the pit lane, teams might stay out, gambling on clean air and track position to stay ahead of those who pitted. Even a car as good as the Bud machine might not be able to make up all of those positions while fighting in traffic.

"How would you like to stay out?" Tony Jr. asked.

"They're all staying out?" Dale Jr. replied, putting in a vote for four tires. "We can beat 'em with four."

"Pit now! Pit now!" Tony Jr. hollered, instructing the team to put four new tires on the car.

As Dale Jr. peeled off the track, many of the lead lap cars stayed out. Several others chose to change only two tires.

With less than 20 laps remaining, Dale Jr. was in ninth place, the deepest he had been all day.

"That really sucked," he sighed.

"I knew it would," Pops answered, disagreeing with his son's decision to pit.

"But, if we woulda stayed out," Dale Jr. countered, "they all might have got four."

"Everybody else in front of you got two tires or stayed out," Norris said, trying to get the driver to focus on the task ahead. "You've got a car that can do it. Remember last time. We can do this right here."

"I'll get what I can," said Dale Jr.

As the field raced away, it was apparent the Bud car wasn't as fast as it had been, fighting for grip in heavy traffic.

"This is like a punch in the gut," Dale Jr. muttered with 12 laps to go.

"It's junk! Junk!" he hollered as he gained a spot into eighth. "I'm driving as hard as I can!"

"You're runnin' 'em down, babe," Norris answered, trying to keep Dale Jr. calm.

"It just won't turn," Dale Jr. replied, before going silent for the rest of the race.

At the finish, Jarrett, who had also taken four tires and restarted in sixth place, made it through traffic to earn the win. Park followed him across the line in second, while the Bud team ended the day eighth.

"The 88 won," a dejected Tony Jr. said, before reiterating the strategy that won the race. "He took four."

"What're ya gonna do?" Dale Jr. answered. "It was a bad set [of tires] at the end. We didn't think two [tires] would win the race. It wasn't a good match on the last set. I was better than Jarrett. That was the way to go."

After leading 108 laps in the win last year, the Bud team had to console themselves after leading another 107 laps this afternoon. A frustrated Dale Jr. tried to keep a positive spin on the finish.

"Four tires won the race," he told several reporters who questioned the team's late-race pit strategy. "Stayin' out wouldn't have won. That deal at the end, what are you gonna do?

"We were leading so easily with about thirty to go. I was just relaxing, being patient and driving in my own rhythm. The car was the best it had been all day at that point. It had cooled off and the cloud cover came in and I think that really helped our car. The guys told me we had enough fuel to go to the finish, so we were just cruising. They would have had a real hard time catching us.

"But then the yellow came out . . . " he said, pausing as the sentence tailed off. "What are ya gonna do?"

chapter 19

to pay my bills

Martinsville, Virginia

B eing a race car driver has its perks, and Dale Jr. was excited to spend Monday at a secret locale in Virginia, participating in sniper training with representatives from Remington Arms and the U.S. Secret Service. Remington, an associate sponsor of the No. 8 team, produces many of the weapons used by law enforcement in the United States, and the sniper range allows officers and agents to hone their skills.

"It was so cool," Dale Jr. reported, after working out some of his frustrations from the race the day before. "I was able to destroy a bowling pin from a thousand yards!"

As a gift, Remington presented Dale Jr. with one of the rifles, making him one of only a handful of civilians to own such a specialized and powerful weapon.

It had been a week since Dale Jr. sat with Darrell Waltrip, and he seemed pleased with the results. Segments of the interview were shown on FOX during the Texas prerace show, while longer segments aired on the FOX Sports Network. But, the extensive interview was primarily geared toward diehard race fans.

The next step was an interview with a media outlet that reached a wider audience, and we spent considerable time discussing the options. Dale Jr. wanted the interview to be a serious one that gave him a chance to speak about his father to an audience that might not know much about him.

"The Today Show" was a good fit as the top-rated program on morning television. Its producers had been the most courteous and reasonable when making interview requests in the immediate aftermath of the crash. They were also serious about sending one of their anchors to conduct the interview wherever Dale Jr. preferred.

When the calendars were coordinated, Wednesday seemed to work best. Dale Jr. and the team were testing at a small track in South Carolina known as Greenville-Pickens Speedway, and Eury Sr. signed off on the idea only if it didn't disrupt the test, so we scheduled the interview to take place during the team's lunch break.

Sitting in the rickety press box, Matt Lauer and Dale Jr. talked for 30 minutes.

Though he answered somberly and often struggled to find the right words, talking about his father comforted Dale Jr. It was his way of sharing memories of his dad with as many people as he could.

"Wherever I go, people want to do their part to tell you they're thinking about you, or thinking about the family, or had the same feelings of loss and heartbreak. I mean, that's good," he said.

"When Adam [Petty] was killed, I never said anything to Kyle [Petty], ya know. I thought if I could . . . put myself in that situation, I would rather people not say anything. I'd rather just try to get over it, and deal with it the best way I can, by myself, without hearing about it every day. I didn't ever say anything to [Kyle], and now dealing with something pretty similar with my dad, I was totally wrong about that. It really feels good when somebody comes up to ya and tells ya they're sorry or whatever they say, it helps."

"Driving race cars, it's what I do," Junior replied when asked about the dangers of his work. "I love it. I get up every day to do it, to drive race cars. If the risk was higher, it wouldn't faze me one bit. If the element of danger, I wouldn't be any more convinced that we needed a change or anything like that . . . I feel very comfortable doin' what I'm doin,' and I don't feel any danger. I don't feel at risk when I get in the car.

"When he was alive, I drove to win and to make him happy and to see him enjoy that. Ya know, I drive for different reasons now. I drive to make a living and I drive to be able to afford . . . to pay my bills every week. And for the rest of my life for that matter."

Lauer concluded by asking if Dale Jr. felt pressure to step out of his father's shadow.

"No, not really," he answered. "I never had pictures of my father hanging in my house until now. I do things like that to think about him and try to remember him. And, I think I'll just be me, the best I can."

After their chat, Lauer headed back to New York, and Dale Jr. returned to his race car.

The Bud team was testing components for that weekend's race at Martinsville, Virginia. The half-mile track had been one of the biggest challenges of their rookie season. Their best finish was 26th, including a horrendous race in which Dale Jr. crashed several times and even ran into a tow truck in the garage area. To be more competitive, the race required solid brakes, a more patient driver, and the right pit strategy.

In qualifying, the team applied lessons from the test, and Dale Jr. turned a solid lap to earn the 10th starting position.

During the final practice session Saturday afternoon, everyone struggled in the unseasonably hot weather. Each time the Bud car came to the garage, the massive brake discs emanated waves of heat, which, along with the engine and gear train, made it perilous for the crew making changes to the smoldering machine. Standing within a few feet of the car took my breath away.

The heat was also a problem for the driver, as Junior had to change shoes midpractice, putting on insulated driving shoes to keep his feet and heels from burning. He was happy with the feel of the car, but didn't like being passed easily by Tony Stewart.

"Stewart oughta have new tires to get around me!" he hollered before invoking the name of a hapless former NASCAR driver: "I ain't no pushover. I ain't J. D. McDuffie!"

Race day provided no respite from the sweltering heat, and Tony Jr. urged Dale Jr. to take care of the car for 500 laps. "Be good," he reminded him. "Remember, ya gotta finish to win it."

Even while being cautious, Dale Jr. climbed to sixth place before the first pit stop.

The tiny track always produces exciting and close racing, but as the race continues, debris from the tires ("the marbles" in race-speak) builds, narrowing the groove through each corner. Because driving through the marbles is like steering on ice, passing becomes incredibly difficult, even with a fast car.

A short track also allows a variety of fuel and tire strategies, which jumbled the field throughout the afternoon. When the Bud team chose to pit after 100 laps, a large group of cars stayed on the track, which put

Dale Jr. in 17th place on the subsequent restart.

"We gotta think about pit strategy to get us back up there," Dale Jr. reminded Tony Jr. "We aren't up there no more, so let's think about it."

In the middle of the pack, Junior found the going chaotic.

"I'm just trying not to get run over!" he yelled. "Tony Jr., just get me track position. Nobody can really pass or do anything."

Junior held his position until he scraped the wall as he exited turn two on lap 200.

"Is the right side fucked up?" he asked in a panicked voice.

"It's not bad. It's the fender only," answered Norris, using binoculars from high above the track.

"I can't believe it. The car came clear off the ground," replied a relieved driver.

During a yellow-flag period on lap 269, the team made a stop as Brian Cram placed cold rags in the car to help Junior with the heat. The quick work lifted them five positions to 13th, but the rags weren't cold enough for Junior's liking.

"If I wanted a dry rag, I'd use my hat!" Junior hollered.

"You guys be careful there," Dale Jr. warned, turning more serious. "The pit lane is slick as hell. Make sure you guys don't get hit.

"Damn, it's hot. You guys don't want any of this shit out here," Junior said, kidding the crew, some of whom were looking for any shade they could find between stops. "It's too hot out here for y'all! You just stay where you are."

"It's cooler air up there near the front," replied Tony Jr., more than happy to trade barbs with his cousin.

"Tony Jr., there ain't a track big enough for as hard as I'm wheelin' it!" Junior laughed. "We're so much better than what we had last year.

"Are y'all drinkin' lotsa cold water and using wet rags there?" he asked, with envy.

"It's the only luxury we get," replied Tony Jr. before needling Dale Jr. about hitching a ride to and from the track each day in Dale Jarrett's helicopter. "We don't get to ride the paddle-whomper home," he said, to the delight of the Bud crew, who would have to fight the post-race traffic jams all the way back to Mooresville.

The team made their final pit stop on lap 414, which dropped them to 16th.

"You've got what you got," Tony Jr. said. "We're not planning to see you here again."

The strategy paid off when the yellow came out again on lap 451. Seven of the cars in front of Dale Jr. came to the pits, moving the Bud car to ninth place.

Racing as hard as he could to finish in the top 10, Dale Jr. lost a spot to Stewart, then lost another to Jerry Nadeau. Dale Jr. crossed the finish line 11th, 15 spots better than his previous best at Martinsville.

Jarrett grabbed his second consecutive win, passing his Robert Yates Racing teammate Ricky Rudd for the lead with five laps to go. As the Winston Cup points leader, Jarrett extended his lead over Jeff Gordon to more than 120 points after eight races.

While many of the cars looked as if they had been pelted by baseball bats, the Bud car rolled into the hauler with surprisingly little damage as driver and crew celebrated a competitive run.

"I wanted a top-10 so bad," he told reporters. "The team was telling me on the radio to go get Nadeau those last couple of laps. I really could have spun him out the last couple of corners, but I don't want to race that way and I don't wanna earn spots like that.

"Before the race, Tony Jr. told me I couldn't win it if I didn't finish, so I tried to take care of the car. I still wheeled it as hard as I could. Everything gets so hot in there, imagine sitting inside that thing for 500 laps."

Before anyone could ask another question, Junior threw his backpack over his shoulder.

"I'm outta here," he said as he walked away. "We've got a weekend off!"

chapter 20

i'll take care of you

Talladega, Alabama

Few things are certain on the lengthy NASCAR trail, but twice a year you can confidently make Sunday plans well in advance. There will never be a Cup race on Easter Sunday or Mother's Day. NASCAR won't mess with Jesus. Or Mom.

The Easter break was the first off-weekend of the season, and after such a whirlwind of emotions and constant travel, everyone needed time to catch their breath and get a well-deserved rest. During the break, the Earnhardt family received a personal invitation from President Bush to meet with him on Air Force One while he was in Charlotte several days after the Martinsville race.

Bush, along with brother Jeb, had been supportive of the Earnhardts in their legal battles surrounding the autopsy photos, and met with a grateful Teresa as well as Dale Jr., Kelley, Kerry, and Taylor. After the meeting, the family was given an in-depth tour of the Boeing VC25 jet, posing for pictures with the plane's crew members and Air National Guard staff.

"I left there feeling great and really patriotic," Junior said the following week, describing the meaningful occasion before adding a small punch line. "Then, I got home and my tax bill had arrived in the mail."

The night before the Talladega race weekend, MTV began airing the Dale Jr. "Cribs" episode. The channel also debuted a one-hour documentary, "True Life: I'm a Race Car Driver," which was shot the year before. It originally was scheduled for an early-March debut, but was delayed and reedited after Big E's death. The shows reached a new audience not yet exposed to Junior or NASCAR.

The one-two punch on MTV represented a new paradigm on several levels. The reality-TV craze was still new, which gave both shows a raw, exciting feel that is now taken for granted. (The "True Life" special was produced by Bill Richmond, one of the producers of MTV's groundbreaking "Real World" series.) They showed a behind-the-scenes glimpse of Junior, away from the usual racing action. His likable and easygoing nature and quick wit were ideal for the reality-TV formula.

In the pre-DVR era, most TV shows aired once or twice and then were gone forever. But both shows aired dozens of times on the channel over the course of several weeks. If a viewer missed one airing, another was likely only a few hours away. As the buzz built, fans could watch them again and again. And the buzz wasn't merely inside the NASCAR world—it also drew mainstream media interest, including a feature on "Entertainment Tonight."

Through Dale Jr., the shows portrayed NASCAR in a hipper, younger, and more rock-and-roll light than before. Among the hundreds of feature stories and articles on Dale Jr. during his eight seasons with Budweiser, the two MTV shows, along with a lengthy story in *Rolling Stone* magazine in 2000, had more impact than any others in forming the young driver's image.

Though the "True Life" episode was shot before his dad's death, Dale Jr. had a pointed answer to questions about the pressure that comes with being the son of a legend.

"I'm not my father," Junior said emphatically. "And, I hope people realize that—[the ones] who cheer for me because of my father. If they do it because it's Earnhardt, fine. But if they think I'm that man or gonna be that man one day, I think they'll be disappointed. 'Coz I'm gonna be somebody different."

His spirits were high after watching the shows, adding to his energy level Friday afternoon at Talladega for an event with executives from Anheuser-Busch and Major League Baseball. As the official beer of MLB and NASCAR, Budweiser brought two of its largest properties together and unveiled an MLB All-Star Game paint scheme that would appear on the No. 8 car at NASCAR's All-Star Race in May and again in July at the Pepsi 400 at Daytona.

Junior was excited about the paint scheme, not because of any interest in baseball (his father was much more of a fan), but because the race car was primarily white. White had always been his favorite color for a race car because he believed a clean, white race car looked cooler. And faster. (He also liked orange, which was the color of choice for many of the cars prepared by his maternal grandfather, Robert Gee.)

The Talladega infield area is a notorious party zone akin to Mardi Gras or spring break. While many thought of Dale Jr. as a hell-raiser and partier (which he certainly could be in his downtime, away from the track), he was focused and dedicated once the race weekend arrived. Even at the wild-and-crazy Talladega track, he rarely left his bus from the moment he arrived Thursday evening until the mad dash home after the race. While a number of drivers were frequently spotted carousing during race weekends, Dale Jr. was rarely among them.

Despite the tragedy at Daytona, there was no mistaking how competitive the Bud team was throughout Speedweeks, which gave them confidence for Talladega, the first restrictor-plate race since the 500. The chassis that performed so well in the Budweiser Shootout was the team's thoroughbred of choice for Talladega, and the weekend had gone well as the final practice session began.

Called "Happy Hour," the final practice session prior to the race was always the most stressful for crew members. If the team is struggling to tune a car's handling, Happy Hour is the final shot to make changes before the race. More ominously, a crash during this session forces a team to prepare the backup car without any practice laps. Starting a race from the back of the field with an untested car especially worried Tony Jr.

Within the first two laps of the session, Dale Jr. drove the No. 8 from the back of a pack numbering a dozen or more cars to the front, barreling through the field with abandon, including several moves that put him in the middle of cars running four abreast. The wide Talladega track makes that kind of move slightly less risky than at Daytona, but it didn't make it any easier for Tony Jr. to watch. Following the action from the top of the team's transporter, Eury Jr. had to look away.

"He's scarin' me," he laughed, "and I ain't even drivin'."

A bold Dale Jr. poked fun at Norris, who suggested a little patience from the driver.

"C'mon, Ty! We should be practicing being up front!" he yelled at his spotter as he slung the car into turn one, talking on the radio while running three-wide. "Ya gotta *want* me to be up front!"

On race morning, the drivers' meeting was longer than most. While race car drivers can be cold and calculating, there was no hiding their uneasy emotions several hours before the race. Back on a superspeedway, everyone was concerned about a repeat of Earnhardt's fatal accident, and tension permeated every inch of the crowded room.

The aerodynamic rules meant the cars would once again run in large packs, making another massive crash almost inevitable. The Big One had taken out nearly half the field at Daytona, and previous crashes at Talladega had demolished millions of dollars of machinery in one swoop. To cut down on risky moves, Mike Helton gave the drivers a warning about racing below the yellow line along the inside of the 2.66-mile track.

"This is your only warning about the yellow line," Helton stated, describing a new rule instituted for the race. "If you go below that line to pass, we can black flag you."

Near the end of the meeting, Michael Waltrip spoke up.

"Let's work together and take care of each other," he said. "I'll take care of you, if you take care of me."

After the drivers' meeting, Dale Jr. chose to stay for the church services. Though always well attended on race morning, the service that day seemed particularly crowded, as drivers, crew members, and their families hoped for a small dose of divine intervention to ease their nerves.

While nearly everyone approached the race with caution, Dale Jr. seemed different. With his father gone, it was time for him alone to carry the Earnhardt name into battle at Talladega. His swashbuckling aggressiveness in practice was evidence of his mettle, and as the race neared, he carried himself with a heightened sense of purpose, poise, and confidence.

"I feel like we got the perfect car," Dale Jr. said as he pulled away for the pace laps.

"That's what you got. The perfect car," laughed Tony Jr.

"Just take it easy getting out of the pits," warned Tony Sr. "Be careful leaving your pit box."

"Yeah, I'll try," Dale Jr. replied. "All you pit guys, gimme a push if you can. I need lotsa pushers today. I don't know how much it helps, but it looks cool. Ya know, the teamwork deal looks real good."

"All right," Tony Jr. responded, pointing to his pit crew, "everybody pushes and everybody puts on your 'wannabe up front' attitude. Let's go!"

"Hell yeah!" said the driver, before referring to Joe Gibbs Racing driver Mike McLaughlin, who had won the Busch Series race the day before. "We'll run a hundred and seventy laps stayin' outta trouble and then for eighteen laps we'll drop a McLaughlin on their asses."

As the race began, Waltrip's appeal to take care of each other seemed to have sunk in. The racing lacked the usual cutthroat intensity, though this did not mean a lack of drama or excitement for Dale Jr.

Less than 50 laps in, Junior made a great save, sliding the Bud car sideways after young rookie Casey Atwood made contact in the tri-oval, immediately in front of the Bud pit area.

"Is he outta control there?" asked an alarmed Eury Jr.

"Tell the 19 [Atwood] to stay on my ass in the tri-oval!" Junior barked at Norris, trusting his spotter to pass the message along. "It ain't fun, I know, but just tell him just be patient!"

Just as they had done at Daytona, Dale Jr. and Waltrip found each other in the pack and worked together in the draft until Michael disappeared from the back bumper of Junior.

"I was at half-throttle. What happened to Michael?" Junior asked.

"He was just runnin' hot," Tony Jr. answered. "He just needed to drop back and cool off his car."

"Are me and Michael gonna pit together?" the driver asked.

With no response, he snipped at the crew.

"Talk! I don't care who it is!" he barked. "Just talk!"

"We're discussing it," replied Pops.

"Thank you!" came the testy response.

Separated from his teammate, Junior dropped out of the top 10 and into another encounter with Atwood.

"I'm 'bout ready to knock the fuck outta him!" Junior growled. "Lemme know when he's behind me and I'll just get outta the way!"

Regrouping, Dale Jr. displayed the muscle he had shown in practice, slicing into the lead on lap 68 as seemingly all of Alabama erupted in cheers. It was short-lived, however, as Junior lost drafting help, a problem he attributed to poor spotting from Norris.

Being a spotter—especially at the restrictor-plate tracks—is a thankless task. While the driver is in the middle of three- and four-wide action, he relies on the spotter to help him find minuscule openings in traffic and to predict which line of cars is best at any given moment. A spotter at Talladega can be perfect for 187 laps, but a single mistake or misjudgment on the 188th can not only lead to the destruction of his own car, but a large portion of the entire field. On top of that pressure, the spotter is relied upon to help keep the driver's state of mind positive and calm, which is often the most challenging job of all.

"C'mon, Ty! Let's go!" Junior yelled at Norris. "I'm in the bottom line . . . can you see me?"

Shaking his head at the harsh mood of his driver, Tony Jr. looked over my shoulder as I scribbled madly, trying to keep up with the heated dialogue.

"Write down 'Spotter Sucks,'" he laughed, pointing to my notepad.

Less than five laps later, Junior's venom had a new target.

"Fuckin' Hornaday! I swear to God I wanna punch him out!" he yelled after the two made contact in the draft.

"Ty, tell these fuckers they need to chill the hell out," he said, as if his spotter had the power to calm the other 42 racers. "There's still a long way to go!"

One lap later, a subdued driver decided to take his own advice.

"I guess I need to as well," Dale Jr. said quietly.

With a new demeanor, Junior raced into the lead on lap 96, holding it for three laps. Shuffled back briefly, he surged forward again to lead lap 105. Junior's car was fast at the front, and the rest of the field seemed content to catch their collective breath and follow him single-file. No one mounted a serious challenge for 25 laps, and Junior laughed when he found Rusty Wallace and Sterling Marlin in second and third.

"Hey, we're leading the beer cars," he said.

As the final pit stops approached, it looked like an auction house in the Budweiser pit, as a number of crew chiefs and team members made their bid to stop in tandem with the fastest car on-track. With restrictor plates choking the horsepower, it was crucial to come to pit lane in conjunction with other cars, then form a tight draft exiting pit lane, reaching top speed much sooner than a car traveling alone. Even with a fast car, pitting alone on the final stop could end any hope of a victory.

In the pit box next door was the Square D team of Andy Petree Racing with the veteran driver Bobby Hamilton. Petree's team was part of the RAD program (the agreement between Petree, Childress, and Earnhardt to share data and technology on restrictor-plate programs). Hamilton's crew chief was Jimmy Elledge, who had spent years working on Earnhardt's GM Goodwrench team at Richard Childress Racing. He also happened to be the father of Kelley Earnhardt's daughter, Karsyn.

"Hey, *buddy*!" Pops Eury said with exaggerated gusto as he worked with Elledge to determine the best lap for a pit stop.

Drivers moved to align with friends and family, and Junior now had Hamilton and Dale Jarrett as his temporary best companions. Jarrett's UPS team was in the rival Ford camp, but a fast car overrules sponsor and manufacturer loyalties—at least for a few laps.

Dale Jr. pulled to pit lane with a small gaggle on lap 150 while most of the field stayed out. As the rest of the field began to pit, Dale Jr. climbed from 29th place to 12th by lap 159. Pushing Steve Park, Junior struggled to gain positions, climbing to 10th with 15 laps left. But Park's car simply wasn't as fast, and no amount of pushing from Dale Jr. made a difference.

"Steve's gotta do something here or I'll leave his ass," Junior hollered.

"He's a lap down," Norris said.

"*What*? Nobody told me!" Dale Jr. replied angrily as he quickly pulled out from behind his teammate in search of faster drafting partners.

The move cost Dale Jr. significant distance, and with 10 laps to go, he was running 22nd.

With fury, Dale Jr. gained eight positions in a single lap, climbing to 14th with six laps remaining. He gained another six spots on the next lap, and the crowd rose to their feet, sensing another dramatic Earnhardt charge to victory.

But in his haste, Dale Jr. became blocked in the middle lane and several drafting partners disappeared from his bumper. With no room to move high or low, he dropped several positions before making a final charge in the last two laps, fighting his way to eighth place.

On the final lap, Hamilton passed and then blocked Tony Stewart for the win. Hamilton's fourth career victory gave Elledge his first victory as a crew chief and Petree's first win as an owner. The 188-lap race had been run without a single caution flag, and The Big One had been averted.

"That's a good job, guys. A good clean race," Junior said on the cool-down lap. "We just got caught in the middle there. Damn, no cautions is nerve-wracking. It's a helpless feeling."

"Good job, driver," Tony Jr. said.

"It's so mentally draining to run three-wide all day," he told the crew. "I'm the world's worst at being patient, and it's hard as hell on the nerves.

"I had no help!" he complained, describing some of the treacherous moves in the draft. "I dunno how good I gotta make it to get help. No deals out there. If you screwed somebody, they'd screw you back.

"I was frustrated because I was positioned where I couldn't really make a move. I wanted to stay in the top line because the high side is where it seems to come alive in the last two laps. I just couldn't get there."

chapter 21

nascar is a lot like my daddy

Fontana, California

Los Angeles, an important market for Budweiser, is largely untapped by NASCAR, so Dale Jr. was agreeable to do a brief telephone news conference with the L.A.-area media in the days before the race at California Speedway.

"Keeping everyone motivated has been tough," he said, when asked how hard it had been to continue after his dad's crash. "The team looks to us leaders—me and the Eurys—to guide them and to have a plan."

About his own motivation, Junior shared several thoughts.

"I got friendly advice from a buddy of mine, Kyle Petty," Junior explained. "He said to maintain my focus on driving the race car and let others run the team.

"To see how pumped up my dad was by Budweiser's 'First Win' posters and T-shirts [after the Texas victory] was motivating. The win at the Winston was probably the greatest single moment with my dad. The greatest reward of all was seeing his smile and how much he enjoyed that. After he was gone, I pondered new motivation. Would it be the same? As soon as I got into the car, the motivation was just as strong, just different. Now it's for me."

Was he surprised at the nationwide outpouring after his father's death?

"I had a good sense of what he meant to the racing world," he said. "But to see what he meant to people beyond that—as an icon—was stunning."

And finally, was he looking forward to coming to the Los Angeles area?

"I got a lotta friends in L.A.," he said. "It's cool to catch up and check out a lotta things. For a boy from North Carolina, it's a breath of fresh air."

The boy from N.C. had several options the night before action was to begin at the speedway. One was a *Playboy* Playmate of the Year party at SkyBar in Hollywood; the other was a party thrown by *Maxim* magazine. Junior opted for the latter, leaving me to fend for myself at the *Playboy* event.

On a sunny Friday at the track, Junior's first duty was a fun interview with Jimmy Kimmel and Adam Carolla for a segment that would appear on Comedy Central's "The Man Show." Following the interview, Dale Jr. climbed into the car for the first practice session at the two-mile track.

Only a few laps into practice, the team radios squawked with a harsh metallic blast of sound. It was our first indication Dale Jr. had hit the wall very hard.

"Junior, you OK?" asked Ty Norris.

After an agonizing pause, Dale Jr. finally answered.

"Yeah, I think so . . . that hurt like a sonuvabitch," he said meekly. "Something in the right front gave way."

I hustled to the care center, where the ambulance dropped Junior off for his mandatory doctor's visit. After a few minutes, he walked gingerly to the golf cart.

"What happened?" I asked.

"I was really deep into turn two," he said quietly. "You run along the bottom, right on the yellow line there. Something broke in the right front and the car nosed over. I knew I was gonna hit hard. This track is so wide and the car started sliding toward the wall. It happens in such slow motion . . . sliding along . . . slow motion . . . slow motion. Then, the very instant it touches the wall, it's like FAST FORWARD! FAST FORWARD! FAST FORWARD! It hurts *bad*! That was about as hard of a hit as I've taken."

Lying on the couch in his motorcoach, Junior used several ice packs on his aching body. But something struck me as odd as he nursed the left side of his body.

"Didn't you hit with the right side of the car?" I asked. "Shouldn't you be sore on your right side?"

"I'll teach you about that," he said. "You just have to go limp when you hit the wall. When I'm strapped in the car and I hit with the right side, the seat and the belts hold my torso in place. But all my internal organs slosh to the right, which stretches and tears at the muscles on my left side. So, I might have bruised ribs on the right side if they slam against the seat, but everything on my left side hurts like hell—all my insides."

The crash, caused by a flat right front tire, demolished the car and the team worked to prepare the backup car, trying to set it up as close as possible to the first. Despite soreness on "all his insides," Junior was healthy enough to climb into the backup car for practice the following day.

Surprisingly, the car turned the second fastest lap overall in the early going until another calamity befell the team. In the rush to prepare the second car, an oil line had been installed incorrectly, causing the engine to explode when a rod sailed through the oil pan.

When race day arrived, Dale Jr. awoke to the realization he'd have to start the race from the back of the field, the NASCAR penalty when a team has to switch to a backup car. (Unlike the current rules, the engine change was allowed without penalty in 2001. In that era, teams built separate engines for practice/qualifying and the race.)

The day was also something special. April 29 would have been his father's 50th birthday, and Dale Jr. preferred to remember his dad on his birthday rather than dwell on the day of his death.

The *Los Angeles Times* Sunday edition included a tribute for Big E, and the track honored his memory with a brief invocation and the release of doves. Though Junior didn't particularly understand the significance of the doves, he appreciated that Bill Miller, the track president, and Dennis Bickmeier, the communications director, were the first in their positions to ask him (and Teresa) about their wishes for a tribute.

Junior was clear in his response: do whatever you want, but do it when I'm not there.

Starting at the back, the team and driver began the race in a subdued manner. The driver was still sore from his accident; the team was exhausted from working in the desert heat to prepare the backup car and rush to replace an engine during a practice session. Without much track time, no one knew how well the car would perform, but it proved to be very quick as Dale Jr. gained seven spots in the first three laps and then climbed into the top 20 by lap 46.

The first pit stop failed to cure a loose-handling car, and the driver began a series of complaints before watching Bobby Labonte spin on lap 59.

"Whoooo! Thank God for that yellow flag," Dale Jr. exhaled before scolding his team. "I need some help here. Ya see, he's loose too, and that's the *champion* spinning out! He's the champ and he spun out. It feels like the spoiler's been taken offa my car. We need to take care of that right now before I spin it too."

The driver eventually calmed down.

"The car is close. We're decent," he said. "We can do good here. I'm not mad."

By lap 87, the Bud car had climbed into the top 10.

"That's the fastest lap anybody's run all day," said Tony Jr.

"One at a time fellas!" Dale Jr. yelled triumphantly as he swept into eighth. But his joy was short-lived as the Bud car sputtered down the back straight on lap 106.

"I'm outta fuel!" he screamed. "I think I'm outta fuel!

"Excellent. *Exxxxcellent*. This is just where I wanted to be," Dale Jr. moaned, dripping sarcasm as the car coasted silently around turn four. "How could you guys let the car run outta gas?"

"Both computers figured we could go at least two more laps," Tony Jr. replied. "Maybe it was because you were going so much faster."

The crew sprayed ether into the carburetor to help the smoldering engine refire. As the car stumbled to life, it stalled while pulling out of the pit box. The No. 8 had dropped to 33rd, one lap behind.

"I've just been driving so hard, working *so* damn hard and now we're at the back," Dale Jr. said.

"This whole damn weekend has been hard for all of us," Tony Jr. replied. "We're just gonna get it back. Let's go get 'em and not let it end this way. You just gotta have that same attitude as last week. Ya gotta *want* to get back up front."

"We know how to give one away, don't we?" Tony Sr. groused before the team caught a lucky break when the yellow came out on lap 113.

As the leaders made pit stops, Dale Jr. stayed on the track, allowing him to restart at the front of the grid. He was now on the lead lap, but nearly two miles behind Jeff Gordon.

At the restart, Dale Jr. got a good jump and pulled away, but began to complain of oil on the track in turn four. At first, everyone in the Bud pit area laughed, as it was almost always the driver fighting to stay on the lead lap who was first to report the tiniest debris or oil on the track, hoping NASCAR would throw a caution flag and allow him to catch up with the field. But after a few more laps, it was clear the driver wasn't imagining things.

"It fuckin' sucks out here," Dale Jr. spat. "There's oil everywhere!"

"We let NASCAR know," Norris told him. "Just watch what you're doing and be careful!"

"Oil all over the damn corner, right down in the groove" he answered. "They better listen to somebody before I wreck this damn thing!

"Oil on the track is a potentially dangerous situation at these speeds," he said with mock seriousness. "They're gonna get somebody hurt. What's the point? I'm gonna start thinking this is dangerous!"

To illustrate his point, or because he was pushing so hard to stay ahead of the leaders, Dale Jr. nearly lost it on lap 141, sliding sideways out of turn four before he managed to right the car.

"I guess NASCAR is a lot like my daddy on this deal," he said. "It ain't a good idea unless it's *their* idea."

Finally, with enough drivers corroborating Junior's claims, NASCAR threw the yellow flag on lap 145.

"Hell yeah!" said a relieved Dale Jr., now able to circle around to the back of the field.

"Way to get around 'em. You made up a lap," Norris said.

Now in 29th place, Tony Jr. encouraged his cousin.

"We can win this one from here," Tony Jr. said.

The pit crew rose to the occasion with their quickest stop of the season to date, completing their work in 13.79 seconds.

"Just be patient with me, guys," the driver answered. "It's much harder in the back than in the front."

"I got my cake. And I wanna eat it too," laughed Tony Jr.

"Me too, but I don't wanna get messed up. I don't wanna get caught up going for a win," Dale Jr. replied. "What we wanna concentrate on is twelfth place or better."

This was a reflection of Junior's view of racing for points rather than wins. The championship means so much prestige and cash, it often takes precedence over gambling for a race victory. The team had come into the race on a hot streak, climbing 14 positions to 12th place in the standings.

In Junior's way of thinking, finishing in the same spot (or better) as their points position would help them in the overall standings.

With 100 laps to go, Junior watched as his teammate Waltrip crashed hard.

"Oh, shit!" Junior exclaimed.

"What happened?" Tony Jr. asked.

"He just got loose," Dale Jr. said.

"I wanna stay out. Leave me alone," Dale Jr. said. "Lemme know about Michael, please."

"We'll let ya know on Michael, but let's get gas real quick," Tony Jr. said. "Now you can race as hard as you wanna go. We would have been in trouble on fuel otherwise. We would have been a few laps short if we don't stop."

"They didn't cut off the roof, so that's good," Earnhardt Jr. said. "He's a big boy so it must take awhile to get him out of the car."

Tony Jr. assured him Waltrip appeared to be uninjured.

If driving a race car can be considered art, Dale Jr. soon created an instant masterpiece, taking his Chevy high and low, passing anything in his way in the next 30 laps.

"Uh, Dale Jr., I know you wanted to finish twelfth," Norris deadpanned, "but I think I'm gonna raise that bar now, babe. That's twelfth place there right in front of you."

"Hell *yeah!*" Junior yelled as he sailed by Sterling Marlin with a daring pass. "Look at me goin' by! We got us the high side workin.' We're vers-a-tiiile!"

"Go get 'em!," Tony Jr. cheered.

"OK, my car is neutral now, so don't fuck with it," Dale Jr. replied.

Since the team made the extra stop for a splash of fuel, they stayed out as the rest of the leaders began the next round of stops. As the others peeled off, Dale Jr. stayed at speed, earning bonus points for leading the race on lap 200.

After their stop on lap 202, Dale Jr. asked for the fuel status.

"Can we make it now?" he asked.

"Ten-four," Tony Jr. replied.

"You guys ask a lot of me," Dale Jr. chuckled.

With 30 laps remaining, Dale Jr. reached fifth place, cursing and yelling at the lapped cars. Three laps later, Junior grabbed fourth.

"That's fourth-place hero shit right there, boys!" Norris proclaimed.

The yellow came out on lap 224, leaving Junior behind only Tony Stewart, Jeff Gordon, and Rusty Wallace.

"Tell me something," Dale Jr. said to his cousin. "Make a decision and we'll stand behind it."

"I'm doing what the 20 [Stewart] and 24 [Gordon] are doing," Tony Jr. replied.

"I want two tires and then I'll drive the shit out of it," the driver said.

"We're staying out," Tony Jr. said emphatically.

"That's just as good for me," Dale Jr. answered.

When the green flag went into the air with 18 laps to go, Dale Jr. wasted no time passing Stewart for third. He then made another bold move, going to the outside of Wallace and Gordon to make it three wide for the lead.

But with worn tires, the pass was simply too daring, and Junior slid high into the marbles. With no traction, he had no choice but to ease off behind the leaders.

Wallace beat Gordon to the finish for his first win of the year, then celebrated his victory with a salute to his late friend by taking a victory lap holding a black No. 3 flag.

As Dale Jr. pulled onto pit lane, he was met by his crew, happy for such a good result after a long and trying weekend. The strong finish meant they had gained two more spots in the standings.

"It would have been a miracle if we would have won this race," Tony Jr. laughed as Dale Jr. helped push the car to the garage. "You wanna talk about overcoming adversity? We crashed one, we blew up a motor, and then we ran it outta gas. We worked hard for that one."

The two were sharing such a great moment, I was hesitant to remind Dale Jr. he was required to go to the media center as a top-three finisher.

"Ha! Hell yeah," he laughed. "It's been so long I forgot all about that."

In the media center, Dale Jr. didn't show any ill effects of the weekend.

"I'm real happy with that," he started. "We had a race-wining car, but we ran out of gas and had to fight back the rest of the day. I wheeled 'er hard all day. We have been waiting for something like this to have a reason to celebrate a little bit.

"We had a horrible weekend," he continued, then listed all of the mishaps. "It was just a mess. We didn't know what were going to do in the race, and sure enough, we ran out of gas. I thought it just wasn't worth trying there after awhile. But you stay after it and stay after it and eventually we got back on the lead lap."

How did he feel after Friday's wreck?

"I stretched my neck a little bit when I hit the wall, and it got sore real early in the race. I thought to myself, 'Man, this is not going to be too much fun,' but we had enough cautions where I could ride it out."

Finally, someone asked his thoughts on his father's birthday.

"I didn't know how I would feel on his birthday. It was emotional for me. But it made me feel good. I guess I'd like to celebrate it a bit. Seeing Hank [Parker Jr., one of Junior's best friends] win yesterday [in the Busch Series race] really gave me an incentive. It inspired me to try and do something really good," he smiled.

"Today would have been my dad's fiftieth birthday, so it's kinda cool. It's made me feel even better to run so good. I want to celebrate with a couple of beers back home, and I think we'll pour one out on the ground for him like they do in all the rap videos."

chapter 22

sandstorm in turn two

Richmond, Virginia

"**I**just remember that, at that time, I could have quit driving race cars for the rest of my life and been happy," Dale Jr. said, recalling his fondest memories of winning the Winston All-Star Race in 2000. "At that very moment, I felt like I would never enjoy another win as much. That race is my proudest moment as a driver."

Dale Jr. was in the Speedway Club, high above Lowe's Motor Speedway, helping promote the 2001 edition of the Winston, less than three weeks away.

"The way it happened was cool inside the car. I've watched it a hundred times, and it's just as cool. It will always be special to me. [I've had] nothing close to that feeling since . . .. The last ten laps is like being thrown to the wolves. It's highly intense. I think it's the most fun race no matter what they pay to win because it's all-out, no hanging back, no messin' around. It would be just as fun to win if they gave you ten bucks."

In 2000, Dale Jr. was the first rookie to earn a starting spot in the no-points, all-glory race. The format, a series of short segments leading to the final 10-lap dash, suited the aggressive style of the team and driver, and the Eurys developed a unique setup that was very fast on short runs. After bouncing off the turn-four wall and overcoming several pit-lane mistakes, Dale Jr. drove the Bud car like a madman, passing Dale Jarrett on the outside with less than two laps to go. The win paid more than half a million dollars, but the post-race celebration meant more to Junior than any amount of money.

"The winner's circle last year was the happiest time I think I ever spent with my dad. I felt like I had really done something, you know, something like a 'Hell yeah, I did this!' and I knew Dad felt the same way. He said 'This is cool,' and he didn't have a plane to jump on, so we threw beer around on each other and jumped around and hollered and made fools of ourselves on national television. It was a lot of fun, a time I'll never forget."

The questions turned to more recent, painful memories.

"I get sad less often," he said about his state of mind.

Earlier in the week, an emergency medical technician contradicted NASCAR's claim of a broken seatbelt, saying he had released the belts when he reached the car. The autopsy results had also been released, listing several injuries (namely collarbone and hip abrasions), which some experts suggested were inconsistent with a broken seatbelt. When asked about NASCAR's investigation into his father's crash, Dale Jr. replied emphatically.

"I know in my heart what I feel happened and I feel very comfortable with that," he said. "I don't lose any sleep over it. I know NASCAR is doing what it can do and doing the right things as far as they feel, but my faith is more behind Mike Helton than anything else . . . .. I've got one-hundred-percent confidence in Mike to make the right decisions, do the right thing, and handle the situation the way it needs to be handled.

"I know what the facts are. I am not going to tell you what I know, don't ask me what I know, but I know what the facts are. I am not sitting here waiting for an answer like you all are. And I'm OK with it."

When pressed further on the issue, Dale Jr. relented.

"I believe the belt broke, and I will always believe that."

The focus shifted to the future as he was asked about NASCAR making it mandatory to wear a HANS or Hutchens Device.

"I think it should come down to preferences," he said. "Drivers shouldn't be mandated to wear this or do that. We've been racing for years and years and years with what I feel is adequate equipment."

Not wanting to sound completely callous about safety issues, he described how his approach to safety had changed.

"When I get in the car, I look at how my seatbelts are mounted, and I look to see if maybe it's rubbing on a sharp surface," he said. "I look and see if it's outdated and make sure they bolt the seat in and use the right grade bolt or the right size washers and just make sure nothing is in a bind or pinch or anything like that. Something like that is going to open your eyes to these things."

What would he think about winning the Winston a second year in a row?

After a pause for effect, he said, "I'm down for that."

Next up was the race weekend at Richmond, Virginia, where the three-quarter-mile track was a favorite for Dale Jr. He won twice there in the Busch Series and was the defending race winner in the Cup ranks. The track offered close racing with multiple grooves, and it was a night race, which Junior preferred. As a night owl, he loved racing under the lights, and it meant getting home in time to enjoy a Sunday off with his buddies at the house or on the lake. What was not to like?

After the third place at Fontana, the team's confidence was back, and with that confidence returned fun at the racetrack.

Starting 14th, Dale Jr. spent the first half of the 400-lap race struggling to keep up, nearly going a lap down to Rusty Wallace before a fortuitous yellow flag allowed them to remain on the lead lap. When the caution flag fell on lap 197, for fluid on the track caused by a blown engine, team and driver began a comedic give-and-take.

"I love these tires this year," Dale Jr. reported. "They're like the tires they used a long time ago. We can really race with these tires."

"If ya love 'em, why aren't ya up front?" teased Danny Earnhardt, normally a quiet member of the pit crew.

"How do your gauges look?" asked Jeff Clark, the engine tuner, concerned about the oil and water temperatures.

"Nice," Junior replied. "They're silver with nice red needles on 'em."

The caution, initially expected to be a quick one, was extended when safety crews poured too much Speedy Dry on the track. Similar to kitty litter, the substance soaks up oil and other liquids but must be swept away before the race can continue. During the delay, Dale Jr.'s mind wandered.

". . . and six hours later, your winner is Ricky Rudd, after 200 laps of caution!" Dale Jr. announced, showing a knack for commentary that might serve him well when his driving career is over.

"It's the slowest and closest race ever at Richmond!" answered Norris, getting into the spirit. "No one could get away from anyone else at 50 miles per hour!"

The trucks vacuuming the Speedy Dry created a large cloud of dust.

"*Sandstorm!*" Dale Jr. yelled with mock alarm. "Sandstorm in turn two! Sandstorm!"

The green flag finally appeared on lap 215, ending 18 laps of caution. The racing lasted only two laps before a multicar crash on the front straight created a chaotic and smoky scene. Unable to see down the track, Dale Jr. stuck to the rear bumper of Bill Elliott's car.

"If Bill was gonna hit anything, damn sure I was gonna hit something!" Junior laughed before referring to a decal on the back of Elliott's car that read "Your Friendly Dodge Dealer." "My Dodge dealer is one friendly SOB to help me through there."

Less than 20 laps later, Dale Jr. threw the car sideways toward the inside wall as Elliott and Michael Waltrip crashed immediately in front of him.

"Helluva job!" Pops Eury yelled.

"That was like a bomb went off in front of me!" said a breathless driver. "I saw the roof of Elliott's car. We were just racing along nicely and he ran into the back of Michael. I about spun into the inside wall there. I thought I was going to hit it."

"Me too," Tony Jr. laughed. "I thought you was coming to see me."

For the next 100 laps, Dale Jr. climbed from 16th place, passing cars until only the top four were ahead of him. But, having abused his tires and brakes to get to fifth place, he dropped to seventh in the closing laps.

A multicar crash with less than 10 laps remaining prompted NASCAR to throw a red flag to prevent the race from ending under a caution flag. (The current green/white/checkered rules didn't reach the Cup Series until 2004.) Stopping the cars on the backstretch on lap 394 allowed crews to clean the track before a final frantic dash to the finish.

"C'mon, NASCAR," Dale Jr. yelled during the stoppage. "Let's go! Let's *gooo!*"

After the cars restarted, the green flag was delayed, leaving only three laps of racing to the finish. Concerned that his tires had cooled too much under the red flag, Junior hung back on the restart to finish seventh as Tony Stewart won the Pontiac Excitement 400. Stewart was followed by his Bristol nemesis, Jeff Gordon. Wallace was third, ahead of Steve Park.

"We almost had a fast enough car to win the thing, but we weren't as good on long runs," Junior said on pit lane. "With a little over a hundred to go, they made some changes and then the car was really loose. I like a loose car because it's fast, but if you're not careful, it'll try to spin out every lap."

Junior explained his reason for hanging back on the final restart.

"I wanted to just have some space to hold onto my position," he said. "But the car was actually pretty good so I suppose if I had been more aggressive we might have been able to catch the 10 car [Johnny Benson]. With two to go, though, the only way you're gonna get around somebody is to really hit 'em, and I had already run into Johnny earlier. That's a good finish so we can enjoy a weekend off before the Winston."

chapter 23

did i look pretty?

Concord, North Carolina

During the weekend off, Dale Jr. and I took advantage of an invitation from Michael Waltrip and his wife Buffy to join them at an NBA playoff game between the Charlotte Hornets and Milwaukee Bucks. With front-row seats along the baseline, Dale Jr. was interviewed by TNT's Cheryl Miller, then received more onscreen time when the Hornets' Jamal Mashburn wasn't able to reach a loose ball as it knocked over our drinks like bowling pins, soaking Junior with cold Budweiser.

A few days later, we flew to Los Angeles for the E3 Electronic Entertainment Expo. A hardcore computer gamer, Dale Jr. had a sponsorship deal with Interact, a company that made inexpensive steering wheels for video games. As their guests, we were allowed sneak previews of several games, including "Rogue Spear" and "Soldier of Fortune 2." Dale Jr. also received a top-secret glimpse of Microsoft's Xbox gaming console six months before it was released. Several of its designers were big Dale Jr. fans.

After a skateboard exhibition inside the cavernous hall, Junior was also able to sit down with Tony Hawk, the skateboarding legend with a very successful series of video games. Hawk impressed us with his seemingly effortless charisma and laidback demeanor. Because of a NASCAR license with EA Sports involving all of the Cup drivers, Junior was unable to lend his name to a game as Hawk had done, but was happy to spend a few moments with an athlete who was also a successful businessman.

With so much focus on safety since Earnhardt's death, a new idea was thrust into the limelight at Lowe's Motor Speedway before the Winston All-Star Race. Track president Humpy Wheeler introduced what became known as the Humpy Bumper, an energy-absorbing bumper designed to lessen the impact on a driver in case of a head-on crash. While Wheeler generated considerable attention developing and testing the bumper, it was never seriously considered by NASCAR, which was conducting its own driver-safety studies.

At the track, fans continued to present Dale Jr. with Dale Earnhardt memorabilia. While he was continually gracious, he struggled behind the scenes with many of the items given to him, including a meticulously prepared scrapbook with news clippings reporting his father's death.

"What do I do with this?" he asked, shaking his head. "How am I supposed to feel? It's tough. Man, it's tough."

He was also confused by fans who wanted him to have their most prized Big E items, such as old Goodwrench hats and well-worn T-shirts.

"I can't understand why they want me to have it," he said. "I mean, if it's their favorite item, why would they want to give it to me? Don't they want to keep it themselves?"

Dale Jr. did find comfort in hearing from others who had lost their fathers at a young age. Junior would listen intently, asking questions of friends or fans of a similar age who shared their loss. He seemed determined to understand the many emotions that coursed through him.

The Winston All-Star Race marked the first of two weekends of racing only a few miles from Mooresville. For the teams, it was a home game, a rare opportunity to sleep in their own beds. Because nearly all of the teams are located within a 50-mile radius of the track, it also meant family and friends could easily watch the action in person.

The Winston is as much a party as it is a race, and as the sun went down the excitement built. Unlike the usual driver-only introductions, the Winston also focused the spotlight on the crew members. Introduced en masse amid swirling smoke and fireworks, Tony Eury Sr. led the Budweiser team through the giant stage doors, striding forward with three fingers held aloft, their hats turned backward, Dale Jr.–style. As they walked to the race car, lightning bolts flashed through the sky, a hint of what was to come. Behind the crew, Dale Jr. was introduced, wearing a white uniform with red sleeves and the MLB All-Star logo on the back, matching the car's white paint scheme with red numerals.

Rather than the grid on pit lane, the cars were lined up along the front stretch where the fans could get a good look before the race began.

Instead of a 43-car field, the event started only 21 entrants—all recent race winners or former champions—for 70 laps of action. There would be two 30-lap segments divided by a break, then the final 10-lap dash for the winner's purse of $500,000.

Dale Jr. rolled toward the green flag from the inside of the eighth row. As the 21 monsters began to accelerate, a sudden burst of rain fell on turn one. With cold tires on a suddenly wet track, one car after another spun or slid into the wall as if the track was covered in petroleum jelly. Chaos on ice!

Kevin Harvick, Jeff Gordon, Michael Waltrip, and Jeff Burton all sustained major damage; Dale Jr. slid through sideways but unscathed.

"Whoa, man, we missed that one!" he yelled as he slowed on the backstretch. "It was so wet you wouldn't believe it. Everybody was just wheelin' it . . . sliding and turning back and forth. That was some *crazy* shit! If that's what it's like dirt racin', then that's all right with me. Slidin' and hangin' on, I'm down with that! Nobody was hooked up there, every last one of us.

"Hey, Tony Jr., did you see me on TV?" Earnhardt Jr. asked. "Did I look pretty?"

"Yeah, man, you looked *real* professional," Tony Jr. replied with a big laugh.

"Crazy, man. Every damn last one of us," Junior said, pulling the car down pit lane as NASCAR stopped the race. "I knew it was going to be slick, so I shifted to second gear early at the start. We chugged along. Park was beside us and then he disappeared."

Because the Winston was a non-points race, NASCAR made the unprecedented decision to allow the teams whose cars were damaged to pull out a backup car. The Harvick, Gordon, Burton, and Waltrip crews rolled their second machines out of the haulers.

Watching a replay of the start, Dale Jr. told the live television audience, "It was the craziest thing I ever saw! Everybody was slidin.' I was just trying to hang on to mine. Luckily nobody came down across the track and hit us."

After a lengthy delay to dry the track, NASCAR brought the cars back for a complete restart, only to see the precipitation return.

"Don't let 'em throw the green flag here. It'll happen all over again," Junior yelled, turning to heavy sarcasm as the cars crawled around behind the pace car. "Let me explain it to ya: when it's raining, the ground gets wet, OK?"

NASCAR waved off the start, and the cars came to pit lane for another delay.

The clock inched past 11:30 p.m. as the field lined up two-by-two for the rerestart, two and half hours after the initial green flag.

"Dale Jr., you got your adrenaline back?" Norris asked.

"Hell yeah. I'm young. I got plenty," he replied.

Dale Jr. climbed as high as eighth place until lap 18, when he tried to go three-wide into turn one only to get into the marbles and nearly hit the wall. At the end of first segment, the Bud car had dropped to its original starting spot, 15th place.

"It's weird. Ninety percent of the corner, it's fine, then it's loose," Dale Jr. reported.

Well past midnight, the second 30-lap segment began and Dale Jr. held his position for five laps before complaining the car was "loose everywhere," followed by a series of vivid expletives in no particular order.

"I got a really, really bad vibration," he said. "Something's really wrong. I'm gonna wreck."

By lap 43, Dale Jr. dropped back to 20th in an act of self-preservation.

"Just take care of it," Norris told him. "No sense trying to catch anyone."

At the end of the second segment, Junior tried to describe the trouble he was having.

"I'm afraid it's in a brake rotor or something," he said. "The whole car jumps when I hit the pedal. Really, really, really, loose in . . . really, really, really loose off."

After a stop for major adjustments, Dale Jr. started the final 10-lap segment in a familiar 15th place. Dale Jr. displayed faith in his team on the restart as he bravely carried what had been an evil race car past several cars into 11th place.

With five laps remaining, Dale Jr. grabbed 10th and then ninth. With two laps to go, he was eighth, turning the quickest lap of any car. Then he passed Todd Bodine on the final circuit to finish seventh.

"That race was a total blast!" Junior proclaimed as he crossed the finish line. "The fans were going crazy. I think all of the races should be like that. Line us up right out there by the fans and crank it up!"

"Good comeback, driver." Tony Jr. told him. "You finished seventh."

"No shit?" he replied. "Who won?"

"Jeff Gordon. In his backup car," Tony Jr. said.

"The last ten laps felt like old times out there," Dale Jr. said. "We were great, easily the fastest car on the track, and I could pass cars on the outside line. Until then, I was just doing all I could to keep it off the fence. The car would roll over so hard in the corners my eyes hurt from trying to see my way around. It felt like I was looking out the passenger-side window. I'm worn out."

When a night owl like Dale Jr. is tired, you know it's been a long night at the track.

chapter 24

business

Concord, North Carolina

The week began with a surprise when beer executives in St. Louis learned, via a news release, their star driver would replace Joe Nemechek in Saturday's Busch Series race, one day before the Coca-Cola 600, the longest race on the NASCAR tour.

Nemechek had broken a shoulder blade while testing at Dover, and called Dale Jr. to ask if he would drive for his small, family-owned team in the Busch race at Lowe's Motor Speedway. Junior quickly said yes, without consulting anyone at DEI or Anheuser-Busch, assuming it's easier to ask forgiveness than permission.

The Anheuser-Busch contract with DEI restricted Dale Jr. from racing outside of the Bud car without expressed permission. The reasons were simple. They did not want to see their spokesman representing other sponsors or brands beyond those of the No. 8 team. The more he appeared in colors other than Bud red, the more it weakened the equity they had spent tens of millions of dollars developing. They also did not want to lose him if he were injured (or worse) while driving someone else's race car.

By Tuesday, one of Junior's custom seats had been fitted in Nemechek's chassis. Without an agent or manager to negotiate for him, he had happily accepted a relatively small share of the team's winnings for the weekend. He had never negotiated a driver contract outside of his family, and even that was a handshake deal he had made with his father. He had trusted his father completely with all of his business dealings—but now he needed to learn a lot very quickly.

But this was not about money. Junior agreed to drive as a favor for a fellow driver. It also represented a chance to have fun in a race car without the pressure of sponsors or point standings. He loved racing in the Busch Series and looked forward to returning for the first time since 1999. Junior was adamant about driving Nemechek's No. 87 car, so DEI and Anheuser-Busch reluctantly signed off on the deal.

The night before the Busch race, Dale Jr. made an appearance on the QVC shopping network as part of his agreement with Action Performance, the company that produced much of the Earnhardt-licensed memorabilia. As a tie-in with the MLB All-Star race car, his two-hour appearance on the show "For Race Fans Only" was broadcast live from Fieldcrest Cannon Stadium in Kannapolis. The year before, the minor league team that played there was renamed the Kannapolis Intimidators when Dale Earnhardt bought a small share of his hometown franchise.

Amid baseball-themed tchotchkes, one segment of the program opened with a hideous porcelain sculpture of his father. Though he remained cool on the air, Junior was furious offstage to have been surprised by such an awful item. He demanded to be notified in advance of the items being featured during his time on air.

Dale Jr.'s history with QVC was another example of his inexperience in the business world. He appeared on the network several times a year, and after each show the QVC staff would regale him with tales of record sales, eventually topping $1 million per hour. He struggled to comprehend how he could generate such massive numbers, yet see such a small portion of the proceeds. He understood the royalties he received, but I struggled to explain basic retail principles such as overhead and inventory in a way he could grasp. Yet, despite this lack of acumen when it came to the specifics, he showed the street smarts of his father by later demanding (and receiving) substantial fees for his QVC appearances.

Junior hoped driving Nemechek's car would be fun and relaxing, but it turned out to be anything but. After qualifying a disappointing 33rd, Junior struggled mightily with the unfamiliar car during the race, falling two laps behind by lap 100. He was embarrassed to finish 29th, three laps behind winner Jeff Green.

Since the 600 didn't begin until late afternoon the following day, we piled into one of Junior's vehicles and headed to Winston-Salem to see one of his favorite bands, Tenacious D. At that time, comedic actor Jack

Black's band was known primarily in the underground for infrequent TV appearances and a network of vast Internet downloads. As someone who surfed the 'net many hours at a time, Junior had developed a large collection of their music and comedy, and was always happy to share with anyone who would listen.

The show was the highlight of the weekend for Junior, who watched from a private nook beside the stage. When we were brought backstage, Jack Black was predictably funny, as was his bandmate Kyle Gass, but neither registered a flicker of recognition when introduced to Dale Jr.

The Coca-Cola 600 marked the two-year anniversary of Junior's debut in the Cup Series. In 1999, there had been so much prerace hype and media coverage that Junior nearly gave himself an ulcer with worry that he would disappoint millions if he wasn't able to qualify for the race. He managed to hold his emotions long enough to qualify 8th and then finish 16th in a successful debut.

The 600 is the largest event for what is known as "The Coca-Cola Racing Family." Rather than sponsor a single driver, as Pepsi had done with Jeff Gordon, the Coke brand chose to be an associate sponsor for a number of drivers, giving the brand more opportunities to be on a winning team each week. The brand had a long relationship with Earnhardt and DEI, and each DEI driver was part of the family. Coke had also been the primary sponsor for Dale Jr. when he raced against his father for the first time in the exhibition race at Motegi, Japan, in 1998. Since that time, they continued to hold a personal services contract with Junior.

Because of Budweiser's primary sponsorship beginning in 1999, Junior was no longer able to participate publicly in any of Coca-Cola's promotions or advertising, but he was permitted to make several appearances for the brand each year. (Even though Coke is a soft drink, Budweiser considers them a direct competitor for what they call "share of stomach.")

Prior to driver introductions for the 600, large flatbed trucks circled the track, each with a massive banner featuring the name and photo of a Coke Family driver. As the trucks streamed past, Dale Jr. looked for his name.

"I'm a Coke driver," he joked as his name and likeness was nowhere to be found. "What am I, the ugly cousin?"

He was relaxed as he climbed in the car. The team learned several things near the end of the Winston the week before and had the fastest car in the final 10 laps of that race. They were also racing DEI chassis No. 005, which had carried Junior to his maiden win in Texas and was spectacular in the previous year's 600, winning the pole and leading 175 laps before fading at the end, finishing fourth.

On the pace laps, Junior had an unexpected hazard.

"Wassup, guys?" he asked, echoing a popular Bud ad from a few years back. "You guys have fun tonight, all right? Whoa! Somebody just threw a beer bottle at the car!"

"Yeah, NASCAR is talking about it," said Norris.

"It musta been Sterling Marlin that threw it," Junior laughed, " 'coz it was a damn Coors Light."

The race was slowed after two laps when Tony Stewart spun out after starting at the back of the field. Stewart had missed the mandatory drivers' meeting because he was in Indianapolis, where he finished sixth in the rain-delayed Indy 500. He then flew to Charlotte in an attempt to complete 1,100 racing miles in one day. Stewart's helicopter landed in the infield grass just a short time before the green flag.

"I am just chillin'. . . . chillin'. . . ." Junior described during the caution. "Just waiting for the chance to pounce and just take this damn race over. I want 'em all to think we're just dead and gone back here, but then we'll spring to life and show 'em all that we're far from dead!"

As he started the third lap, Junior noticed the crowd, 170,000 strong, waving three fingers in honor of his father.

"That lap-three deal is pretty cool, huh?" he mused.

The first pit stop on lap 52 foreshadowed the rest of the evening when Junior was forced to back up because he was blocked by the car in the stall ahead.

"I thought I needed to back up," he said about the confusion. "Then I thought, 'Damn, I don't,' but by then I couldn't get the car outta reverse."

Frustrated with the changes to the car and having lost so many positions in the delayed pit stop, his mood turned.

"Are we gonna talk about what we changed," he yelled at Tony Jr. "Or are we gonna be separate all night?"

With the sun beginning to set, the track's grip level began to change. With each inch of shade crawling across the track in turns one and two, the Bud car handled worse. Junior dropped to 27th place by lap 73.

"Do all ya can. Just hang on," encouraged Norris as the driver became more agitated.

"I can't hang on! I'll go a lap down!" he answered.

Just past lap 100 of the 400-lap grind, Dale Jr. fell off the lead lap and dropped to 36th.

"I can't drive the car like this all night now!" Junior hollered.

"Babe, we're doin' all we can do," replied Eury Sr.

"Look, I'm coming in, and y'all are gonna fix this race car," Junior answered.

During their rookie season, the team and driver struggled during races to improve an ill-handling car, often finishing with heated arguments. Now, they seemed committed to dig in and work together to make the car better.

"Just because the car is running like shit, we don't have to go to shit ourselves," Pops Eury instructed the crew in a less than subtle manner.

After a series of pit stops, the car began responding as darkness covered the track.

Although they dropped two laps behind the leaders by lap 252, Junior began gaining positions, climbing to 29th place. Their teeth-grinding frustration was beginning to ease.

"I'm hammer down!" the driver reported as the race entered its final 100 miles.

Jeff Burton won the 600, providing a bright spot in what had been a poor season for Burton and his Roush team. Harvick was second, while the ironman Stewart completed his 1,100-mile marathon with a third-place finish.

By the checkered flag, Dale Jr. had climbed to 25th. It wasn't a good result, but the team seemed encouraged about fighting through their troubles and improving as the race went on.

"That was rough," Dale Jr. said. "The car didn't drive too good, but we finally got it close about three-fourths of the way through, and we were able to keep pace with the leaders."

chapter 25

school of hard knocks

Dover, Delaware

In his monthly column for NASCAR.com that appeared in the days before the race at Dover, Dale Jr. took readers on a nostalgic trip to some of his favorite moments growing up around the NASCAR circuit. He was too young to remember any of the races from the 1970s, but a friend had given him a stack of tapes—in the now-defunct Beta format—with race footage from several decades. Junior devoured the footage, watching the tapes over and over again. (The tapes also provided the inspiration and raw material for his 2006 TV series, "Back in the Day with Dale Jr.")

"I remember riding down the road in my mom's 1978 Monte Carlo, Fleetwood Mac playing on the radio, and nothing mattered but ice cream," he mused near the end of the column.

"I will always miss those times as they fade away. Twenty years from now, these will be the good ol' days. 'I remember when I was only 26 and we ran only 38 races a year,'" he wrote before signing off "from the school of hard knocks, Dale Jr."

Junior's fond memories of his mom, Brenda, are primarily from his youngest years. Struggling to make it as a divorced, single mom with two children, she was forced to leave her kids (both under age 10) behind when her small and aged millhouse burned to the ground. With no money, Brenda moved to Virginia to stay with her extended family while Kelley and Dale Jr. moved in with their dad and his new young wife, Teresa. Brenda later remarried, but was able to see Dale Jr. and Kelley only several times a year. When Kelley became pregnant in 2000, it provided the perfect excuse for Dale Jr. to spend some of his newfound wealth to move his mom and stepdad to a new home in Mooresville. (Since then, their relationship has become close, and his mom is one of his trusted employees at JR Motorsports.)

The team had struggled in both previous Cup races at the one-mile, high-banked Dover Downs Speedway, and they hoped to regain some of the confidence and momentum they seemingly lost for much of the 600.

When rain washed away the Cup qualifying session, NASCAR used the current owners point standings to grid the starting lineup, which placed Dale Jr. 11th. (Junior was 10th in the driver standings, one spot ahead of Harvick. But when adding his father's finish in the 500, the No. 29 Richard Childress Racing team was slightly ahead of the No. 8 in owners points.)

Jeff Gordon took advantage of his front-row starting position to rocket away, putting much of the field a lap down before the halfway point of the race. Dale Jr. was able to hang on the lead lap, but wasn't thrilled with his car.

"This thing is sooooo fucking loose, y'all," he said on lap 80.

"This is a four-hundred-mile race," Tony Jr. replied. "There's a long way to go. We'll get it fixed."

"Do whatever you have to do, but I'm about ready to spin out," the driver answered.

Less than 100 laps later, almost as predicted, Dale Jr. spun the Bud car coming off of turn four. Miraculously, he was able to catch the car without making contact. Considering the heavy traffic, steep banking, and an inside wall, he was lucky to limit the damage to four wrecked Goodyears.

"Uh, I guess you can only go so fast at this place," he deadpanned. "I was just hangin' on until the rear end just stepped out on me."

"Can I get an 'attaboy' for that save?" Junior asked as he crawled toward the pits to receive four new tires.

"I'll give you a high five when you leave," replied Tony Jr., who jokingly extended his hand toward the race car as Dale Jr. pulled from the pit box.

Despite the spin, quick pit work meant the Bud team remained on the lead lap. The crew made major adjustments to the car, and the changes turned out to be correct, as Junior restarted in 15th with a much-improved car.

Making their last stop with less than 50 laps remaining, the team caught a break when the yellow flag came out several laps later. While many of the other cars in the top 10 made another stop during the caution period, the Bud team remained on-track, allowing Junior to restart in fifth place. Without much lapped traffic to contend with, and in relatively clean air, Dale Jr. continued his march, climbing to third position.

Gordon scored a dominating victory, leading 371 of the 400 laps, followed across the line by the DEI cars of Park and Dale Jr.

It was a happy driver who went to the media center as a top-three finisher.

"Things got a lot better after that spin!" he chuckled. "It somehow stayed off the wall, which was mostly luck. After that, we made some dramatic changes to correct the car, and it was great the rest of the day."

"It was fun," he said when asked about his charge from 15th to 3rd. "We had the best car there at the end, and we were even closing on the 24 car and Steve. We had a decent car all day, but we just couldn't get the track position. Gordon just ran off and left us, but from second place on back it was bumper-to-bumper. It makes it fun when you're running that close. Plus, if you're slightly better than the car in front of you, that's really fun."

"We're happy with anything in the top ten right now," he said, when told he was now in ninth place in the standings. "To have Steve Park up here with me makes us all happy. We're trying to run better than our points position each week, so finishing better than tenth was the goal. We just need to find a way to get Michael [Waltrip] up here at the front again. I think they're just a new team trying to gel. It took Park and his guys several years, and it's looking like the Bud guys and I are starting to gel as well, so we just need to give Michael's team a little time."

After finishing last at Dover, Waltrip was mired in 28th place in points, only 12 races after winning at Daytona. The victory was his only finish in the top 10, and the struggles at Dover meant the NAPA team's crew chief, Scott Eggleston, was fired less than 48 hours later. Despite Junior's plea to give the team more time, the decision by DEI management to fire Eggleston was an example of the pressure in Winston Cup to constantly perform. Less than four months after winning the biggest race in the sport, Eggleston was replaced by Steve Hmiel, DEI's technical director, on an interim basis.

chapter 26

every night is saturday night

Brooklyn, Michigan

"Every night is Saturday night at the dirt track," insisted Ken Schrader, although the calendar said it was Wednesday.

As the owner of I-55 Speedway in Pevely, Missouri, Schrader had invited Dale Jr. and Kenny Wallace to join him at the 1/3-mile dirt track outside of St. Louis, signing autographs for two hours before the late-model racing action began. We flew from North Carolina in Schrader's plane, dropping off our luggage at the local Drury Inn before heading to the track.

A sold-out crowd queued for signatures in a massive line despite the wicked heat and oppressive humidity.

"I gotta get psyched up," said the gregarious Wallace, laughing and yelling as he hopped out of the van. "I've gotta be KENNY WALLACE for two hours!"

Amid the procession, a diabetic woman collapsed and an ambulance was summoned. After the medics arrived, she refused to leave until she received her autographs, which were quickly procured.

While Schrader and Wallace raced in their own late-model stock cars, Junior relaxed in the small suite above the track, conducting an interview with a reporter from the *St. Louis Post-Dispatch*. Although the *Post-Dispatch* was the hometown paper for Anheuser-Busch, their sports staff had been lukewarm at best toward Dale Jr. while effusive in their coverage of Rusty

Wallace, who had grown up in St. Louis. That brief interview, however, helped lead to several major feature stories in the paper in successive years.

Following the races, Schrader demonstrated what he meant by his "Saturday night" comment, providing massive amounts of ice-cold Budweiser. Hours after the stadium lights had gone dark, several dozen of us laughed, drank, and told racing stories until an obscene hour of the morning when the Bud finally ran out. Unfortunately, each of us believed someone else was the designated driver. Somehow, 10 of us (a motley mix of stars and civilians) piled into a large van with an inebriated off-duty policeman at the wheel. He drove us slowly to the hotel and we tottered out, walking across the parking lot to a 24-hour diner. Only after walking back to the hotel lobby did we realize he had driven us to the wrong Drury Inn.

With scant sleep, it was a much quieter group that flew with Schrader Thursday afternoon, arriving in Jackson, Michigan, the nearest airstrip to Michigan International Speedway.

Going into the race, the team had a lot of momentum—Dale Jr. had gained 17 positions in the point standings in the previous seven races. In that span, only Tony Stewart had scored more points.

At the Michigan race the previous August, Dale Jr. set the track record for Winston Cup cars, winning the pole position with an average speed of more than 191 miles per hour. His brother Kerry had made his Winston Cup debut that weekend, making the Earnhardts the first father-and-two-son trio to start a Cup race in 40 years. Photos of the three Earnhardts, posing together before the race, now hung in Dale Jr.'s home.

After qualifying seventh on Friday, optimism grew in Saturday's first practice, where the Bud car was second quickest overall. It was then third quickest in the second session before a blown engine ended their day in a repeat of the engine woes suffered before the California race, a track nearly identical to Michigan. Jeff Clark and Pops Eury expressed concern for the race, but Dale Jr. expressed full confidence in the DEI engine builders.

On his way to the motorcoach lot, Junior stopped to sign autographs for nearly an hour. Large groups of fans lined the fence near the walkway between the garage and the private motorcoach lot, hollering for signatures as each driver and team owner walked past. Because the crowds seemed to be there no matter the time of day, we began calling them "waffle bellies," referring to the shape of the marks the chain-link fence left as they leaned forward each time a driver came near.

Away from the waffle bellies, Dale Jr. was still building intricate RC cars in the stillness of his coach each weekend. He was also watching a lot of movies. His favorite actor had long been Tom Hanks, and Hanks' film *Cast Away*, about a FedEx executive stranded on a remote island, resonated deeply, reflecting the isolation and loneliness Dale Jr. felt.

He also enjoyed Cameron Crowe's near-autobiographical film *Almost Famous*. Junior connected most with the character Russell Hammond, played by Billy Crudup. Hammond was a rock star, playing to huge crowds each night, but he too felt disconnected from the people around him.

When a reporter asked Junior if the mustache he had grown in recent weeks was in honor of his father, he was quick to answer.

"Nah, man. I grew it because of the character Russell Hammond in *Almost Famous*," he said, before adding a hilarious afterthought. "I don't care what anyone says, that's a handsome man."

The Michigan track is one of the widest on the tour, and the mustached Dale Jr. utilized every inch as he pointed his red car to the inside at the start, sweeping from seventh to fourth with a four-wide move before the first lap was complete.

During a yellow-flag period on lap 17, the team decided to follow the leader, Jeff Gordon. If the No. 24 pulled in, Junior would follow, but Gordon chose to remain on the track.

"That's cool. I didn't want to come in anyway," Junior laughed, happy with his car. "I have a minute here, so I'm just talking to you guys. The car is good. I like it. Don't change it at all."

When the race resumed, Junior swung low, aiming inside Gordon in turn four. The turbulent air from Gordon's car swirled around Junior's rear spoiler, drawing the Bud car into a lurid slide, but Junior never lifted his right foot, and he took the lead on lap 23.

"Man, that was cool as hell!" Junior said as soon as he pulled ahead of Gordon.

"Yeah, I thought the fans were gonna tear the seats out," said Norris.

The yellow came out on lap 40 as Dale Jr. and Gordon were pulling away.

"The track is gonna tighten up, don't y'all agree?" Junior asked.

When no reply was heard, Dale Jr. pushed the radio button on the steering wheel again.

"Did y'all hear that? Am I talking to myself? Can you hear me?" he asked.

"Ten-four," Pops Eury answered, but that wasn't good enough.

"Then tell me what I just said," Dale Jr. yelled. "Are those headsets working? Y'all aren't talking to me here. Are y'all nervous or something?"

The Eurys chose to take only fuel on the stop, which put Junior in the lead on the restart.

Gordon, aware of Junior's wild slide earlier, pulled close to the bumper of the Bud car, then quickly pulled to the outside in turn four, taking the air from Junior's spoiler again. As Junior fought for control, the crafty veteran went around and retook the lead.

"Wooooooo!" Junior hollered. "I was really loose there, and when Gordon was on the outside, it made it worse!"

"He didn't need to do that," said Norris from the spotter's stand.

"We're just as fast as them," Tony Jr. reminded his cousin. "Wait until we get ours right again and then you can do it to him."

Gordon and Junior pulled away easily from the field. After a pit stop on lap 82, Dale Jr. gunned the engine, sending billowing smoke from his rear tires.

"I'm worried about that motor," Clark told me as I waved away the smoke. "He really turns it hard."

As the race sped past the 100th lap, Junior dropped to fourth.

"The motor didn't seem like it ran that good," Junior explained. "It won't pull up in the draft."

"We might have the wrong gear selection," Tony Jr. said.

The concern was much more than gear selection when Junior suddenly slowed on lap 127.

"It's blown up!" Junior screamed. "Burnt another piston? Damn, is it out of fuel? I might be out of fuel."

As he rolled silently to the pits, the field sped past, dropping the No. 8 to 32nd place, one lap down.

"It sounded like a burnt piston," Dale Jr. said after the team had refueled the car. "It seems OK now. I'll stay out here."

It was the second time the car had run out of fuel this season, and the Bud crew hoped Dale Jr. could make a similar furious comeback like he had done in California.

Fighting to regain the lead lap, Dale Jr. radioed as he slowed on the backstretch on lap 170.

"It's blown," he said with finality. "Big time."

He pulled the smoking heap off the track and steered straight to the garage. After being one of the fastest cars all afternoon, a frustrated driver had very little to say to reporters after he climbed out.

"We ran outta gas, then burnt a piston," he told them tersely. "We'll go home and figure it out."

With his toughest competitor in the garage, Gordon easily won his second consecutive race. The win allowed Gordon to take over the points lead from Dale Jarrett, who finished 18th. The early retirement meant Dale Jr. finished 39th, his worst tally since the lap-one crash at Rockingham.

chapter 27

death sits a couple of rows back

Long Pond, Pennsylvania

A typical autograph session for Dale Jr. meant sitting at a table for at least two hours as a long line of people shuttled past quickly. After several years of the sessions, Dale Jr., dreaded the mind-numbing routine but did his best to at least seem somewhat interested. Sometimes a fan would say something surprising to keep his mood light.

During an appearance for Coca-Cola at Hershey Park in Hershey, Pennsylvania, a six-year-old girl told Dale Jr., "My dad likes Jimmy Spencer."

"What do you think?" Junior asked, knowing Spencer was a native of the area.

"I think he stinks," she replied, earning big laughs from Dale Jr.

We had killed time on the flight to Pennsylvania with several card games between us. After two games, Junior had trounced me soundly, and he laughed at me when I said I enjoyed playing.

"How the hell can you enjoy it when you lost?" he asked seriously a few minutes later.

His need to win extended from the race car to his video games and even to our shared love of music. I had a long history as a musician and paid my way through college working at a record store. Junior and I had an unofficial game of one-upmanship to be the first to find the newest artists with the latest and greatest songs.

Driving from the appearance to Pocono Raceway, Dale Jr. played a new song he had discovered, "Life on a Chain," from the debut CD by Pete Yorn. I had to admit it was a pretty damn good tune, and he hit "repeat" several times to rub it in. Score another win for Junior.

We stopped along the way to search for the latest issue of *Rolling Stone* magazine, which included a lengthy feature story on Dale Jr. written by contributing editor Touré. It was cool to spot the magazine with a sultry photo of Angelina Jolie on the cover, but we quickly turned past the babe to read the story.

It was the second major feature in the magazine for Dale Jr. In March 2000, Touré had been sent to North Carolina knowing very little about Junior and even less about NASCAR. Most of his major stories had been about hip-hop artists, but the writer and the racer became fast friends. After hours and hours of interviews, the first story generated a lot of interest and laid the groundwork for the MTV shows later in the year.

Junior had done several interviews since his father's death, but felt Touré would be best suited for him to discuss sensitive topics and emotions he hadn't shared with anyone else.

Junior had a good relationship with nearly all of the full-time NASCAR and sports media, but he believed their histories with his father, some dating to before he was born, meant they always saw him as Big E's son rather than his own man. *Rolling Stone* and Touré provided something altogether different. Dale Jr. felt more at ease because Touré had no such history, was close to his age, and shared many of the same interests in music and culture. The resulting interviews, conducted in the days after the California Speedway race in April, produced a story filled with raw emotions in which Junior explained how his complex and often difficult relationship with his dad had developed.

"He didn't say he loved me often, but he said it as soon as he got to the car [after Dale Jr.'s first win] in Texas. 'Good job, I love you. Get the fuck out of this car.' Our relationship was primo from then on out. We talked like equals almost. We had conversations that were a whole lot fuckin' cooler," he told Touré.

It was the first interview where he shared his state of mind immediately after his father's crash.

"I was really nervous. I did not like the fact of not knowing. That was the worst part. Still . . . .." He pauses and is silent for awhile, the words are hard to say. "Him dying hadn't crossed my mind at that time. I just thought that it was maybe a little more serious than his past injuries had been."

He also answered questions about the risks involved in his occupation.

"I don't wanna die," he says. "But I *like* the fact that it's dangerous. It's treacherous. The possibility of hittin' the wall is exciting. That's some of the draw for me. I'm ballsy enough to do it. When I'm in the car, I feel macho, like I can bench press 350 pounds."

The story closed with a poignant quote, summarizing Junior's emotional roller coaster.

"Death is closer than it was," he says. "If I'm sittin' on a plane, death is sitting closer than it was before. It's a couple of rows back now."

The article was an unqualified hit in Junior's eyes, and, unlike a few months earlier, he no longer worried if his rough language and honesty would upset Budweiser or NASCAR.

To prepare for the race at Pocono Raceway, the Bud team tested there for several days in May. They had struggled at the strange track in 2000, destroying a car during testing and another in a practice crash during the race weekend. Each of the three corners is unique, which meant setting up the car for speed in one corner would hamper its handling in another. Developing a fast car meant finding a compromise through at least two of the three corners. The many laps of testing paid off right away, as Dale Jr. set the sixth best time in qualifying.

The following day, Dale Jr. was second quickest in Happy Hour, and the car was consistently fast on longer runs. The team was so pleased with the car, they ended their practice session early so Dale Jr. could strap into the No. 29 car for five laps. Before being chosen as Earnhardt's replacement, Kevin Harvick had committed to race for the championship in the Busch Series with AC-Delco sponsorship (the same sponsor that backed Dale Jr. during his championship seasons). Most weekends, the Cup and Busch races were held at the same track, which made it easy for Harvick to race both cars. But this weekend the Busch Series was racing at a new speedway in Nashville, which meant Harvick was forced to miss the final practice at Pocono. To help out, Dale Jr. agreed to drive the No. 29 for a few laps to make sure it was handling well. Harvick won the Busch race that evening in Nashville before flying to Pocono for Sunday's Cup race.

Race day was Father's Day, another difficult milestone for Junior to discuss. But, as usual, his demeanor didn't show the sorrow he must have felt.

"I'm telling him to conserve fuel now," Ty Norris said on the first pace lap Sunday afternoon.

Fuel conservation was often a key to race strategy at Pocono, and it was never too early to save fuel.

But conservation wasn't on the mind of the driver as he swept into second place by the second lap, then took the lead on lap 16. After he turned several scorching laps, Dale Jr. backed off slightly to conserve his car.

"All right, we know what this car is capable of, so let's just chill out now and just hang with these boys," he said. "Let's keep the leaders in sight until the end. The car is great . . . really good. But hang on, because I'm sure I'll think of something to start bitching about sometime soon."

During a pit stop on lap 48, Tony Jr. had trouble with one of the lug nuts on the left front tire, which allowed a number of cars to go by as the Bud car sat a few seconds longer than usual.

Restarting ninth, Junior found the going a little tougher but gradually worked his way into second place by the halfway point of the 200-lap race. Junior raced hard with Jarrett and Gordon, dicing for the lead with the top two drivers in the point standings. Ricky Rudd, Jarrett's teammate, joined the battle as the top four cars pulled away.

Fuel strategy soon took center stage for the Bud team, as they opted to make an extra stop for a splash of fuel during a caution on lap 123. Their fuel mileage had fallen short of the other leaders, and they used the opportunity to fill the tank. The strategy meant they could now go farther than most of the other leaders, but it also dropped Dale Jr. to 16th, the last car on the lead lap.

The strategy proved to be a disaster, as the top three pulled away on a clear track while Dale Jr. was stuck at the back of the field, fighting with slower lapped cars. Frustrated with a lack of progress, Tony Jr. decided to bring Dale Jr. back to pit lane on lap 155 for four tires and fuel. He hoped it would allow Junior to make up time on a clear track, gaining positions when the others pitted. But, the risky strategy put them one lap behind as Junior pulled out behind the leader Jarrett, who had yet to pit. Soon after the two crossed the start/finish line, the yellow flag came out, the worst scenario for the Bud strategy.

In the days before the current "free pass" rule (which freezes the running order immediately and allows the first car not on the lead lap to gain back a lap), the entire field would race back to the line to complete the lap. It often meant a frantic thrash as lapped cars tried desperately to pass the leader even as they approached a wreck. In certain circumstances, the leader would slow down, allowing a friend or teammate to regain a lap.

"Go hard!" Norris yelled. "You did not take the yellow flag!"

"Jarrett's spotter says he'll back off," Norris told Junior as the two cars screamed out of turn one.

"He's not backing off enough!" hollered a frantic Dale Jr. "Tell 'em *please* back off!"

"I'm talking to his spotter right here," Norris answered.

It was common for spotters to communicate with each other when their drivers were racing together on the track, but sometimes discussions between spotters don't translate into actions on the racetrack. Clearly, Jarrett had seen how fast Junior's car had been and didn't want to allow such a potent competitor the luxury of getting his lap back without earning it.

"He ain't backed off shit," Tony Sr. groused.

"Fucker," Junior yelled in frustration about the man who had graciously offered Junior a seat on his helicopter to travel to races such as Martinsville. "Two-faced SOB right there."

As the two crossed the line to take the yellow flag, Junior expressed his displeasure by slamming into the side of Jarrett's car.

"I wouldn't have let us back on the lead lap," Tony Jr. said, the voice of reason. "Why should he? We outran him on all of the earlier restarts."

"Just stay out there," Tony Sr. interjected. "He still has to pit. You'll either be at the tail end of the lead lap or the first car one lap down. Maybe he needs a wheel mark on the side of that car."

"I already got him," Junior replied. "Don't worry about it. I gave him a good wheel mark. I'm going to be right here. On the lead lap or one down, I'll be right here. He'll have to deal with us one way or another."

"There's forty to go, it ain't over yet," Tony Jr. reminded him.

"I *know* it ain't over!" Dale Jr. snapped. "But we have too good of a car to be in this position."

"Let's get serious now," Tony Sr. said. "No more talk. Let's just see how good we can do in these last laps."

On the restart, Dale Jr. was in front of the leaders on the track, but still nearly a full 2.5 miles behind. The team hoped another yellow flag would allow Junior to make up the distance. As the race restarted on lap 162, Dale Jr. used his aggression to pull away from the field.

As he streaked away, Junior was still angry, believing Jarrett's decision was rooted in a rivalry between their two small North Carolina hometowns.

"Jarrett . . . he's a Hickory guy," Junior said. "He'd do anything to get Kannapolis out of the way."

For 15 laps, Junior held off the leaders, but fresher tires began to make a difference, and Junior fell one lap down as Rudd, Jarrett, and Gordon went by.

"You did all you could," Pops told him.

Rudd led the final 24 laps to grab his first Winston Cup victory since September 1998. Gordon was second, followed by Jarrett in third. After a late stop for another splash of fuel, Dale Jr. finished 20th.

"If he [Jarrett] would have let me go, he would have had clear sailing. But, we're even. It's all forgotten now," Junior said, clearly still stewing from the incident.

"I'm frustrated. The finishing position doesn't show how kickass that car was today," he told the team. "We could really race with those guys."

The team had solved the mystery of going fast at Pocono, and led 11 laps to prove it, but could they close the deal sometime soon?

chapter 28

did he hit you?

Sonoma, California

The trip to Sonoma, California, for the Cup race at Sears Point Raceway was highly anticipated by many in the NASCAR garage because of perfect weather, beautiful vistas, and copious amounts of wine. However, the 10 turns of the undulating road course were anything but inviting for Dale Jr. Besides, he preferred beer.

Despite several days of coaching by Boris Said, the road-racing tutor for most Winston Cup drivers, Dale Jr. wasn't confident in his ability to get around the Sears Point track. The 24 Hours at Daytona experience helped, but it was difficult to translate what he learned in the Corvette to his lumbering Cup car.

To save some money, Dale Jr. chose not to have Shane Mueller drive his motorcoach to northern California. Staying with the team at their hotel, Junior drove himself crazy with boredom in his room. My role became social director, finding things to do and places to go when practice and qualifying ended.

Luckily, Junior could go nearly anywhere in Marin County and not be recognized or bothered. We had recently become friends with Robby Gordon's sisters, Beccy and Robyn, so we invited Beccy to join us as we headed to the mall. Wearing his Rage Against the Machine T-shirt and a ratty ball cap, Junior was able to relax and enjoy shopping for CDs and clothes.

The three of us piled into an old-fashioned photo booth, mugging and laughing for the camera before heading to the nearby cinema.

We were happy to tell the Gordon sisters about our new "waffle bellies" terminology, and Dale Jr. decided we needed to come up with an alternative to the term "pit lizards."

"That's old shit from my dad's days," he said. "We need something new."

After a long list of ideas, we knew we had our winner when someone suggested "helmet licker." It was funny, it was simple, and the multiple inferences could apply to a male or female, describing people whose sole mission was to be near famous athletes.

Since my role often included half-assed attempts at being Junior's security guard, we also decided my new title would be "Licker Blocker."

As we laughed about the new lingo, Beccy kidded Dale Jr., telling him his mustache made him look like the cartoon character Yosemite Sam. The mustache was gone within days.

Despite a fun and relaxing time off the track, the racing action was anything but. After a minor practice crash bent the Bud machine, Junior worked off his frustrations by crawling under the rear of car and helping the crew repair the damage. While he was certainly qualified to fix the bent bodywork, his efforts were more a product of his embarrassment at crashing so early in a practice session. By crawling under the car, he was out of the reach of reporters asking him about the incident. Besides, it couldn't hurt morale if he offered to help the crew repair the damage he had caused.

Junior started the race 37th, with a solitary goal: finish without a major incident.

The poor qualifying effort relegated the team to what was known as "Gilligan's Island," a separate pit area for the nine slowest-qualified teams. Located inside the final hairpin turn, it meant the team was stranded there once the race began. To mark their spot on the island, several team members ran to the Budweiser souvenir trailer and purchased Gilligan-style "bucket" hats for the entire crew. Tony Sr. was appointed the role of Skipper, while Dale Jr. was nominated as his Little Buddy, Gilligan. Not surprisingly, no one volunteered for the roles of Ginger and Mary Ann.

The twisting circuit kept Dale Jr. busy, shifting gears many times on each lap while braking and accelerating through right- and left-hand turns. The first yellow flag fell on lap 33, allowing Junior to stay on the lead lap.

"Stay ahead of that 24 car!" yelled Joey Meier, the secondary spotter.

"I'm just tryin' not to hit anything!" Junior replied as he took the caution flag.

Having dropped to 41st place, the team made several major changes on their stop, and when the race restarted, the adjustments proved helpful as Junior aggressively climbed to 27th.

"Can we pit now?" Dale Jr. asked when the second caution came out on lap 53.

"No," was Tony Jr's response.

"It was just a thought," said Dale Jr. "Hey, we're doing better than last year."

"I just remember a lot of cussing," Tony Jr. laughed.

"It's cool. We're all grown men here," Dale Jr. replied.

Because of the location of the flag stand on the circuit, Junior wasn't able to see the flagman on the restarts, so he asked for help.

"Green flag! Green flag!" Tony Jr. yelled. "Pass only on the right . . . or left . . . or wherever you can pass!"

"Can I pass on the inside or not?" Dale Jr. hollered.

"To be honest, I don't know," Tony Jr. replied. "That's why I said 'Pass 'em wherever!'"

"Now I'm really confused," said Gilligan/Dale Jr.

"It's always to the right," the Skipper/Eury Sr. interjected. "Even though it's a road course, it's still on the right. They don't change it. They try to not confuse you guys."

As Dale Jr. climbed into the top 20 on lap 71, Tony Jr. encouraged his cousin.

"I'm proud of you," he said. "You're doin' great, and there aren't any marks on the car."

That changed on the following lap when Junior was slammed by Ken Schrader in the tight hairpin. In a frantic bid to regain ground he had lost, Junior slid off the track at turn two on lap 73. The next lap, he spun off the course again.

"I think I set a record," Dale Jr. bragged. "I'm the first guy to spin out twice and not lose a lap. *Gotta* be a record."

One lap later, Dale Jr. apologized to his crew.

"I wasn't thinking . . . spinning out like that," he said. "I guess I just turned into an idiot for a few laps. But, now I've changed back into my real self."

"Yeah, way to go. Nice job," Tony Jr. said with sarcasm.

"Thanks. I was running too hard, trying to stay with those guys who had fresher tires," Dale Jr. replied in a surprisingly positive tone, considering his off-course excursions.

"Damn, the fan and these air vents inside this car are nice," he laughed, explaining why his mood was so good. "I've got air coming in the right side, I got a tube in my suit and fresh air down the back of the seat. This is crazy, but it's the best ever. It might even be too cold out here to have it on."

Junior pushed hard to the finish, avoiding a series of spinning cars to pass Stacy Compton on the last lap for 19th place.

"God a'mighty!" Dale Jr. laughed during the cool-down lap. "Those last couple o' laps were crazier than hell! I came into the hairpin coming to the white flag and it was just a wall of dirt and smoke and shit all over the place. I just tried to get through it."

"Good job today, Dale Jr.," said Jeff Clark. "A mere mortal would have given up."

Tony Stewart earned his first Winston Cup road-course victory, leading the Gordons, Robby and Jeff (no relation), across the finish line.

As Dale Jr. pulled toward the hauler, I had a cold bottle of water for him, but he asked for a towel instead. In the hot, dry weather, he would occasionally get a nosebleed after a race. Still in the car, he peeled off his goggles and helmet, then wiped away a small amount of blood.

"Here comes Stacy Compton!" he said urgently. "Stand right here, just in case!"

Just in case of *what* I was unsure, but I suspected the possibility of post-race aggression.

On his last-lap pass, Junior made contact with Compton, who dropped to 24th. Compton walked quickly to the No. 8 car as I braced to leap into action.

"What the hell was that?" Compton asked as he stuck his head inside the window. "I don't race you like that!"

"I didn't mean to get into you," Dale Jr. replied. "I was just holding my line!"

"Well, we don't race each other like that. That's bullshit!" Compton said. "We've always raced each other clean, and I'll remember that."

As Compton stormed off, Junior chuckled and began to unhook his seatbelts.

"Oh, no, here comes his little crew chief," he said to me. "Stay right there."

Enter Chad Knaus, Compton's rookie crew chief. Notebooks in hand, Knaus saw Dale Jr. with the bloodied towel.

"Did he hit you?" Knaus asked.

"Naw," Junior drawled, bracing for a tongue-lashing from the tightly wound crew chief.

"I wanted to say, 'Thank you,'" Knaus said, to our astonishment. "We need our driver to get up on the wheel, and if he's in your way, you just move his ass over! Thanks, man."

Climbing out of the car, Junior shook his head and laughed about the encounter. "That was . . . strange," he said.

chapter 29

the return

Daytona Beach, Florida

"I don't associate that with my dad," Dale Jr. said, pointing as the helicopter flew us over his father's private gravesite a few weeks after his death. "I won't visit it much. I feel much closer to him in turn four at Daytona. That's much more a part of his life . . . and the lives of my family."

The Pepsi 400 marked the return to Daytona International Speedway. Rather than wait until the start of the race weekend to confront the track where his father perished, Dale Jr. came to Daytona early to relax with a number of his close friends.

Tuesday afternoon, two days before the on-track action began, Junior and his buddies piled into a large SUV and headed to the Speedway. Finding an open gate, Junior drove them onto the track, eventually coming to a stop in turn four where the crash had occurred. They sat on the banked asphalt for more than an hour.

"We sat there, joked a bit, and just came to peace with it," Junior explained later.

The previous Saturday, Dale Jr. faced another emotional moment when he stepped into the role his father would have taken as he walked his sister Kelley down the aisle in her wedding to Ray Holm, a mechanic at Robert Yates Racing. He was happy to take the role, repaying in some small way the many things his sister had done for him through the years.

Kelley was two years older, and had always been his closest confidant. From the sad days of seeing their small home burn to the ground, she had always played the role of his protector. A late bloomer, Junior had grown up shy and frail (he didn't grow past five-foot-six until after high school), and had always relied upon his sister. When he struggled with severe homesickness in his first semester alone at military school, Kelley chose to join him, enrolling in the same school.

After Junior and his stepbrother Kerry began racing, Kelley also got into the act. Early on, it was clear she was the most aggressive and talented driver of the three. However, even with her famous last name, many crew members refused to help a woman driver, so Dale Jr. became her crew chief. When college beckoned, her driving career was over. Kelley's education helped her move up the ladder and become an executive with Action Performance, the company that produced NASCAR souvenirs and merchandise.

Since their dad's death, Junior had come to lean on her even more. Because Junior had trusted his father so completely with his business affairs, his company, JR Motorsports, was little more than a name and a small office. Now that she was married, Kelley was willing to take a cut in pay by leaving her position at Action to manage Junior's fledgling business efforts.

The Daytona race was the first to be televised by NBC, and Dale Jr. was asked if he would read his "I Know a Man" column in turn four for their prerace show. Junior refused, but the network persisted, trying to pressure him to read the column. Their insistence aggravated Junior, and NBC didn't help its cause when it hosted a mandatory meeting for team owners and drivers, insulting them all by instructing them how to act in victory lane. Junior already hated how the tightly structured procedures dampened his elation after a win, and now a television network was telling him how to act?

With so many emotions so close to the surface, Dale Jr. and the Eurys asked me to inform the media they would not grant interviews during the weekend, allowing them to focus on the race.

Every day since the Daytona 500, Tony Jr. and his father had spent an hour or more tweaking and perfecting this race car. They wanted nothing more in the world than to return to Daytona and win in honor of their former boss, uncle, and brother-in-law. When the team unloaded the car, detailed in the white MLB All-Star scheme, it was the most refined and prepared chassis they had ever brought to a track.

As practice began, the team and driver seemed quiet and tense, but once the session got rolling, they loosened up, working hard to put the final adjustments in place.

Even though Dale Jr. qualified 13th best Friday afternoon, he had the fastest and best-handling car during the evening's final practice session. It was a continuation of the confidence and swagger Junior showed in April at Talladega. With his father gone, he pushed himself to be the new generation's best restrictor-plate racer.

As the Saturday-night race approached, attention shifted from Dale Jr. to the evening's grand marshal, the spandex-wrapped songstress Britney Spears and her matching pair of massive bodyguards. Junior autographed a number of items for her family, who were longtime Earnhardt fans. Dale Jr. also met Lance Bass from N'Sync at the drivers' meeting, sans bodyguards and spandex.

Walking to his car on the starting grid, Junior was focused, wearing his hat backward like days of old, and posing for photos with baseball executives in his white driver's uniform. Before he climbed in, Junior agreed to a brief interview with NBC.

The flurry of activities immediately before such a huge race was a prime example of the difference between NASCAR and other sports. The week before, Junior and I flew to Chicago, where he threw out the first pitch before a Cubs game at Wrigley Field. Hours before the game, we met several players but were unable to meet with the starting pitcher, Kerry Wood. Though Wood was a big Dale Jr. fan, no one was allowed to speak with him before a game. Now, Junior was glad-handing and answering questions until the very moment he crawled into his race car for perhaps the biggest and most emotional race of his life.

For the 160-lap race, the team added a second spotter just as they had done for the previous race at Sonoma. Joey Meier, one of DEI's pilots, was an extra set of eyes for Dale Jr. along the backstretch, helping Ty Norris with a closer view of crucial areas such as the exit of turn two.

"Ty, tell me what you want from me tonight," Meier asked during the pace laps.

"I told you not to ask me that until we're back at the hotel," joked Norris as the two spotters calibrated which areas of the track each would be responsible for during the race.

"Dale Jr., I can see you clearly down the backstretch, but I may be guessing everywhere else," Norris said.

"That's OK. I'll be guessing a lot myself," Junior answered.

As he drove past the Budweiser pit area on the final pace lap, Dale Jr.

poked fun at the crew and his publicist standing on the pit wall, saluting and waving at their driver.

"Hey, y'all get off that wall there! You guys need to get ready to work tonight," Junior laughed. "We've got some work to do. And tell Jade to get the hell back. He's in the way there."

As the race began, the pace was frantic, a clear departure from the caution-free Talladega race. Surprisingly, Dale Jr. chose to drop back, falling to 31st by the seventh lap.

"It's gonna be a mess there," Norris said. "You don't need to be in the middle of all that shit."

Not satisfied to ride near the back, an impatient Dale Jr. soon switched to his usual aggressive strategy, pushing into the top 10 by lap 20.

"This sonuvabitch is fast," were the first words from Junior since the green flag.

With Kevin Harvick ahead of him and Michael Waltrip behind, the three Chevrolets snaked to the front. Free of traffic on lap 27, Junior swept to the outside of the No. 29 car, taking the lead for the first time.

When time drew near for green-flag pit stops, the driver had a small request.

"The car's pretty good," Junior said. "I need maybe a quarter-pound more [pressure] in the left rear [tire] to loosen it up."

After the stop on lap 51, Dale Jr. was silent for several laps.

"I'm really loose off of turn two for some damn reason," he said. "I feel like I'm gonna spin out back there every lap. Tony Jr., what did you change on this?"

"We added a pound in the left rear," he answered.

"A pound? I said a *quarter*-pound!" Dale Jr. hollered. "You won't listen to me?"

"We can't make that small of an adjustment," Tony Jr. answered.

"What? Are you sayin' I can't tell the difference in a quarter-pound of pressure? 'Coz I can!" Dale Jr. said with exaggerated hurt in his voice. "I asked for it and you didn't listen. Damn, man. I am more valuable to you than you'll ever know."

"No, he meant our tire gauge won't read that small of a change," Pops interjected with a chuckle.

Though the bickering between cousins could become a dominant theme during races, there was always a subtle underlying sense they were merely needling each other, replaying small injustices or inside jokes from when they were young. Though Dale Jr. probably could recognize the small distinction between the adjustment he had asked for and the one he received, his exaggerated complaints were done without malice, with a hint of a smile or a wink in his voice. Through the years, newcomers to the team were shocked at the bickering between the two, but soon learned it was more akin to the fights of an old married couple who loved each other very much.

"Hey, you're all worth a lot to each other, my brothers!" Norris said, trying to keep driver and team focused on the track.

The lengthy green-flag run ended on lap 88 when Andy Houston crashed the McDonald's car, sending nearly the entire field down pit lane several laps later. No team was quicker than the No. 8 crew, and Dale Jr. left his pit box in the lead, followed by Park in the No. 1 car.

"Awesome. Fucking awesome," Dale Jr. yelled as the crew celebrated with high fives.

"One more, boys," Jeff Clark reminded them. "One more stop to go."

At the green flag on lap 93, Dale Jr. wanted to make sure he and Park could stay together to fend off challenges from Matt Kenseth, now third in the No. 17 car.

"Ask Steve what he wants to do," Junior told Norris. "Does he wanna run high or low? Let's pretend I'm driving the 1 car right now. You tell me when the 17 car has a run on the 1 car."

"He has to run high to stop the 17 car from passing him," said Norris.

On lap 100, Kenseth made the predicted move to the outside, pulling a line of cars with him. Along the backstretch, Dale Jr. momentarily dropped to fourth, but utilized the preferred inside line in turn three to inch back to the lead.

"They're racin' like hell back there!" Junior laughed, after weaving aggressively to stop another passing attempt. Determined to lead the race as many laps as possible, Junior had been swerving his car back and forth on the backstretch, blocking the momentum of his challengers in the middle and outside lanes.

"That looked like a pretty nice save there, driver," Tony Jr. told him.

"What can I say?" replied Dale Jr. "I got a good car here. I'm just showin''em my ass. They can run over me pretty easily if I don't."

The action dissipated for a few laps until lap 129, when a surprising new drafting partner, Rusty Wallace, pushed Junior free of the pack. The beer-backed rivals ran nose-to-tail, pulling away from the field.

With pit stops looming, intense negotiations began. Since Junior's teammates had been shuffled backward, the team had spirited debates about which cars would be best to join the No. 8 on pit lane. What about the No. 18 car of Bobby Labonte? Or Ken Schrader in the M&M's car? What about staying with Wallace in the No. 2 car? He was a rival, but the two cars seemed to be very fast when hooked together.

Scanning the radio frequencies of other teams, Norris heard speculation the Roush Ford cars might choose to make a stop for fuel only, not taking time to change tires.

"What do you think about not taking tires?" Tony Jr. asked his driver.

"I believe my tires are good if ya wanna try it," he replied. "Whatever ya want, I'll drive it."

The stops began with 20 laps remaining, as Labonte and teammate Stewart took two tires. The following lap, Schrader's team took gas only, while Johnny Benson and Dave Blaney took two tires.

"It's starting to push real bad," Dale Jr. reported, not as confident as before in his tires.

"The 2 [Wallace] and 6 [Mark Martin] are not taking tires," Norris reported.

"If they're not, then neither are we," Dale Jr. replied.

Suddenly, trouble struck.

Behind Dale Jr., a violent shower of sparks, smoke, and car parts spread across the track, as a dozen or more cars bashed and slid along the straightaway just past turn four. The cars of Terry Labonte, Sterling Marlin, and Martin were heavily damaged. Jeff Gordon careened through the grass while Jarrett avoided the crash by using pit lane as an escape road.

The accident started when Kurt Busch and Mike Skinner collided, launching them into the path of the cars speeding past on the outside. Because of the debris field, the pits were closed, which presented a new concern for the Bud team. If pit lane was closed for more than two or three laps, the white car could run out of fuel.

"OK, calm down," Dale Jr. said. "Let's do things like there are a hundred laps to go. What d'y'all think? Two or four?"

"Everyone else seems to be saying four," Norris reported.

"I think we can beat 'em with two," added Tony Jr.

"If I get four tires, I'd like it," Dale Jr. replied. "But if I need to race these guys with no tires or two tires, I dunno about that. I'm pretty comfortable now, but . . . no matter what, I'll drive my ass off.

"Any danger of running out of gas?," Dale Jr. asked. "I'm on the apron now."

"Might be a good idea right about now," Pops replied, before breathing a sigh of relief as the NASCAR official in his stall indicated pit lane was now open. "Pit this lap. Pit this lap."

"Four tires," Tony Sr. said to the crew.

"Four tires," he repeated as the car rolled toward them with 15 laps remaining.

Teams that had already stopped chose to stay out, while others changed only two tires. The Bud crew made a quick, clean stop for four new Goodyear tires, sending their driver back on track in seventh place. The six cars ahead, including the leader Benson, had four worn tires or only two fresh skins.

"Try to see if we can talk to the 2 and the 7," Dale Jr. asked, wondering if the Wallace brothers, Rusty and Mike, would be willing to tuck behind him to force their way to the front. "I know we can fly by these guys. See if they'll help, or if they're full of shit."

"The 2 and the 22 [Ward Burton] will hang with us until we get rid of the trash," said Norris. This was the nature of the drafting partnerships: drivers were happy to help another only until they were able to make a move of their own. "Eleven laps to go at the green. Nobody can beat ya."

"I dunno. It'll be hard," replied Dale Jr. "Just count down the laps. I don't wanna run outta laps."

As soon as the gaggle gained speed, the yellow came out again for fluid on the track, slowing the pack on lap 150. Junior gained a spot to sixth, but he wasn't pleased.

"Y'all can look at the track. There's no oil out here!" he yelled. "I'm out here frustrated.

"I wanna win this race pretty bad," Dale Jr. said, in a matter-of-fact tone. "If we don't, we shoulda. I'm sorry."

"Junior, you've been great," said Meier from his perch on the backstretch. "The cars in front of you haven't been able to keep up with you all night. If you can believe it, it was the 31 car [Skinner] that started that big crash."

"Why wouldn't I believe that?" Junior asked.

"I was being facetious," Meier said.

"Yeah, so was I," said Dale Jr.

With six laps remaining, Dale Jr. wasted no time, pulling to the high line to go past Stewart.

With Mike Wallace pushing, Dale Jr. climbed to third as he completed lap 155.

The cars at the front were racing each other two and three wide, slowing them enough to allow Dale Jr. to pull close behind the leader, Benson, and Blaney in second.

As Junior swung to the outside lane, Jeremy Mayfield pulled out from behind Blaney to push the No. 8. As they screamed into turn four, Junior maintained his momentum on the outside, sweeping past Benson, who had lost his drafting help. The field behind Junior scrambled wildly, and Stewart drove below the yellow line to force his way into second place.

The crowd, estimated to exceed 170,000, erupted with a deafening roar. In the Budweiser pit area, the team made their own noise as their car took the lead with authority. Raw emotions were flowing, and I was barely able to write in my notepad, scrawling "P1!!" in large, shaky letters that looked as if a four-year-old had written them.

The only voice on the radio was Norris.

"Four to go. They're two-wide behind ya. The 20 [Stewart] is comin' with ya," he said calmly.

Stewart was soon passed by his teammate Labonte in the No. 18 car. (Stewart had been given the black flag for passing below the yellow line, but refused to bring his car to pit lane, leading to a heated post-race shouting match with NASCAR officials.)

"You've got your teammate behind the 18. The 15 [Waltrip] is behind the 18," Norris said.

Tony Sr., standing atop the pit box, swung his arm as Junior drove past, willing him forward.

With two to go, Junior ran wide off turn two as Waltrip made a dramatic dive below Labonte. The two bumped as they fought down the backstretch, but Labonte had no drafting help and Waltrip sped past with a push from Elliott Sadler.

With less than five miles to go, the positions were now reversed from the Daytona 500.

"That's the 15 car right behind you!" Norris said, his voice rising. "That man is committed to you, I know it. He is committed to help you."

As the field jostled behind them just as they had in February, Junior and Waltrip pulled away in the inside lane.

"All right buddy, white flag. You got your teammate behind ya," Norris said coolly. "He's gonna stay with you . . . just protect the bottom of the racetrack . . . just like he did in the 500 . . . protect the bottom."

As the cars slung around turn four, past the spot of such tragedy five months before, Dale Jr. headed to his first Daytona victory.

"You got it! You got it!" Norris said as the Bud car crossed under the flagman waving the checkered flag.

"That's unbelievable," Norris said. The NBC in-car camera caught a jubilant driver, punching his fist in the air triumphantly.

"I love you, man," Norris said. "You guys celebrate, you did it."

"Hellllll yeah! HA HA!" yelled Dale Jr. "We got us a win!"

On his victory lap, Dale Jr.'s celebratory banshee yells were heard over the engine noise on his in-car camera. As they rolled down the backstretch, Matt Kenseth pulled alongside and slammed his car into Junior's, an automotive version of a manly fist bump and an homage to Big E. The collision left huge tire marks on the door of the Bud car.

chapter 30

victory

Daytona Beach, Florida

The entire Budweiser team surrounded Tony Jr. on pit lane in a massive group hug. Emotions that had been bottled since February came rushing out as if from a high-pressure fire hose. After so many agonizing close calls, the team had finally earned a victory of its own. Waltrip's NAPA team soon joined the scrum.

Pops held his emotions long enough for a brief TV interview, but he too was soon swallowed by the moment. So much of the public scrutiny had been on Dale Jr., but the Eurys had suffered quietly alongside their driver. Both men had massaged the chassis everyday since February, looking forward to a semblance of redemption. As the crew lifted him in the air, Tony Jr. wiped tears from his eyes as Pops and Steve Hmiel basked in the second DEI one-two finish of the year.

Waves of sound from the grandstands washed over the team. This seemed the NASCAR equivalent of the arrival of the Beatles in the United States: an explosion of joy several months after the assassination of President Kennedy. The NASCAR Nation had been in mourning, and now it was time to celebrate again.

Junior pulled onto the infield grass just past the start/finish line, spinning the car in a bid to replicate his father's celebratory donuts from the 1998 Daytona 500. He spun to a stop in the middle of the massive Winston Cup logo painted in the grass.

Leaping from the car, Junior stood on the doorsill, pumping his arms high in the air as he drank in the noisy adulation from his devotees. Waltrip pulled his car alongside, climbing out to give Junior a massive hug.

Across the infield grass, the first person to reach the duo was Danny "Chocolate" Myers, who had been one of Big E's most prominent RCR crew members for many years. Myers was followed by a multicolor stream of uniforms as Bud, Pennzoil, NAPA, and GM-Goodwrench crews converged. One by one, Junior hugged each of his team members.

Waltrip climbed atop his car, celebrating in a way he had been unable to enjoy at the 500. Junior ascended to join him for a massive, lingering hug before they waved to the crowd in tandem. From atop the NAPA car, Junior launched himself into the air in his victory tradition of diving into his crew members' outstretched arms.

NASCAR officials interceded, asking Junior to drive the car to victory lane. Junior pulled straight to the hallowed ground then climbed atop the doorsill again as confetti swirled around him. He held a can of Budweiser in the air like a chalice, taking a massive gulp before waving the can wildly. He grabbed a second beer and poured some of it on the car in tribute to his father.

"I gotta thank my buddy Tony, my crew chief, for hangin' in there with me," he breathlessly told NBC's Bill Weber while reaching over to pulls Pops near. "All my friends. The guys on the crew. Budweiser. I could talk all night! I had a great car. It was all car. One hundred percent."

Weber reminded him it was 11 years to the day of his father's first points-paying Daytona win.

"I dedicate this win to him," Junior replied. "I mean, there ain't nobody else to dedicate it to that would mean more to me. I wanna say 'Hey' to Teresa back home. I hope she's lovin' it!"

Junior sat down on a Budweiser cooler, as if overwhelmed by the moment, with Steve Park sitting alongside.

The next to join him was Danny Earnhardt, Big E's quiet younger brother who had been a part of Junior's crew for years. Dale Jr. handed him the baseball-design helmet he had worn in the race. Major League Baseball executives were on hand, intending to place hologram decals on the helmet and uniforms in order to auction them off in the coming weeks, but Junior insisted no one other than his uncle Danny would ever hold the special helmet.

Junior walked to a small stage to answer questions for a gaggle of TV cameras.

"I wanna dedicate this one to my dad," he told them. The joy pumping through his body caused him to speak quickly, his sentences running together. "The thing that crossed my mind was Tony's face, Tony Jr.'s face, my grandmother's face, my sister's face, ya know, Teresa's face. And you can't wait to see them, to see their expression, 'coz that's the reward from winnin' somethin' like this."

One by one, drivers and team owners stopped by to offer congratulations, including Dale Jarrett, Richard Childress, and NASCAR's president, Mike Helton, who embraced Junior.

"That reminded me of someone else I used to know," Jarrett told Junior with a smile.

After the ceremonies, Dale Jr. and I climbed into a van with Pops for the ride to the post-race news conference. Putting a hand on his uncle's shoulder, Junior exhaled.

"Whoa," he said. "This is huge!"

Walking into the press box near the top of Daytona's massive tower, Junior peered down on the tire tracks in the infield grass before starting what is likely one of the longest and happiest news conferences in NASCAR history.

"I wanted to really do some good donuts," he laughed. "It seems like that's a competition here lately . . .. When Matt Kenseth won at Charlotte last year, he did some sort of high-speed slide though the grass, so I was kinda going for that, mixed with some donuts.

"You *have* to do stuff like that after you win because you've got so much energy that you have to let it out," he insisted, taking a subtle dig at NBC's effort to stage-direct victory lane. "You gotta let it out like that by spinning around and jumping out of the car and letting out some yells! Otherwise, if you don't, you get to victory lane and you'll just get outta the car and fall over or lose consciousness."

"Tony and the guys work harder than any other team," he said, putting his hand on his uncle's shoulder once again. "There's more dedication in that shop right now than you'll find in any other shop. Every once in awhile, you'll have a car that'll do that. It'll just dominate."

It wasn't long before the questioning turned to his father, and what it meant for Junior to come back to Daytona.

"The very first lap I made around the racetrack felt different. It was kind of tough," he said. "After the first practice qualifying run, I really didn't think much about what happened here in February . . . I was more nervous about how good my car was than anything else. It's really hard to stay calm because you're thinking about each car, how good they were in practice and all. You're picking apart each car in front of you. You try to play out every scenario that can possibly happen. I just think you always get real nervous on the cautions. I was saying to Tony, 'Whatever happens, if we win, we should have and if we don't, we should have.' If I didn't win then I made the wrong decision somewhere."

As Junior spoke, he would occasionally turn to look at the 2.5-mile speedway, still gleaming under the bright lights far below his perch in the media center. It was as if he were trying to soak in every moment, replaying each pass for the lead and each lap to the finish.

"When Michael pulled behind me with two laps to go, I just knew that he was going to help me," he said. "I knew he wasn't going to make a move because I helped him in the Daytona 500 and I told him that I helped him, so he *owed* me. He was so happy when we were jumping on the cars. He's had a rough year, so I was happy for him as well."

Beyond what the win meant for him and his team, he also had a larger sense of what it meant for the fans who had been cheering for him all season. For years, his motivation to succeed was seeing his father's smile. Now, he drew inspiration from the crowd.

"When I'd pass people for the lead, I'd see that everybody has their arms raised and that kind of pumps you up," he explained. "But all year long, people have been pushing and pushing for us to do well. Then you start to feel a little pressure that you won't win for them and give them reason to root for you. So it's a good feeling tonight. That's why I pulled down on the front straightaway and jumped out. That was for the fans and nobody else .. . I really wanted to jump up there and hear them cheer. It felt good."

More than an hour after the checkered flag, Dale Jr., still in his beer-soaked uniform, made his way to his bus where the party was well underway. Budweiser had delivered a large iced tub of beer, and his friends were already several brews ahead of him. Waltrip, Park, and musician Edwin McCain were there to congratulate him. It was surprisingly low key. Everyone seemed content to relax, savoring the glow of victory.

With ESPN banned from the track, reporter Mike Massaro called several times to ask if Junior would drive outside for an interview. With his buddies and his brew in hand, Junior was in no mood to leave, prompting Massaro and his crew to sneak in sometime after 2 a.m. to track down the winner for an interview.

Around 4 a.m., the Budweiser finally ran out and the party came to a close.

After sleeping off the aftermath, Dale Jr. was on a flight to Seattle where he would spend the next few days with Budweiser at the MLB All-Star festivities.

While they were thrilled with the victory, Budweiser executives had a serious matter to discuss. Before Saturday night's race, Junior had slipped one of his favorite skull-and-crossbones decals to a crew member, asking him to put it somewhere inside the car. Unfortunately, the decal was placed immediately next to the Budweiser logo on the dashboard, in full view of the in-car camera. For any food or beverage product, the skull-and-crossbones mean one thing: poison. Budweiser demanded no more skulls anywhere near their logo.

In Seattle, Junior spent several hours Monday afternoon at the Bud World display, signing autographs before going on the field with the players before the Home Run Derby. Everywhere he turned, he was congratulated on his emotional win. Budweiser arranged for a series of interviews with CNN, MSNBC, and ESPN.

In the middle of one of the interviews, Junior was asked about claims the race had been fixed. Unknown to Dale Jr., his victory had been questioned, starting with Jimmy Spencer's post-race comments to ESPN.

"I knew going in the 8 car was going to win this race." Spencer spouted. "Something was fictitious and, uh, he was real fast the other night and, uh, and they were fast down here in February, and I mean, ya know, it's not ironic the 8 car would win with what happened here in February."

Johnny Benson, who Junior passed to take the lead for the last time, also suggested something didn't seem right. "You don't go by yourself on the outside and make that kind of time up," Benson said.

Their comments fed a series of cynical stories, including a *New York Times* piece questioning the victory and a column by Eddie Pells of the Associated Press, who suggested "Gentleman, start your conspiracy theories." *USA Today*'s motorsports writer Chris Jenkins quoted Spencer and hinted the race was determined in advance, much like pro wrestling.

None of the theorists had an explanation for how NASCAR could rig such a massive event. Nor could they explain why the sanctioning body would risk its millions of fans and hundreds of millions of sponsorship dollars to skew an event or somehow orchestrate the results of a 160-lap race with 43 entrants. With the sport still overcoming public scrutiny after the loss of Earnhardt, it was a risk they couldn't afford to take. A storybook ending is not evidence of a fix. Sometimes real life exceeds what a scriptwriter could conceive.

The skeptics failed to remember DEI's dominance in the Daytona 500, and how much Junior had improved on the restrictor-plate tracks. In the three years following the Pepsi 400, Waltrip and Dale Jr. would win 12 more Cup races at Daytona and Talladega, including Waltrip's second Daytona 500 win in 2003 and Junior's own 500 victory the following year. Their continued dominance at restrictor-plate races squashed any claims the 2001 Pepsi 400 victory had been somehow rigged or even that it was a fluke.

More than anything else, the theories were an insult to the team and driver who had dedicated so much heart and soul to the victory. With so much on the line, Dale Jr. and the Eurys would be the first to reject any sort of favoritism from the sanctioning body. Doing so would have tainted or diminished the joy of a true, hard-earned victory.

Junior had been blissfully unaware of these whisperings until Monday afternoon. At a news conference held later in the week at the new Chicagoland Speedway, Earnhardt Jr. described his anger.

"I couldn't believe it," he said. "I was in Seattle for the All-Star Game and this guy asked me what I thought about people saying the Daytona race was fixed. I coiled back to knock the hell out of the guy.

"It's really bothered me pretty bad. It's the biggest win of my career and, for somebody to question its credibility, it's a slap in my face, in my father's face, in Tony Eury Jr.'s face, and in the faces of the whole team.

"I never drove any harder in my life," Earnhardt Jr. said, anger building with each syllable. "We won the race so convincingly, it raised questions. But I don't understand how anybody could think that NASCAR would do that. Why would they? They've got so little to gain and so much to lose.

"Now, I feel like everybody I talk to about the race, I have to prove to them it was real," he spat. "It's a shame. It's a great moment in NASCAR history and it was ruined, pretty much."

Junior insisted on asserting his restrictor-plate abilities in his father's absence.

"If you watched the past two or three restrictor plate races that I raced with him, we were competitive and we ran up front. I learned a lot from him and I know how to drive in those races. I learned how to work the air and how to get by people by yourself without help, and things like that.

"Without him in the race last weekend, I felt invincible. I had everything that he had, the knowledge and confidence, and what he took to those races. I just felt I couldn't be touched."

chapter 31

bad vibrations

Joliet, Illinois

After dealing with the media probes for Pepsi 400 conspiracy theories, Dale Jr. was happy to climb in the race car and begin learning the new Chicagoland Speedway. The 1.5-mile track looked much like many of the other 1.5-mile ovals (this led to the term "cookie cutter tracks"), and was actually located in Joliet, Illinois, rather than the Windy City.

After practice, the team focused on more pressing needs, such as finding the best hobby shops in the area to buy RC cars and parts. Junior's enthusiasm had spread and several crew members got into the model car craze.

Without any history at Chicagoland, the team made educated guesses about the best setup, but they were too aggressive and Dale Jr. qualified 36th. On his qualifying lap, the car suffered coil binding.

"We're going into the corners with so much speed and so much g-force, the left front spring compresses to its maximum and the coils of the spring touch," Dale Jr. explained. "That makes it feel like you have no suspension at all, and then it bottoms out."

Starting the race so far back, Tony Jr. preached patience.

"Let's gain a spot on each pit stop," he said. "Let's gain one at a time. We've got 267 laps to get to the front."

By lap 40, Junior had crawled into the top 20 and the team chose to pit for fuel only at the next yellow flag. The strategy pushed them forward to fourth place. On their next stop, several lug nuts fell from the left rear wheel, causing a lengthy stop and pushing them back to 22nd.

On lap 109, Dale Jr. suddenly slowed with a misfiring engine. He was able to switch to the secondary ignition box, which seemed to solve the misfire, but the engine was still not to the driver's liking.

"This motor sucks," he said, more than once.

To regain the track position they had lost, the team chose to take two tires on their next stop, exiting the pits in eighth, but the choice soon began to backfire.

"I have a bad vibration. I need to get that tire offa here," Dale Jr. explained, before he began speaking in a trembling voice as if he were sitting on a paint shaker. "Evennnn underrrrr theee yellowwwwww flaggggggg, badddddd viiiibrationnnnnn."

With the tires changed and the vibration cured, Junior's complaints refocused on the engine.

"OK, from now on *nobody* complains or says anything about the engine," Tony Sr. said with authority. "We are going to try and get the car as good as we can, and we're gonna do the best that we can!"

"I almost backed into the wall," Junior groused, as NASCAR failed to throw a caution flag due to oil on the track. "That ain't my favorite feeling. That just makes me mad. Their mindset has gotta change. You remember back, like ten years ago, when they'd blow the hell outta an engine and a big cloud of smoke would go up, and then NASCAR would throw the yellow right away? Now, the fluids on the track are just as bad, but they wait around to see if somebody's gonna crash before they do anything.

"There's a pretty little line of oil all over this turn," he described the next lap. "Weeds will sprout up out of the asphalt before they find it."

When NASCAR finally threw the caution flag, Junior returned to badmouthing the powerplant.

"This motor still ain't running right," he said. "It's not turning any RPMs. If I'm in the draft, I haul ass, but when I'm by myself on the track, it feels like I'm up against a two-hundred-mile-per-hour wind. It's so bad, it feels like the wind is whipping in around my feet."

"Uh, oh yeah . . . we forget to tell ya," Tony Jr. said with perfect comedic timing. "We put a new duct in the car this week that blows fresh air on your feet to try to keep you cooler."

"Oh, that may be why I was feelin' that," Dale Jr. laughed.

On the following lap, he began another rant.

"This ain't no fun," he said. "They need to consult with me on the design of these tracks. They need to speak with me."

"*Now* you're sounding like an Earnhardt," Norris interjected.

"Hah!" Dale Jr. replied, then spoke as if he were an adult scolding a toddler. "Everybody that's a lap down needs to line up. Get up here! C'mon! Let's go!"

Amid the bitch session, the team closed on their goal of a top-10 finish, ending the day in 11th place.

"I could wheel the hell out of it," Dale Jr. said on the cool-down lap. "It was good at the beginning and good at the end. It was crap in the middle. This is the car that won Texas, right? Maybe it's time to retire it."

Kevin Harvick earned his second victory lap of the season, winning the inaugural Tropicana 400. Robert Pressley grabbed a career-best second-place finish, while Ricky Rudd closed to within 18 of the points lead with a third-place tally. Jeff Gordon and Dale Jarrett were now tied for the Winston Cup points lead.

"I thought it was a long race. I'd get kinda tired and then I'd catch a second wind," Junior said. "Then I thought, 'I need to finish this thing and go have a cold Bud with the guys.'"

chapter 32

time to go

Loudon, New Hampshire

Junior's Daytona victory continued to receive media attention, including articles in *Sports Illustrated*, *People*, and *Entertainment Weekly*, plus the covers of *Stock Car Racing* and *Racing Milestones* magazines. But, the emotions of that week, combined with jetting back and forth across the country, wore on Dale Jr.

For more than a week, Junior was in a continuous bad mood, and his confidence seemed low before the race at New Hampshire Motor Speedway near Loudon. From the 29th starting spot, Junior worried about the struggle to pass cars on a flat, aging surface. To help the track surface survive the rough New England winter, the one-mile oval was covered by sealant. The sealant initially provided extra grip, but tended to disintegrate on hot days with 43 cars pounding over it. Less than 50 laps into the race, the sealer began to deteriorate, narrowing an already thin groove.

Despite his worries, Dale Jr. found a good rhythm early in the race, patiently passing his way into the top 10 in only 80 laps. He was able to pass cars under long green-flag runs, but struggled when forced to make restarts in the outside line.

On a lap 95 restart, Dale Jr. and Kevin Harvick tried to make their way around the lapped car of Jason Leffler. As the meat in the sandwich, the nose of the Bud car suffered damage, followed several laps later by more metal-banging when Todd Bodine ran into the No. 8, bending the right front fender. The damage caused the handling to suffer and the engine to overheat.

"I have a bent fender! It's tore up!" Junior said. "Damn, these lapped cars race the shit out of ya!"

"You're faster than that 66 car [Bodine]," Norris said. "Watch out, he slammed you good to get by. Just be careful getting back around him."

"That fucker is driving like he doesn't have a spotter up there helping him," Dale Jr. replied.

"You're right," Tony Jr. said. "I don't think he has a spotter today."

"Yeah, I guess their team is one man short," Norris said.

"But your lap times still look good," said Tony Jr.

"The lap times don't matter now," spat Dale Jr. "What matters is passing people. I need to pass people! I can't do that if the nose is all screwed up."

Exiting turn two, Ron Hornaday's green No. 14 car climbed the wall, sending it onto two wheels.

"Whooo! Ol' Hornaday looked like Joie Chitwood back there," Tony Jr. said.

"The water is at two hundred forty-five degrees now!" said Dale Jr., not appreciating Hornaday's thrill show. "How can y'all be comfortable with that shit? Are you guys complacent?"

To counteract the damage to the car, the team decided to make two pit stops, the first to force water into the pressurized system to cool the engine, and the second to change four tires.

Dale Jr. restarted 26th, the last car on the lead lap, but with more fuel than everyone other than Harvick and Jeff Burton, who had also stopped.

As the others began making green-flag pit stops, the No. 8 skipped upward in the scoring, following Harvick and Burton in the top three when a caution came out on lap 235, allowing the team to make their final stop.

"Where are we at?" Dale Jr. asked. "How many laps are left? Can we go to the end?"

"We're done. You're on your own now," said Tony Jr. "You're in ninth and there will be 60 laps to go when you take the green. The guys in front of you have tires that are fifteen to twenty laps older than yours, so this is your time. This is your time to race. Time to go!"

Needing a long green-flag run to move forward, Junior was frustrated as four caution periods dampened his charge. When he had to brake suddenly to avoid Bodine's spinning car, he lost three spots. With less than 20 laps to go, he was in 10th.

"Sorry," he told the crew. "I missed that damn deal on the back straightaway. I didn't wanna T-bone the 66."

With five laps remaining, Dale Jr. got past Mike Wallace to finish ninth.

"If they asked me, I'd tell them to leave it slick! No more sealer!" Junior said.

Dale Jarrett and Jeff Gordon came into the New England 300 tied for the lead in Winston Cup points, trailed closely by Ricky Rudd. The trio did their best to keep the others out of their chase for a title, with Jarrett winning the race, followed by Gordon and Rudd.

"Ninth place is a good comeback," Dale Jr. said. "We passed a lot of cars on a track that's hard to pass on. Once I bent the nose, it never turned quite as well again.

"The sealer tore up almost immediately and the track became one-groove after that. They had three other races here this weekend, so even at the start of our race you could see the areas that had started to come up. There were patches in the corners that made those areas undriveable. It looked like someone had taken wide strips of rubber and just glued it to the track. You had to straddle those areas with the car—you either had to be above or below it if you wanted to hang on."

chapter 33

save fuel

Long Pond, Pennsylvania

For several years, Dale Jr. had donated time and money to support a program in Philadelphia called the Urban Youth Racing League. The group built and maintained small "mini-Cup" cars, teaching inner-city kids an array of mechanical skills. To show their appreciation, the group planned an event called The Dale Jr. Shootout, to draw media attention and give Junior a chance to meet the kids in the program.

Robin Roberts of ABC attended and sat with Dale Jr. for an interview that aired on "Good Morning America." Unfortunately, the weather was horrendous and a steady rain dampened the proceedings in front of the massive Memorial Hall building. When the rain slowed, several of the youngsters drove onto the makeshift course in their mini-Cup cars. One of the teenagers swerved to avoid another, steering off the pavement into the soggy grass. With no traction, he slid straight into a police car parked nearby. Paramedics were exceedingly cautious, putting the youngster on a stretcher, and Dale Jr. made certain the kid was all right before we departed for Pocono for the weekend's action.

The constant travel can have an effect, and I awoke Friday morning in a confused state. For the first time, I was uncertain what city I was in. The hotel room looked exactly like others I had been in the past few months, and looking out the window wasn't much help as I saw the same McDonald's and Arby's or Lowe's I had seen over and over again. While it soon dawned on me I was in Wilkes-Barre, Pennsylvania, I couldn't help but shake the realization of the country's complete homogenization. It's as if every city or town we visited had lost its local or regional identity.

Everywhere I went, it all looked the same—except for the decrepit Pocono Raceway, which looked nothing like any other track.

Having raced here only a few weeks before, it was hard to muster the energy to get excited about 500 more miles of racing, but Dale Jr. did his part to energize his fans by rocketing from 12th to 8th place on the first lap. By lap nine, Junior made an exciting but risky move, going three wide to earn fifth place.

At the first Pocono race, the DEI cars suffered poor fuel mileage. Since then, chief engine builder Richie Gilmore had worked tirelessly to improve the miles-per-gallon performance of their Chevy engines.

Just as the tricky Pocono triangle forces a team to compromise on car set-up to get through each of the unique corners, engine building is an artful compromise between horsepower, fuel mileage, and reliability. Gilmore couldn't sacrifice the other elements to make better mileage, so the challenge was immense. To test their findings, Steve Hmiel and Gilmore took Kerry Earnhardt and a small crew to Kentucky Speedway for several days of testing. Would their hard work pay off?

The Bud team was running eighth after a pit stop for fuel and four tires on lap 144, when Dale Jr. heard the two words he dreaded most.

"Save fuel," Tony Jr. said.

"Awwwww, man," he groaned.

"Coast around, and use second gear," said Jeff Clark, the team's engine tuner. "The low idle on yellow helps mileage."

"I can't put on the gas, brake, and clutch," Junior protested. "I only have two feet."

"Use your third leg," suggested Clark.

A few laps after the restart, a multicar crash took place inches behind Junior, slowing the field again.

"Talk to me on our fuel mileage," Dale Jr. asked. "Can I make it?"

"Negative," was the answer from Clark.

"Whoa!" Dale Jr. exclaimed as he rolled onto the front stretch and saw cars strewn across the track. "How many cars were in that one?"

"About six or seven," Tony Jr. replied.

"That looked like a big, big wreck," Dale Jr. said.

The team chose not to bring the Bud car down pit lane, fearing Junior would drop to the back and, like the earlier Pocono race, never make up the lost ground.

"We're gonna have to pit with a few laps to go," Tony Jr. said. "We're two gallons short. We'll just take a splash pretty much."

"I'll make the call. I'm drivin'!" Dale Jr. joked.

The team caught a huge break when the yellow came out again as Dale Jarrett crashed in turn two. Jarrett entered the day tied for the points lead, but his car had been damaged in the multicar crash and then wrecked a second time as the right front tire went flat.

"What do you think?" Dale Jr. asked.

"C'mon, let's pit!" Pops Eury called out. "Fuel only!"

"How many laps on those tires?" asked Tony Jr.

"Ten, but only four under green," Pops replied. "Ten total."

"Let's be good here!" Tony Jr. said, urging his crew.

On lap 159, most of the lead lap cars came to pit lane. The Bud crew fueled the car quickly and Dale Jr. was the first to leave pit lane. He would restart second behind Johnny Benson, who did not stop.

Six weeks earlier, the DEI cars ran 30 to 32 laps on a tank of fuel, but now the Eurys were gambling the new and improved fuel mileage would carry them 41 laps to the finish. A lot of chewed fingernails in the Bud pit showed they weren't certain the fuel would last.

"Just keep those butterflies closed under yellow," Clark reminded. "Save what you can."

"How do I get around if the throttle's closed?" asked a frustrated driver.

"Just don't spin the tires and run in second gear. You'll do great," Clark answered.

"We're OK on fuel if we get two more laps of caution here," Tony Jr. said, looking at the latest fuel figures.

"Tell me about the calculation because I want to know if we can make it to the finish," Dale Jr. requested. "I don't want to be the only one that doesn't know a thing."

"Let's win this race and then we'll send a wrecker out to get ya if you run out on the backstretch," Pops told him. "We're gonna go with the computer on this one. It says you can make it."

"Hell yeah!" was the reply from the car.

As the green flew on lap 162, Tony Jr. cautioned his cousin.

"Just sit and draft that 10 car [Benson] for a while," he said. "Do that for a few laps and we'll be good."

Tucked in the draft behind the No. 10, Junior followed Benson's tire tracks for seven laps. Finally, Dale Jr. impatiently swept into the lead on lap 169.

One lap later, another caution came out when Kurt Busch lost his right front tire and it careened down the front stretch as if it had a mind of its own.

"Does this *really* mean we can make it now?" Dale Jr. asked.

"Ten-four," was the immediate response from Tony Jr. "We're good from here on out. Without a yellow, we would have had two-tenths of a gallon left."

Marty Snider came to the pit box to interview Pops about the strategy.

"If it'll pick it all up, it'll make it. It's gonna be close," Eury told the television audience. "It's just a gamble. We didn't want to be back there in that traffic. If you get behind on this racetrack, you can't make it up . . . We're gonna take a chance."

Dale Jr. pulled away easily on the restart, opening a lead of more than four seconds. With 20 laps to go, Bobby Labonte moved into second place. The defending series champion had yet to win during the 2001 season, and set sail for the Bud car.

With 15 to go, Junior could see Labonte closing in his mirror. "How much faster was he on that lap?" he asked.

"Only a tenth [of a second] quicker," Norris told him. "You maintain that two-point-four-second lead and we'll be fine."

As Junior began to encounter lapped cars, the lime green car of Labonte loomed closer.

"Keep your rhythm, buddy," Norris said calmly.

"The car's getting tight," said the driver. "That lap, it was just that last corner. I'm losing it all in that one corner."

"Bobby's moving up in turn one like you were," Norris said.

"I can hear ya, but you ain't tellin' me shit!" was Junior's terse reply.

"Stay focused, we're fine," Norris said. "We're fine. Eight to go. Eight."

A victory at Pocono would go a long way toward silencing critics who questioned his win at Daytona. He pushed as hard as the car would go, forgoing fuel conversation to preserve his lead. As Labonte reached 10 car lengths behind, the dirty air behind the No. 8 meant the two raced at a similar pace for four laps until Junior slowed slightly to go around the lapped car of Stacy Compton in turn three. As they crossed the line, the No. 18 was right on the bumper of the No. 8

"He passed the 10 by faking high and going low," Norris said.

With three to go, Junior pushed too hard in the treacherous turn two, sliding just enough for Labonte to pounce.

As they crossed the line side-by-side on lap 198, Labonte inched into the lead. As the two dove into turn one at more than 200 miles per hour, Junior stuck the nose of his car to the inside of Labonte. Somehow, the car gripped the pavement enough to give him a tiny advantage. Crushing the throttle pedal as if he were trying to force it through the firewall, Junior violently pulled into the outside lane, blocking Labonte. The champion countered by swinging quickly to the inside, then back to the outside.

The two were again door-to-door at top speed, and turn two, known as the Tunnel Turn, was ahead. There was no way the two could get through it two wide. Neither wanted to be the first to lift, but Labonte's outside position gave him the favored line and he swept past the Bud car as they entered the turn. Labonte pulled away as Junior fought for control in turn three, before completing two of the most exciting laps of the season.

"It won't run," Dale Jr. said as he rounded turn two on the last lap. "I'm outta fuel!"

The leaders had such an advantage that Dale Jr. still finished second as his starving engine sputtered and stuttered across the line.

"Helluva run, man," Norris said, but there was only silence from the driver.

Junior led 31 laps and finished second at a track that had vexed him the year before. After climbing from his car, Junior fought through a crowded victory lane area to shake hands with Labonte.

"I ran out of fuel on the last lap," Junior told him, prompting Labonte to react in mock disgust.

"All that for nothing?" joked Labonte. "You shoulda told me you were gonna run out of gas!"

As a top-three finisher, Junior made his way to the post-race news conference.

"I did all I could do to hold him back," he said. "If we ran that same thing ten more times, he would get by me each time because he was faster. He must have wanted this one more than me, and I wanted it pretty bad. He went into the Tunnel Turn like I've never seen anyone do it before. He went about fifteen, twenty car lengths deeper in that corner than I did, and he was gone. I had a lotta fun with him because I respect

Bobby. I kinda played a little dirty. I wanted to win and I was trying to block or make him hit me in the rear bumper, but he wouldn't have none of that . . .. Congratulations to Bobby. He was awesome.

"If you would have asked me last year if I was looking forward to going back to Pocono, I would have looked at you like you were crazy. We really struggled on tracks that were relatively flat like this one, and there were a lot of smashed race cars after we were done . . .. With about eighty laps to go, I would have given anything for a top-three finish, but once you get up there in the lead and then lose it with [two] to go is disappointing. I thought we would be all right up there because we had clean air on the car, but it just kept getting tighter and tighter, and I just couldn't hold Bobby off. Even though I had a big lead, I was never cruising out there. I was going as hard as I could."

chapter 34

the finger

Indianapolis, Indiana

In the days before the race at the historic Indianapolis Motor Speedway, Junior's lengthy *Playboy* interview with writer Kevin Cook hit the newsstands, but, to our surprise, another magazine caused much more of a firestorm.

The September edition of *Racer* featured Dale Jr. standing defiantly on the cover, along with a story by Ben Blake. It was not one of Junior's more sparkling performances in print, as Blake had the misfortune of interviewing him on a day when he was agitated and irritated. But the controversy began as readers turned to page 41 and found a full-page photo of Dale Jr., wearing his uniform and dark sunglasses, giving the middle-finger salute. The photographer, Tony di Zinno, had snapped a few frames as Junior gave me the finger for something I said during the shoot. The image was so strong the magazine decided to run it.

Anheuser-Busch executives were nonplussed by the image; several smaller sponsors were incensed to see Junior make (in the words of one) "such a vile gesture." In the days that followed the magazine's release, Dale Jr. had to write an apology to the president of one of the companies whose tiny decal rests amid the dozens of others on the No. 8 car.

Racer editor Andy Hallberry said he never had such a response to any other photo. More than 120 readers canceled their subscriptions, many suggesting Dale Jr. would have never gotten away with the gesture were his father still alive. Hallberry resisted the urge to print a similar photo of the

Intimidator the following month, laughing that "flying the bird" was one of Big E's most used gestures, especially in the race car.

~

"Hey, where's my pit?" Dale Jr. asked on the pace lap of the Brickyard 400.

"We're on your left," Tony Jr. joked, doing his best to relax Dale Jr., who was starting a disappointing 36th.

The rectangular Indianapolis Motor Speedway has four distinct turns with very little banking. While lithe IndyCars rocket through the turns with their wide tires and massive downforce, getting a 3,500-pound stock car through the corners is a dilemma the Bud team had fought. But, they were anxious to apply some of their recent discoveries on the similar flat turns at Pocono, where they had nearly won seven days earlier.

"I got brake problems!" Dale Jr. yelled on lap two. "The fucking brakes don't work! The pedal went right to the floor!"

"It pumps up, but it goes down," Dale Jr. said in the next corner, just as a yellow flag came out for a crash.

A stop under the green would have certainly put them a lap (or more) behind, but under the yellow, they could be more deliberate in their repairs. As Junior crawled cautiously to a stop in his pit box, the crew lifted the hood, checking all of the lines and the brake-fluid levels. Because they were already at the back of the field, they stopped twice for additional adjustments and fuel.

Dale Jr. was relieved to report the braking issues seemed to be gone ("for now" he groused), as he restarted in 40th place.

Junior was able to pass 13 cars in 13 laps, and when the caution came out on lap 22, the team chose to take only two tires, hoping to gain track position. However, as Dale Jr. cruised past in the far lane, Hut Stricklin shot wildly out of his stall, careening into the left side of the Bud car. The impact forced Dale Jr. into the pit-lane wall, damaging the right side as well.

"I got a bent left front fender, and I got into the outside wall," Dale Jr. hollered.

The team stopped three times under yellow to try to repair the body damage and straighten the alignment of the front tires.

"Be careful. Your alignment is still three-sixteenths off," Tony Jr. reminded Dale Jr. as he restarted 40th, just as he had less than 20 laps earlier.

Surprisingly, the damaged car was still fast, passing cars with ease on the long front and back straights.

"I'm surprised!" Dale Jr. reported. "It's not too bad. Just a lil' less aerodynamic."

After another stop for fuel, Dale Jr. continued to pass cars, reaching the top 20 by lap 44.

"Guys, we're gonna win this fucker," Jeff Clark insisted after a quick pit stop.

"Hell yeah! I'm pumped up, and drivin' like hell," answered Dale Jr. "We're in this motherfucker. It's funny, when I go down the straight, it's wiggling around."

"You're as fast as anybody right now," Norris told him.

Since the team had repeatedly filled the gas tank during the early stops, they could go farther than nearly any other car, and, to his amazement, Dale Jr. drove his beaten Bud mount into the lead by lap 65. By pitting later than the rest, the team was on a different fuel sequence than most of the field except for Tony Stewart and Steve Park.

"Wooohoooo!" Dale Jr. bellowed as he completed a three-wide pass, moving by Stewart into second place.

With Park leading easily, Dale Jr. and Stewart ran in tandem for 20 laps. Communicating through their spotters, Junior waved Stewart past on lap 94 to see if the duo was faster with Tony's car in front. One lap later, Stewart waved Dale Jr. back into second.

"Tony says that he is just too loose with you right on his back bumper like that," Norris reported. "He says that one of you needs to give the other some space so you can both run in clean air. He doesn't care who, but you guys need more space in between each other."

The crucial moment came on lap 132, when the race was slowed for debris on the track. With less than 30 laps remaining, the team chose to change four tires, setting themselves for the finish. However, a number of teams chose to take only two tires, which pushed the Bud car to tenth place.

"It's damn hard to pass in traffic at the front," Dale Jr. explained. "What do ya think about our chances to get these guys with two tires?"

"Slim to none," Tony Jr. replied.

"Well, my car won't turn now," Junior reported. "Something feels different, maybe following these sorry-ass guys. These tires just aren't the same as the others. I'm tight. Tight, tight, tight."

With his car no longer in clean air, Dale Jr. hung on to finish 10th, while Jeff Gordon became the first man to win the Brickyard 400 three times. Gordon was followed by Sterling Marlin in second and Johnny Benson in third. In a similar tire situation to Dale Jr., Steve Park fought back to finish seventh.

"We passed more cars than I can imagine," an overheated Dale Jr. said. "It was almost easy moving up after we got the brakes fixed, and then Hut [Stricklin] just ran into me. He hit me so damn hard I slammed the pit wall. After that, the car wasn't as aerodynamic. It seemed like just a few laps later the crew told me we had five bonus points because we were leading the race."

chapter 35

metal to metal

Watkins Glen, New York

A busy week for Dale Jr. began in Baton Rouge, as he made another appearance for Coca-Cola. In the center court of a large mall, fans packed the railings three stories high. Junior was stunned to see several thousand people willing to come out on a weekday afternoon. The turnout was another example of the interest in NASCAR in regions of the country without a race nearby.

Junior flew to upstate New York Thursday afternoon to visit an Anheuser-Busch brewery in Baldwinsville, then hopped on a flight to Chicago, where he made an appearance that evening at a banquet held by the Rainbow/ PUSH Coalition. Junior was recognized for his efforts supporting the Urban Youth Racing League before he took the podium to present a special-recognition award to Morty Buckles, a promising African-American NASCAR Late Model series driver.

Soon, he was back in the air, flying to the Finger Lakes region of upstate New York, where practice began Friday morning at the Watkins Glen road course. Because Junior had won a Busch Series race there in 1999, his confidence at the Glen was much higher than it had been at Sears Point Raceway. He had a top-10 run going in his first Cup race on the 2.45-mile NASCAR course when a broken shift linkage ended his day and Steve Park earned his first career Winston Cup victory.

Saturday night, Dale Jr. and Tony Jr. raced late-model stock cars against each other at Tioga Motorsports Park, a half-mile paved oval near Oswego, New York. Tony Jr. "nudged" (his term) his cousin, giving Junior a flat left rear tire on lap three. After being allowed to change the tire, Dale Jr. eventually prevailed in the 18-lap dash for charity. Had he lost to his cousin, Earnhardt Jr. might never have heard the end of it.

It would not be as simple to make up ground in Sunday's Cup race, starting the day from the 27th position. The team knew their best chance to gain track position was to make their first pit stop as early as possible, putting them on a different sequence than the cars ahead of them just as they had done at Indianapolis.

As soon as the first caution flag of the day appeared on lap 19, Dale Jr. made a stop while most of the field stayed out. This allowed Dale Jr. to run as high as second place when the leaders began to make their stops 10 laps later.

When the second caution came out on lap 39, Dale Jr. was anxious to pit again for fresh tires.

"Are we gonna pit here?" Dale Jr. asked.

"We're staying out," Pops told him.

"Are you serious?" Junior replied.

"Ten-four. We're staying out," Pops repeated.

"Awwww, I'm just hangin' on!" Dale Jr. said.

Though not the fastest car, and despite protests from the driver, the pit strategy worked to perfection. As the laps counted down, Dale Jr. and Ricky Rudd, one of the best road course racers in Winston Cup, waged a fierce battle for fourth place. The two made contact several times before Junior launched the Bud car into the air, climbing the curb in the chicane along the backstretch to avoid hard contact with Rudd.

"We're going metal to metal and wheel to wheel!" Junior yelled in his best announcer voice.

With seven laps remaining, Dale Jr. lined up fourth for a restart, immediately behind Rudd. At the green flag, Rudd was slow to gain speed, which forced Dale Jr. hard on the brakes to avoid a penalty for passing before the start/finish line. As he fought to regain traction, six cars streamed past him before turn one.

Now battling for each position, Dale Jr. slid off the track in turn one on the next lap while racing Boris Said, his road racing tutor. The near-crash dropped Junior to 12th, where he finished the race. He was lucky, however, to have avoided the deep gravel pit just outside of the turn. Had he become stuck in the gravel, he could have dropped as far back as 29th place.

It wasn't nearly as dramatic for Jeff Gordon, whose victory extended his Winston Cup points lead and made him the all-time leader in Winston Cup road-racing victories with seven.

Dale Jr. was pleased with the best road-course finish of his young Cup career, but frustrated about the late restart.

"That restart was way too slow. I don't know what Jeff [Gordon] was thinking," he told the team. "Everyone was bottled up, so when I let off the gas to keep from hitting the 28 car, I lost momentum and everybody was all over us, three and four wide. It was crazy.

"To have run so bad in practice and qualifying and then to run so well in the race feels good, but it's still frustrating because I feel like we should have had a top five."

chapter 36

junior finally listens

Brooklyn, Michigan

One of the most crucial moments in the growth of NASCAR was the 1979 Daytona 500. It was the first NASCAR race televised live in its entirety, and it earned huge ratings as Cale Yarborough and Donnie Allison crashed each other going for victory on the final lap. Then, joined by Donnie's brother Bobby, the drivers extended their disagreement in a flurry of angry punches live on CBS. The passionate fight gave NASCAR a level of national awareness it never before had.

As the sport's popularity grew, so too did the number of major sponsors. Now the scrappy and scruffy daredevils were representing major corporations that preferred their spokespeople not be involved in nationally televised assault and battery. Thus, as sponsor dollars grew in million-dollar increments, the very element that drew so much attention was now strongly discouraged.

In the same way, the primal allure of a dangerous sport that killed Dale Earnhardt drew many new viewers. FOX, TNT, and NBC reported average ratings gains between 30 and 35 percent during 2001, the highest numbers in NASCAR's history. Yet, the scrutiny that followed Earnhardt's death forced the sport to examine and improve safety in as many areas as possible, decreasing its thrill-seeker appeal.

Diehard NASCAR fans began to complain the sport had lost its appeal without Earnhardt, and the bare-knuckle rivalries of the past faded.

NASCAR driver rivalries are vastly different than rivalries in almost any other sport. In most college or pro sports, teams see a hated opponent

223

once or twice per season. But NASCAR pits rivals head-to-head 38 times a year. This is part of what makes the sport great: no matter where the race is held, fans know every all-star will be in the starting field.

Yet, rivals or not, each driver must share a level of respect and trust for the others. Each driver's life is in the hands of the other 42 drivers on the track. That level of mutual trust isn't a factor when a player stretches for a fly ball or leaps for a rebound. Certainly there are examples of heated retaliation and roughhousing between drivers, but because such serious harm can result, a driver with a reckless history must mature or improve in order to remain in the sport.

Another new element had been introduced to NASCAR in the previous decade: the motorcoach lot.

Reserved for drivers and team owners (and now crew chiefs), the private, fenced-in mobile communities fill each week with million-dollar-plus buses, creating a smalltown dynamic that exists nowhere else. In what other sport do you spend three or four nights a week living three feet away from your competitors? The (relatively) quiet oasis is a place where drivers and their families can relax away from fans, media, and sponsors. It's tough to maintain a rivalry at full boil when the other driver sleeps in the next motorcoach. This doesn't mean everyone is friendly with everyone else— far from it—but it does make it difficult to hold a white-hot disdain on track when your wives and kids are friends.

For Dale Jr., the motorcoach community was a huge influence after Daytona. Many veteran drivers he respected came to his bus, encouraging him to reconsider his stubborn opposition to wearing a head and neck protection device. Dale Jarrett was the most insistent, appealing to Junior more as a friend than competitor, reminding him the entire sport needed him around for years to come, and that he was risking his life by not using all of the safety gear available to him. Jeff Gordon, Jeff Burton, and others took a similar tack, quietly lobbying Junior to try one of the options. Junior's resistance seemed to finally weaken when Terry Labonte, one of his father's rivals and normally a quiet presence in the garage, came to see him one evening.

Before the final practice session Saturday afternoon at Michigan International Speedway, Dale Jr. finally chose to wear the Hutchens Device in his race car.

"I was surprised that those guys took the time and the interest to approach me about it," he explained. "When they are that serious about it, you have to listen and give it a try."

Junior chose the Hutchens Device over the HANS because of his loyalty to Bobby Hutchens, who had developed the system at Richard Childress Racing. It took much of the day to get the straps adjusted to Junior's liking, especially the crotch strap that wrapped around his groin. Junior was also frustrated with the location of the hooks mounted on his helmet, and was concerned they would pull his open-face helmet backward rather than hold it down. With the help of the team, which was thrilled he had finally changed his mind, the hooks and straps were fine-tuned when he climbed in for the 400-mile race at Michigan.

Starting from the 12th position as a light mist fell on the two-mile track, Dale Jr. hovered near the top 10 early in the race but began to struggle when the dark clouds, swirling winds, and cooler temperatures didn't agree with the No. 8 car.

Dale Jr. had dropped to 13th position when rain prompted a yellow flag on lap 98.

"You guys need to speak up, especially Tony Jr.," Dale Jr. insisted as the field slowed. "I wanna ask all o' you guys if you can hear him when he talks? Is it just me? I mean, it's like he's on AM radio and everyone else is on FM."

"Ten-four," Tony Jr. replied with a resigned tone.

"C'mon, Tony Junior! Speak up!" Dale Jr. yelled, teasing his cousin. "It sounds like you're using some sorta megaphone. I just can't hear it over this screaming engine. Or is it that your voice is just not masculine enough?"

The crew got a good laugh from the banter as the rain increased, stopping the race for an hour and 45 minutes on lap 100.

During the delay, Junior answered questions about the Hutchens Device.

"It was a little uncomfortable in a few places, but we'll work on making it fit me a little better in the race car," he explained. "Overall, I didn't notice it too much, and we'll be using it from now on. It's cool."

During the delay, Pops and Tony Jr. studied the radar closely and decided to gamble the rain would stay away long enough to complete the full distance. When the race restarted, they brought Dale Jr. in for a splash of fuel, which meant they could make it to lap 200 with one less stop than many of the leaders.

Now running deep in the pack, Junior struggled.

"My tires feel like they're made of concrete," he yelled.

"It's starting to drizzle up here," Norris reported from atop the tower above the front stretch on lap 150, dooming the team's fuel strategy.

"I know," said Tony Jr. "We're staying out. We're not stopping here."

As the rain intensified, NASCAR threw the red flag on lap 162 with Sterling Marlin leading. When it was determined the race could not be restarted before darkness, Marlin had earned the first Winston Cup victory for Dodge since 1977. Ricky Craven was second, while Bill Elliott finished third. With their strategy foiled, Dale Jr. and the team settled for a 12th-place tally.

"We would have been in good shape if the race would have gone the distance. It was really starting to work for us," Junior said, walking under a Budweiser umbrella through a water-logged garage area. "I think the last five laps before it rained were our best laps of the day. The car was starting to work well and we were able to pass some guys before the rains came. I guess twelfth is decent, but it could have been better."

chapter 37

shelly and
ol' man elliott

Bristol, Tennessee

Dale Jr. was a part of NASCAR's Winner's Circle program, which paid bonus money to winning drivers who made appearances to help sell advance tickets. Dale Jr. was selected to travel to Darlington Raceway for a Wednesday-afternoon news conference. Before the questioning began, Cathy Mock (née Elliott), the track's public relations director, read an excerpt from the Dale Jr. *Playboy* interview. He had been asked which track was NASCAR's worst.

"Darlington. It's old. It's egg-shaped. It's full of seashells," Dale Jr. said. "They use crushed rock and seashells in the asphalt mix. It's so coarse you get an awesome grip for four or five laps, but then your tires wear off and you're just sliding around, trying not to hit something. Go out on that track and rub your hand on it—it'll actually cut you."

Andrew Gurtis, the track's president, approached the stage carrying a trophy with a large seashell on top. Laughing heartily, Dale Jr. received the first-ever Shelly Award. The trophy was inscribed: "Darlington Raceway Day at the Beach. 'The Shelly' presented to Dale Earnhardt Jr., Aug. 22, 2001."

"I hear you've sold more tickets since that interview came out," Junior joked.

As the questioning turned to his father's death, he was asked if he had moved on.

"I don't know if you can really say you can move on from this. I really don't know how you're supposed to grieve. Is there some sort of guidelines you follow? I've been able to deal with everything well. You handle it however you handle it, and I think I've been able to do that well."

That afternoon also saw the release of NASCAR's official report on the Earnhardt crash. The study reinforced the findings NASCAR had released in the days after the crash, concluding Earnhardt died of a basal skull fracture, which likely occurred either by contact with the steering wheel or on "rebound" from the impact with the wall. Their research revealed Earnhardt died "as a result of a series of factors coming together at the same time."

The collision with Schrader's car added to the severe angle of wall impact, which, combined with the rotation of the helmet on Earnhardt's head, contributed to his death. The broken seatbelt exacerbated the impact, throwing Earnhardt into the steering wheel, causing the broken ribs. "No single factor can be isolated as the cause of Dale Earnhardt's death," the study concluded.

Prepared by Dean Sikking and Don Reid, Ph.D.s from the University of Nebraska, and Drs. James Benedict and James Raddin from the Biodynamic Research Corporation, the report contained more than 320 pages of data and details. (Sikking also led the team that created the Steel and Foam Energy Reduction system, commonly known as the SAFER barrier. The barriers dissipate the energy of a wall impact and are now installed on most major NASCAR tracks.) The study also concluded there was no way to determine if a HANS device or other restraints would have prevented the same injuries.

Having come to his own understanding of the crash, Dale Jr. didn't seem overly interested in delving deeper into the details of the study.

If Junior selected Darlington as the worst track, Bristol Motor Speedway would have to reside on his list of favorites. Years earlier, he had learned the appeal of watching a Bristol race from high above the corners, now surrounded with towering grandstands.

"When I was a kid, I remember playing on the side of the hill above the banked turns," he explained. "You could look right down into the cars, and I remember paying attention to Dad's arms and all of the other guys as they steered past me each lap. I think a lot of the fans that sit in the grandstands above the turns can still do that now."

But, the media were much more interested in his decision to finally use the Hutchens Device.

"I have a friend who is a state trooper, and he said it's like wearing a bulletproof vest," Junior said. "You don't have to wear it and you can be a badass and walk around without it if you want to. But why not wear it while you can?"

In the final practice session, the team struggled to find speed.

"It's snug and comfortable," Junior said, describing his car's handling. "But I don't want to be snug and comfortable in last place."

The team made several changes to try and help the car, but when the race began, it was way too loose and Junior slipped and slid. When the first caution came out on lap 15, the team made a stop to fix the handling, restarting in 39th. It would be the first stop of a long evening, as Junior clawed his way to 15th place by lap 150.

"It's jumping like a bronco off the turns," Junior complained after nearly slamming the wall in turn two.

When his progress slowed, frustration and aggression began to take hold, and Junior made contact with Bill Elliott, sending the No. 9 car for a spin, causing one of the 16 caution periods in the 500-lap race.

"The sonuvabitches were cutting me off!" Junior yelled. "Ol' man Bill Elliott, it's like he's falling asleep out here."

After contact with the ol' man, Junior dropped back, losing a lap as Jeff Gordon got by on lap 320.

For 70 laps, Junior pushed hard to stay near Gordon, eventually finding the speed to pass him before a yellow flag on lap 395. It was the second time in two Bristol races Dale Jr. passed the leader to regain a lap.

With renewed intensity, Dale Jr. had less than 100 laps remaining to get back into the top 20. He bounced and banged his way through the field, climbing to 14th place at the checkered flag. It had been a frustrating night, but their perseverance meant a career-best finish at Bristol.

Tony Stewart won the Sharpie 500, holding off Kevin Harvick as the final 98 laps were run without a caution. Gordon was third, stretching his ever-increasing lead in the Winston Cup standings.

"I'm beat," Junior said, as he found a place to sit at the back of the hauler. "It's such a rough track, it just beats up your body every lap. You're always in traffic, there's nowhere to relax or rest. At some points during the race, you're just trying to hang on and survive. You're really not racing anybody."

"When we'd put on new tires, the car would stick like glue," he explained to Tony Jr. "But, after a few laps, it felt like I was driving on balloons or something.

"Where are we in points?" Dale Jr. asked.

He was happy to hear he still held sixth place, but didn't look forward to the action at Darlington the following Sunday.

"I guess it will be a lot of the same next week . . . running in single file until someone ahead of you messes up and you can get by 'em. Every position is a fight."

chapter 38

cast away

Darlington, South Carolina

Junior's dislike for Darlington had earned him a funny trophy, but he was in no mood for laughs Friday afternoon. *Newsweek* magazine had sent writers Daniel McGinn and Bret Begun to the track to interview Dale Jr. for a cover story. While Junior had been relatively patient during the interview, he grew increasingly irritated as their photographer tried to get a variety of cover-worthy photos in the brutal Labor Day weekend heat. After several poses, Junior decided he had enough and walked back to the garage. They begged me to bring him back, but my pleas had no effect until the *Newsweek* writers convinced Junior they needed backup photos just like his team needed a backup car. He begrudgingly agreed to stand inside of turn one, posing with his back to the track he despised.

The mood wasn't much better Saturday as the Bud team huddled after the first practice of the day. The cumulative effect of a nonstop summer of racing had taken a toll on everyone's emotions, and struggling to find a balanced setup on a treacherous track only added to the stress. (A grouchy driver didn't help either.) They had several hours before the next session, which was scheduled to start after the completion of the Busch Series race. That race had been stopped for nearly 30 minutes due to rain, and no one in the Bud hauler was paying much attention as the field lined up for the restart.

"Hey, isn't that Park?" someone yelled, and we all turned toward the TV to watch a replay of a horrific crash.

Steve Park was making a rare Busch Series start in the No. 31 car for team owner Ted Marsh, and his car had suddenly snapped to the left as he exited turn two behind the pace car. At that moment, a lapped car driven by Larry Foyt was running at high speed on the inside line, attempting to double-up for the restart. Unable to stop or swerve, Foyt's car T-boned Park's car in the driver-side door at more than 100 miles per hour.

Everyone on the Bud team huddled around the screen, hoping to see Park climb out. He was wearing a Hutchens Device, but how would it protect him in such a vicious hit from the side? After safety crews arrived, Park remained in the car as they brought in the Jaws of Life, which allowed them to cut through the roof of the car and remove an injured or unconscious driver. After nearly 20 minutes, another crew unfurled a large blue tarp around the crash scene.

The last time NASCAR had used the tarps was Earnhardt's Daytona crash, and everyone in the hauler fell silent. This was serious.

"Do you know where the hospital is?" Dale Jr. asked.

"Yeah," I said. Each week's emergency plan included a map with directions to the nearby hospital in case of a major accident.

"Someone named Earnhardt should be at that hospital," he said as we walked from the hauler.

The medical helicopter transported Park to Carolinas Hospital in Florence, South Carolina. Dale Jr. and I climbed into his Camaro SS, not knowing what we would find when we got to the hospital. There was an apprehensive silence between us as Junior drove through the deserted streets of Darlington and Florence.

We were met at the emergency room by Danielle Humphrey (née Frye) of NASCAR's communications department. She assured us Steve was all right, which was a huge relief, but Junior insisted on seeing Park.

"Hey, Junior," Park murmured. But, after recognizing his teammate, Park uttered a nonsensical stream of numbers and words, an indication of the seriousness of the head injury that would eventually end his promising Cup career.

Thankfully, Park was alive, but he was far from OK.

NASCAR put out a news bulletin saying Park had been alert and conscious as he was airlifted, and would be kept overnight for observation. The initial diagnosis indicated his injuries were a possible fracture or dislocation of the left sternoclavicular joint (collarbone) and a "moderate" concussion. Foyt hit his right knee on the steering column, but was otherwise uninjured.

We drove back to the track before the final practice, where Junior shared the news with DEI executives and crew members. Paul Andrews, Park's crew chief, arranged for Kenny Wallace to practice the No. 1 car in Happy Hour, hoping Park would be cleared to race the next day. When Sunday arrived, Park remained in the hospital and Wallace was tapped to race the Pennzoil car.

Before the race, Dale Jr. described what made Darlington such a challenge.

"You have good grip in the tires for maybe five laps, and then you spend the rest of the run, whether it's thirty laps or sixty laps, just holding on, trying not to crash, praying that the yellow flag comes out and you can come in and get new tires. I think I spend most of the race praying."

Worried about his hospitalized teammate and pessimistic about the 367 laps ahead of him, Junior started on the outside of row nine. Making matters worse, the first caution period didn't arrive until lap 56, long past the time his tires had given up their grip. Driving cautiously, Dale Jr. had moved up two spots to 16th, but was far from happy about it.

"I'm sorry if I'm hot under the collar, but this ain't what I want to do for a living; just riding around," he said.

"Just give us a chance to work on it," Tony Jr. replied.

"I just don't see how we can keep off the wall," Dale Jr. continued.

On lap 78, Junior made contact with Hut Stricklin, spinning him into the wall. Was it retaliation for the pit-lane incident at Indy? Junior was tightlipped during the caution.

With significant changes under the next two caution periods, the Bud car began to respond. As others slowed their lap times dramatically, Junior was able to move up to eighth place by lap 110.

"How many laps until we stop?" he asked.

"Twenty laps to go," said Tony Jr.

"Twenty?" Junior said. "Fuuuuck."

"It may not feel like it, but you're gaining on the guys in front of you," said Norris.

Soon after, Junior nearly hit the wall, sliding sideways off turn two. He managed to save the car, but dropped 14 spots to 22nd place. His in-car camera caught a glimpse of him giving Mike Skinner the finger after another close call.

Luckily, the caution flag came out on lap 182, giving him a chance to pit for fresh tires.

"Sorry I dropped back there," Junior apologized. "I tried to adjust my belts and the [Hutchens Device]. I wanna have children someday, and that belt wasn't cooperating. We just gotta fix it so I'm more comfortable. The way the belts are set, my whole ass went to sleep."

"So the loss of grip is out of your ass . . . not the car?" Tony Jr. asked.

"Half and half," Dale Jr. laughed. "Don't get too happy."

Soon after the restart, Junior made contact with Stacy Compton in the No. 92, sending Compton spinning down the front stretch. The contact prompted NASCAR to issue a stern warning to Dale Jr.

"Maybe he needs to raise his seat up," Compton suggested. "Apparently, he can't see over the hood."

Though Dale Jr. insisted the incident wasn't his fault, he acknowledged NASCAR's scolding.

"I know what they're saying," he replied. "I don't know what's getting into me. I'm just not having fun. I've been in a bad mood lately."

"Time to get in a good mood," Tony Jr. urged, referring to the next race at Richmond, where the team was eligible for Winston's million-dollar bonus. "We're gonna go bust their asses next week for a million."

"I am amazed anyone can finish five hundred miles without crashing," Junior said. "I'm out here slipping and sliding lap after lap after lap, and I feel so stranded. You know, all alone. '*Help! Somebody save me! Anybody!*' Y'all just make me feel like Tom Hanks out here, all alone. I should just get a volleyball to keep me company."

As the race entered the final 50 laps, Dale Jr. moved forward, climbing to 10th place. When a crash slowed the field on lap 350, the cousins decided to gamble.

"We may not win this thing, but I say we stay out," Tony Jr. said. "You were four-tenths faster than anybody on the racetrack."

"I can't believe we're in the top ten! We're talking about Darlington," Dale Jr. said, marveling at their late-race surge as his nasty mood took a respite.

"Just drive these last laps like you just did those," Tony Jr. urged.

Six laps later, Dale Jr. moved into sixth place behind Gordon and Rudd before all hell broke loose with two multicar crashes, one on the front stretch and another in turn three.

"The car feels good," Dale Jr. said. "I'm better than both these cats in front of me. I can get around 'em!"

"I've been coming to Darlington for twelve years and I've only finished two times," Tony Jr. said prematurely.

Rather than end the race under the caution period, NASCAR threw the red flag, stopping the race for track cleanup.

"Why are they stopping us?" Junior protested. "I wanna go to the house!"

"Be ready to be aggressive here," Tony Jr. encouraged.

"I disagree with them stopping the race," Dale Jr. said. "I know the fans like it, but every time they stop a race like this, half the field ends up getting crashed."

Halfway into the eight-minute stoppage, the Bud machine began overheating, spouting water and steam from the cooling system.

"I'm overheating here!" Dale Jr. reported. "This [red flag] is *bullshit*."

"You'll be fine once you get going," Tony Jr. said. "Looks like you'll have four laps to go when they throw the green."

It was a mad dash, with Junior stalking Rudd and Gordon for two laps. Both veterans slowed when Jeremy Mayfield, running third, bounced off the turn four wall. This was the opening Junior needed as he swept past Rudd and inside of Gordon. Dave Blaney saw the same opening and pulled his Dodge to the left of the two Chevys as they approached turn one.

As the track narrowed, Blaney's car touched the apron and veered to the right, taking Dale Jr. with him as they slammed the outside wall. With the track blocked, the rest of the field became bowling pins, bumping and bouncing in all directions. Amidst the chaos, Dale Jr. was able to restart his car, then limp it across the finish line in 17th.

Ahead of the cacophony, Ward Burton grabbed his first Southern 500 victory. Somehow Gordon had escaped the Blaney–Junior mess to finish second with Bobby Labonte in third.

As Junior climbed from his smoldering heap, he spotted Blaney. I followed closely to referee any heated confrontation, but Junior began laughing as he approached.

"Wow! We were three-wide and running hard," Junior laughed.

"Yeah, that was a helluva try," Blaney said. "We *almost* saved it."

As he walked back to the Bud hauler, Junior was asked about the crash.

"I guess I'm more disappointed than pissed-off about that crash. I mean, we coulda finished third on a day when we struggled and fought and scrapped for every position," he said.

"Dave Blaney is one of the best guys, one of the best people out there, but he made it three wide where ya just can't do it. I almost saved the car, and I even came to a stop and started rolling again when the 40 car [Sterling Marlin] blasted into me. It knocked my hands clean off the steering wheel. It looked like a fireworks show trying to make it around that last lap, sparks and smoke and shit flying off."

Before leaving the track, Dale Jr. stopped by the NASCAR hauler to express his displeasure with the red flag which he believed cost him a top-five finish.

"It's the dumbest thing I've seen," he said.

chapter 39

fast and loud as hell

New York, New York

The buzz generated by Junior's appearances on two MTV shows made it easy to secure him an invitation to appear at the 2001 Video Music Awards in New York. The show, known as the VMAs, seemed a natural fit for a young man with a deep love of music. But, it almost didn't happen.

"Nah, I don't know if I could really do that," Junior squirmed when told about the invite. "I just wouldn't be comfortable among all that."

This was another example of his shyness taking hold when he looked outside his comfort zone. I was much more confident in his ability, and several days of reasoning (mixed with shameless pleading) finally won out. Then, attention turned to his most urgent concern: fashion.

"I ain't goin' up there in a damn Mooresville suit," he complained.

The solution: Sarah Parlow, a cute-as-hell New York stylist we had both flirted with at a *People* magazine photo shoot the year before. Sarah was game for the challenge, and we met her and her long racks of high-fashion clothes several hours before the show.

His second concern? "What the hell am I gonna do up there?"

MTV wanted Dale Jr. to introduce the band Linkin Park, a California combo whose blend of hard rock and hip-hop made their *Hybrid Theory* album the top-selling disc of 2001.

As we arrived in New York, the script appeared, and our stomachs sank. It was awful.

"I'm not sayin' that shit," Junior said as he tried on different looks from the racks of style.

"We should just rewrite it," I suggested with overconfidence, not wanting to show my inexperience at the inner workings of big-time award shows. "It's a live show. What are they gonna do? Stop the broadcast if you say something different?"

With both of us fitted in fine Italian leather jackets (straight from Milan, as far away from Mooresville as you can get), we finalized the script as our Town Car approached the Metropolitan Opera House at Lincoln Center. More than a block away, we saw crowds lining both sides of the street. Behind temporary fencing, they looked just like the waffle-bellies at the racetrack. Tinted windows made us invisible to the spectators, but there were still shrill screams as we approached, just in case Nelly or Kid Rock was inside our limo. We toyed with the idea of popping out of the roof, waving frantically and inciting a temporary frenzy until they wondered, "Wait, who the hell is *that*?"

As we stopped behind a line of identical cars, a young MTV staffer double-checked who was inside. "Dale Earnhardt Jr.?" she repeated while scrolling down her checklist. "OK, Mr. Earnhardt, thanks for coming. Stay in the car until your name is called."

As the car crept toward the red carpet, a loudspeaker barked to the crowd in a makeshift grandstand: "Ladies and gentlemen, Dale Earnhardt Jr.!"

Junior exited sheepishly to the teenaged squeals and made his way across the carpet toward a swarm of paparazzi. He was introduced in a similar fashion before each race, but this was an all-new arena. Like a starter's pistol going off for a 100-meter dash, a photographer shouted Junior's name and suddenly the entire pack began screaming at once: "Dale! This way!" "Junior, look to the right please!" "Dale! Dale! Up here to the left!" "Smile, Junior! Smile!"

After the frenzied photographers, there stretched a massive conga line of video cameras and microphones representing media from around the world clamoring to see what Pink, Jennifer Lopez, and Jon Bon Jovi were wearing. No one, it seemed, cared what a race car driver was wearing. Dale Jr. felt like the 43rd guy on the grid at a Winston Cup race: sure, he's in the show, but no one is quite sure who he is and nobody's clamoring for an interview. They wanted the BIG names . . . Outkast! Mark Wahlberg! Howard Stern!

We soon met our very own MTV personal assistant. A dentist by day, he was one of the many volunteers who worked the show each year and, in our nervousness, we forgot his name as soon as he introduced himself. His job was to take care of Dale Jr.'s "superstar needs" and, more importantly, make sure Junior made it to the makeup room, to his seat, and then backstage at the right time. As he escorted us inside, we watched photographers surround the heavy metal band Mudvayne, who were covered in blood from pseudo bullet holes in their foreheads.

We walked through the ornate auditorium and headed backstage. In small, poorly lit hallways, it was a jumble of familiar faces and music icons. In the makeup room, Junior had to wait as Pam Anderson was made up. Someone whispered, "She's looking like a two-thousand-dollar whore," as her makeup was covered with another layer of powder and paint.

"I sure would like to have the new script on the teleprompter," a jittery Junior reminded me.

It seemed like the perfect job for our eager volunteer, and he led me through the bowels of the opera house to a nook where a woman was happy to enter the "newly approved" (wink wink) script into the computer. Mission accomplished.

In the garage area at the racetrack, we called new fans "swivelheads." Swivelheads are so overwhelmed by stimuli, their glazed stares jump side to side, with no clue where to look next. Now *we* were the swivelheads, as P. Diddy stood beside us with his posse (not much different from Junior's Dirty Mo Posse, except the DMP never dressed exactly alike). Across the aisle, rock gods U2 sat in front of Gwen Stefani and her band, No Doubt.

The show opened with comedy bits from host Jamie Foxx, Will Farrell, and Triumph the Insult Comic Dog, followed by a wickedly brilliant Andy Dick as "Daphne Aguilera, Christina's cousin."

The first award of the night went to the boys from Mudvayne. "This'll be hardcore," we chuckled as they approached the podium to pick up their MTV Moonman trophy.

"We'd like to thank our parents!" the green-haired one blurted out, sounding more like an excited sorority sister than a rocker slathered in fake blood. So much for hardcore.

Sitting to Junior's left was Jessica Simpson, a short lil' thing and not as svelte as she would later become. On the aisle was her sister, Ashlee, not yet known to the world as a lip-synching pop starlet. To my right sat an impossibly gorgeous, lanky beauty in a scoop-neck dress exposing a thin strand of skin from neck to belly-button. Of course, Junior and I were too shy to speak with them.

During a commercial break, our volunteer came to retrieve Junior.

"Who is that sitting beside us?" I asked him.

"The tall one? That's Mandy Moore," he said. "She's seventeen," he added as an afterthought, which made me feel like the dirtiest old man in all of Manhattan.

We circled backstage, where we encountered Destiny's Child having a minor diva spat, while Fatboy Slim, actor Christopher Walken, and director Spike Jonze accepted one of their six awards for their "Weapon of Choice" video, which featured Walken dancing through a deserted hotel. As the actor soft-shoed offstage, Junior wondered if Walken's makeup and complexion made him look as if he were made of wax.

"Yo, Jooon-yahhh!" came a loud voice. "Will you sign this?"

The union stagehands began circling, grabbing Dale Jr. T-shirts, hats, and diecast cars that had been hidden backstage. Despite feeling overlooked among the superstars in the arena, Junior was pleased to be recognized by the hardworking guys and gals who couldn't have cared less about Beyoncé or the other luminaries.

"We're not supposed to ask for autographs," one of them admitted, "but I'm not gonna miss a chance to get Dale Jr.'s signature!"

"The people's hero," I laughed.

Junior happily signed each of the items, but the man who loved going three wide at 200 miles per hour was a ball of nerves. Standing with Linkin Park behind a massive façade, Junior waited for his cue behind a flimsy prop door.

"I like my music like I like my race cars: fast. And loud as hell. Here's Linkin Park . . .."

It was all a shaky blur, and it was over in seconds as Junior escaped from the stage and exhaled dramatically.

With our adrenaline dying down, we learned another award-show lesson: there's no food. Luckily, the fine folks from M&M's/Mars had stocked the backstage area with confectionary. We grabbed what we could before we were led to the backstage media area.

Amassed in a large tent, the print media offered an array of questions when Junior stepped to the podium. "What are you listening to these days?" came the first query. Dale Jr. knocked it out of the park with his response.

"I like it all," he said. "Right now I'm listening to the *O Brother, Where Art Thou?* soundtrack. It doesn't matter what kind of music it is. Good is good."

After the news conference, Junior was led to a row of tents that resembled NASCAR's media day, except the interviewers from E!, VH1, and "The Today Show" were incredibly attractive young women. His jangled nerves a thing of the past, Dale Jr. worked each interview like a pro.

We waited for a commercial break and walked back to our seats, hungrily pulling candy from our pockets. As I grabbed a packet of Starburst, a small squeal of glee came from Mandy Moore.

"Do you have any orange ones?" she inquired sweetly. "They're my favorite."

If there were an entry in the *Guinness Book of World Records* for "Speediest opening of a packet of square fruit chews," you'd see my picture, grinnin' like a madman in my Ferrari-red jacket. Then it dawned on me. I'm feeding candy to a teenager. To her delight (and mine), there were three orange ones in the pack and I had made a new friend, however briefly.

We marveled at live performances from U2, Missy Elliot, and Jay-Z, but after several handfuls of processed sugar, we were soon in search of Budweiser. The bar in the lower lobby had only mixed drinks for the tuxedoed record executives, so we headed up a massive stairway, eventually finding a stash of Michelob. It wasn't Bud, but it was an Anheuser-Busch product, and it hit the spot.

While on the beer run, we missed Michael Jackson appearing with 'N Sync, but Junior's focus had already jumped ahead to Saturday night's race at Richmond. We slid out a side door and called for our Town Car. Once we were rolling to the airport, Junior placed a call to the Dirty Mo Posse.

"Did you see it?" Junior asked. "How was I?"

With the reassurance of his buddies, Junior finally seemed convinced the experience had been a good one, as he laughed and told them of the stars we had seen. His buddies couldn't believe he left early without seeing Britney Spears and her albino snake. But it wouldn't have mattered to Junior if the remaining Beatles had reunited on stage—it was time for him to win a million bucks.

chapter 40

step dad

Richmond, Virginia

His rock star moment behind him, Junior returned to his day job. Victory at Daytona made the team eligible for the Winston million-dollar bonus if they could do the same at Richmond, a track where they had a superb history with a win and three top-10 finishes. Optimism grew when the Bud car recorded the quickest time in the first practice session of the weekend, turning a lap at an average of more than 124 miles per hour on the three-quarter-mile track.

Following Steve Park's accident at Darlington, NASCAR had instituted a new procedure. Most speculation about what caused Park's car to veer suddenly had focused on his steering wheel. To help the driver climb in and out, each steering wheel has a quick-release connection allowing it to be taken off the steering column. The Darlington race had been red-flagged for rain, and many believed Park did not secure his wheel when he restarted. When it dislodged, Park's car took the sharp left turn. In response, NASCAR placed an official on pit lane, requiring each driver to tug on the steering wheel to confirm it was securely attached before going onto the racetrack.

The team had done everything they could to replicate their Daytona mastery, including building a new chassis they called "Step Dad."

During their days in the Busch Series, the team had pulled out an aging chassis they called "the red-headed stepchild" because the entire chassis and interior was painted red rather than the more common grey. Surprisingly, the old hunk of metal became Junior's favorite chassis, and he drove it to 11 victories in two seasons. Now, with so much cash on the line, the team built a new short-track car for Richmond, then painted it red inside and out to replicate their old friend.

The 400-lap race was run on Saturday night under the lights, which pleased Dale Jr., who had chalked three of his four Cup wins on Saturday evenings. Starting eighth, Junior was silent on the radio as he slipped past Ward Burton into fifth place on lap 71. He would remain in the top five for the remaining 329 laps, but could he come home first?

He moved to third place during the team's first pit stop on lap 94, restarting behind Ricky Rudd and Rusty Wallace.

Though it was still early in the race, Earnhardt Jr. and Wallace waged a fierce side-by-side battle for second place, with Junior grabbing the position after ten laps of jousting.

"Yeah!" Junior hollered. "My beer is better than your beer! Rusty and I always race the hell outta each other."

"Yeah, buddy," replied Norris from his vantage point above the front stretch. "That was predictable."

"Hell yeah," Junior chuckled. "It's a lot more fun when my car is better than his."

The Bud car was quick all night, but Junior became frustrated at not being able to take the lead. If he pushed too hard, the right front tire would blister by the end of a run. Trying to improve the handling by adjusting the brake bias from the cockpit, Junior turned the knob in the wrong direction, causing him to lock up the left front tire as he pushed into turn one.

As the race entered the final 100 laps, Junior slid sideways on lap 311, allowing Rudd, Stewart, and Harvick to go past. But quick pit work on lap 346 under caution allowed him to gain a position, and he lined up fourth for the restart.

"What is the holdup?" he asked as the caution continued. Junior needed green-flag laps to catch the cars ahead of him. "Are we waitin' on TV or something? C'mon! Let's *go*."

The restarts allowed lapped cars to line up in the inside lane, and as the field returned to top speed on lap 354, Dale Jr. found himself blocked by slower cars. With no time to waste, Junior forced his way past Ken Schrader.

"The damn lapped cars wanna race, and now ain't the time!" Junior yelled with vigor. "I dunno what my car is doing because I'm behind these SOBs. Tell Kenny I'm sorry, but that was getting ridiculous!"

When two more caution periods slowed the field, Junior's frustration extended to his cousin.

"Speak up, bud!" he yelled at Tony Jr. "You're talkin' in lukewarm tones. Ya gotta want me to hear it!"

"Twenty-seven laps to go at the green," said Norris.

Wallace had been at or near the front for the entire race, but the Miller Beer car began to fade, allowing Dale Jr. to go by into third place. Junior now focused on Rudd and Harvick ahead of him.

With 18 laps remaining, Harvick made his move, pushing Rudd out of the groove and out of the lead. Harvick's shove was straight out of the Big E playbook, and it allowed Dale Jr. to move by Rudd into second. The million-dollar prize was in his grasp.

"Go get 'im!" Norris cheered.

An angry Rudd pushed back, crawling alongside Dale Jr.

"Watch out," Norris warned. "He's pissed off about Harvick."

Junior was unable to hold off Rudd, but pushed to stay close.

"Go hard, man," Norris urged. "These two are gonna crash each other and we're gonna win a million."

Rudd inched closer to Harvick each lap, and with five remaining, he returned the hard contact, using what Big E called the "chrome horn." (Though, truthfully, the Cup cars hadn't used chrome bumpers for many years.) The collision opened the door for Junior to take second on lap 397, but Harvick got back by him on the following lap.

Rudd grabbed the win in the Monte Carlo 400, followed closely by Harvick and Dale Jr. On the cool-down lap, Junior pushed Harvick's car Intimidator-style as they pulled to pit lane. If the fans hoped for angry fireworks between Rudd and Harvick, they were disappointed. Harvick knew the rough pass was a payback for his earlier aggression.

Missing the million pained Junior, but he was pleased to learn the third-place finish qualified him to try again for the Winston bonus at Talladega in October.

"We're frustrated because we really wanted to win that million dollars," he told reporters. "We were good, but never quite good enough to take the lead. It was good team effort. We just missed it slightly."

What did he think of the rough racing?

"That's short-track racing!" he laughed. "I think it was a great race, and the fans must have enjoyed it. I had the best seat in the house to watch

Harvick and Rudd beat and bang with each other there at the end. I was hoping that maybe they'd take each other out and we'd be sitting here with a million bucks. I was pulling for Kevin to win it. It's great to see my daddy's team doing so well, and Kevin's a good guy. But, congratulations to Ricky. They did a good job."

Dale Jr. was insistent on crediting his ever-improving team.

"Our team is getting stronger every week. We're young, but I know that every week my team is going to get me up there near the front. Our strategy, our pit stops, and the whole program is improving all the time. I mean, they may look like any other crew to y'all, but to me, these are guys that I grew up with, so it's a big deal to me."

His post-race media scrum complete, Junior made his way to victory lane to shake hands with Rudd.

chapter 41

9/11

Kansas City, Kansas

Falling just shy of a million-dollar bonus seemed to motivate rather than discourage the team, and the following evening they climbed aboard one of DEI's King Air turboprop planes and headed west to Kansas City. The brand-new Kansas Speedway looked similar to the Chicagoland track, but subtle differences between the two led the Bud team to book two days of testing in preparation for the inaugural race there later in the month.

I rarely attended test sessions, but was along for the ride because we scheduled a media session for Dale Jr. during the Monday lunch break. I had grown up less than an hour away from the track, so it was also a great chance to see a lot of old friends and spend a few evenings with my parents.

Dale Jr. and I were scheduled to fly Tuesday evening from Kansas City to Vancouver, British Columbia, where he had been invited to appear in a music video with his favorite musician, Matthew Good. The Matthew Good Band had a small following in the States, but was one of the most successful rock bands in Canada. The two had struck up a friendship after Junior sent Good one of the limited-edition Dale Jr. Les Pauls.

Like his father, Dale Jr. disliked testing for several reasons. The test driver's job was not to push as hard as he could, but to drive at a fast but steady pace, allowing the team to understand the effects of each change or adjustment. Junior didn't like the monotony of lengthy tests, and worried he was more likely to be injured at a test than at a race. Typically, as the sole car on track, the driver has no other cars to help judge his braking points or

246

racing line, and the constant repetition makes him more prone to a crash caused by a lapse of concentration.

After the Monday-morning session, Junior met with the local media.

"I'd rather the season end as soon as it could," he told the reporters, describing the toll taken by the continual grind of the Cup season. "I like being home as much as anything."

The following morning the team arrived at the track early, then was drawn inside the hauler to view the horrific sight of the World Trade Center in flames. I was still at my parents' home, and sitting with my mom and dad while watching the calamity, the last thing I wanted to do was leave my family, but I had to get to the track to be with the team in case they chose to return to North Carolina.

When I arrived, the track was eerily quiet. Amid the confusion of the morning, all of the medical and emergency workers were on alert, pulling them away from the track and stopping the test entirely. The garage was deserted and the few teams that remained were inside their haulers, watching the news coverage.

The Matthew Good video shoot was canceled immediately, and when all air travel was halted, the team had no choice but to pack into two rental vans and drive 1,000 miles east to the Statesville, North Carolina, airport, where our cars were parked adjacent to DEI's hangar. Pilot Joey Meier stayed behind in Kansas City with the plane, hoping to fly home in the near future.

With everyone in shock, we divided into two groups: Dale Jr. and Tony Jr. wanted to stop and buy compact discs for the drive, while my group chose to listen to newscasts as we traveled across the country. Were we at war? Would there be more attacks?

In jarring contrast to the frightful emotions of the day, we drove hour after hour under glorious blue skies, completely devoid of clouds and air traffic. Wherever we stopped for food or fuel, everyone was in a stunned, quiet daze. Trading driving duties, we made it back to the DEI hangar in less than 15 hours, arriving at 3 a.m.

In response to the attacks, NASCAR initially announced an adjustment for that weekend's race at Loudon, New Hampshire, canceling Friday's practice and qualifying, and setting the starting lineup by points. As the air-travel ban lengthened, it was clear the fans and teams would not be able to get to New Hampshire in a timely manner. With no open weekends the remainder of the season, the Loudon race was rescheduled as a one-day event the day after Thanksgiving. The race the following week at Dover would continue as scheduled.

The week was a whirlwind of emotions, confusion, and patriotism. Teresa permanently forbade Dale Jr. from traveling on commercial flights, while rumors began to circulate that the Dover race (and everyone's hotel reservations) was in jeopardy because the Dover Air Force Base was chosen to hold the remains of those killed at the Pentagon.

Many American companies responded to the disaster by donating vast amounts of cash and supplies. Anheuser-Busch donated $1 million to the American Red Cross to aid victims of the attack, and 10,000 cases of canned water to aid rescue workers in the World Trade Center rubble. Anheuser-Busch also began aggressive efforts to encourage employees to donate blood at Red Cross facilities, and generated millions more in financial donations from employees and beer distributors.

At JR Motorsports, Junior and Kelley discussed what they could do to help. The siblings chose to devote their donations to the Speedway Children's Charities, financing efforts to aid the children of those killed or injured in the attacks.

For the Dover race, Junior committed to $100 for every lap he completed. With a race length of 400 laps, his donation could reach $40,000. He also pledged $10,000 for every pit stop his team completed in less than 14 seconds.

Despite telling the Kansas-area media he was ready for the season to be over, the weekend off didn't sit well with Dale Jr.

"It really didn't feel like a weekend off, because you really couldn't relax," he said before traveling to Dover. "I was like everyone else, watching the news coverage and just staying glued to the television. I think the ones that benefited from the quiet weekend were the guys on the crew. They were able to spend some time with their families or their girlfriends and that's always a positive thing with the insane hours they work week after week after week."

Many already considered NASCAR the most patriotic sport in the land, and as the teams unloaded early Friday morning, 10 days after the attacks, nearly every car carried a sizable American flag or patriotic paint scheme. While the Bud team covered the trunk-lid with an American flag decal, the best look of all was MB2 Racing's No. 36 car. For the Dover weekend, the car was devoid of almost all sponsor decals, which were replaced by a stunning paint scheme that made the entire car appear to be draped by an American flag.

Just as it had been a comforting relief for many to be at the racetrack following Earnhardt's death, many of the type-A personalities in the garage area were thankful for a chance to be back in the garage, working hard and preparing to race. I spent much of the week trying to think of ways to ease the tension for Junior and the team.

Recalling Junior's monologue two weeks earlier at Darlington, when he told the team he needed a volleyball to keep him company, I went in search of a Wilson volleyball like the one in the movie *Cast Away*. Unable to find a replica, I created the best lookalike I could, using a red Sharpie to match the bloodstained handprint on the ball in the film.

The following morning, I snuck the ball into the garage and presented it to Tony Jr. and the crew. They decided it would be funny to stuff it into Junior's helmet before the final practice session. We tipped off a few photographers who were able to catch Junior's outburst of laughter when he found the ball inside the car.

Before the race started the next day, the crew decided to carry the joke one step further, mounting the ball behind the drink bottle on the passenger side of the race car.

Sunday morning, Dale Jr. was honored to meet another famous No. 8: baseball great Cal Ripken Jr. and his family were attending the race as honored guests of the race sponsor, MBNA. Junior spent considerable time with Ripken, his kids, and his brother Billy, exchanging autographs and mutual admiration.

chapter 42

where's that big american flag?

Dover, Delaware

The prerace show was a stream of raw emotions as more than 140,000 fans waved the American flags they had been given as they arrived Sunday morning. NASCAR secured Lee Greenwood to sing "God Bless the U.S.A.," followed by the inevitable chants of "USA! USA! USA!" Never before had the normally rote ceremonies meant so much.

Junior soaked in the huge outpouring of emotion from the crowd during the driver introductions, getting a sense of the catharsis the race could provide for millions of NASCAR fans across the country. As the team stood at attention for the national anthem, Danny Earnhardt stood beside Dale Jr., holding a large American flag over his shoulder. Before the race began, the team mounted the flag on their pit stand.

Earnhardt Jr. started on the inside of the second row, quickly taking the lead from Dale Jarrett on lap three. When the first yellow flag appeared on lap 20, Junior assured the team the car had more speed if needed.

"I eased off to chill out," he said. "It was a piece o' cake there. It's drivin' real good."

"How's Wilson?" Tony Jr. asked.

"I dunno where he's at," Dale Jr. replied.

By lap 70, Junior was struggling.

"I need a dry rag. I got stuff in my eyes," Junior said. "These goggles must not be air-efficient. I'm having to wipe my eyes every straightaway, so I'll need a towel next stop."

As the race neared 100 laps, the two fastest cars were clearly the No. 8 and the No. 28 of Ricky Rudd. When the team made a stop under caution at lap 118, Tony Jr. removed a piece of paper from the nose that had blocked one of the air inlets.

"There was something on the grill," Tony Jr. told him. "Keep your eye on the temps."

"I'm watching the water temp. It's about 220 degrees," Dale Jr. reported. "I was worried because I remember back in the days when 210 was all ya wanted to see."

"Hey, man, Wilson says it's OK," said engine specialist Jeff Clark.

"There ain't no Wilson here," Earnhardt Jr. replied.

"He's there, but I'll bet he's all swollen up from the heat inside that car," laughed Pops. "He's never seen heat like this."

"Seriously? I don't see him," Junior said.

"Look behind your water bottle," Tony Jr. told him.

After a dramatic pause, Dale Jr. replied.

"Hey! There he is!" he said, before mimicking Hanks' character from the movie. "*Wiillllsssooonnnnnn!* He's in here, man! I got a buddy."

Overhearing the strange radio chatter, the NBC crew came to the Bud pit area to ask for more details before incorporating the Wilson story into their broadcast. As reporter Dave Burns told the tale, the in-car camera panned slowly then tilted down to show Wilson strapped snugly in place.

After a multicar crash on lap 130, Junior asked Norris what had happened.

"I think the 24 [Jeff Gordon] got into the 14 [Ron Hornaday]," replied Norris.

"Gordon must be turning over a new leaf," Junior said, poking fun at his squeaky-clean image. "I heard him say 'Damn' the other day. He used it in a sentence, too. That's better than just saying it alone."

When Michael Waltrip crashed at the halfway point, Junior explained his troubles with the car.

"This SOB is just rough . . . bouncy," he said.

"Junior, you said exactly the same thing at this lap last year," said Tony Jr. "It must be the track condition that we can't replicate in practice."

"Hold on a minute," Dale Jr. said. "I was talking to Wilson."

"Well, what did he say?" Tony Jr. laughed.

"He says there's a time and place on every lap where I coulda wrecked or spun," Dale Jr. said.

In the next 50 laps, another piece of trash became lodged on the nose, causing the engine temperatures to increase as Earnhardt Jr. followed Jarrett.

"The paper's still there," Tony Jr. told his driver.

"What the hell can I do about it?" Junior asked.

"Looks like it's wedged in there," Norris reported.

"All right Ty, tell Jarrett I'm gonna get on his ass," Junior said, describing how he was going to follow closely, creating turbulence and a change of air pressure on the nose, hopefully dislodging the paper. "I ain't gonna spin him!"

Before the temps could spike, a yellow flag came out on lap 268.

"We're gonna make some changes on this stop," Tony Jr. said. "It might be a few seconds longer, but it should take care of the bouncing and hopping."

The No. 8 was in second place coming to pit lane, but fell to eighth after the long stop.

By the time he passed Tony Stewart on lap 305, Dale Jr. had climbed back into fourth place.

"Keep it rollin'," Norris encouraged. "Go get the 24."

Rolling past Gordon, Dale Jr. was now third, and faster than any car other than the leader, Rudd.

With 55 laps remaining, the race took a sudden turn when Rusty Wallace, already one lap down, made hard contact with Rudd, spinning the No. 28 and opening the door for Earnhardt Jr.

After the pit stops, Junior lined up third behind Jarrett and Jerry Nadeau.

It took a few laps to get by Nadeau, and then, with less than 40 miles to go, Junior swept easily past Jarrett to take the lead. Pulling away, Junior became concerned about being slowed or blocked by lapped cars. Norris began working with the spotters for the cars just ahead.

"I told the 13 [Hermie Sadler] we want the bottom lane when we get there," Norris said. "I told the 17 [Matt Kenseth] we want the bottom, so he'll go high."

With 25 laps to go, Junior had a 3.08-second lead on Nadeau, then increased his lead further until Jarrett spun in turn two on lap 387.

"Fuck! I knew it," Junior hollered as he slowed for the yellow flag, his huge lead wiped out in a flash. "We can't ever win one of these easily."

Just as when he was leading easily at Texas, the late yellow flag made Dale Jr. vulnerable no matter what strategy the team chose. If the Bud car stayed out, the cars behind could pit for fresh tires, but if the Bud car pulled down pit lane for two or four tires, the same challengers could stay on track, putting Junior deep in the field.

"We're staying out," Tony Jr. said, the opposite strategy of the Texas loss, confident the car was quick enough to win without fresh tires. Six others did the same, which meant cars pitting for tires were now in eighth place and back, a distance nearly impossible to make up in the short time remaining. The real concern now was the car in third place. After his spin, Rudd had fought back with a vengeance and was looming large in Junior's rearview mirror.

"That 28's been good," Junior said.

"It's a ten-lap shootout," Tony Jr. said, though it was actually less. "You're better than anyone."

When the green came out on lap 393, Junior spun the rear tires as he accelerated in first gear. Worried that Nadeau would get beside him, Junior moved aggressively in second gear to block the inside lane. Once they were up to speed, Junior pulled away.

"All right, buddy, great job," Norris said as Junior completed the lap. "It's gonna be yours. Seven to go."

When Nadeau drifted high on the next lap, Junior extended his lead to 10 car lengths.

Other than Norris calling out the laps, the radio was silent until Junior headed toward the checkered flag. Rounding turn four for the last time, the Bud car slid sideways, as Norris cheered him on.

"Way to go, wheelman," Norris said. "Great job!"

Despite the lurid slide, Dale Jr. hung on to cross the line as the winner of the MBNA Cal Ripken Jr. 400. Flag-waving fans went berserk as Junior grabbed his second emotional and dramatic win of the season.

"Hey, where's that big American flag at?" Earnhardt Jr. asked as he rounded turn three on the cool-down lap. Joey Meier grabbed the flag that had flown in the Bud pit area, climbed over the wall, and handed it to Dale Jr.

With the flag flying high from the driver's door, Junior spun the car 180 degrees and rolled around the track in the opposite direction, putting him only a few feet from the fans crowded along the fence.

("That thing is damn heavy at that speed," Junior later joked with me, describing the strength it took to hold the large flag upright with one hand as he drove.)

Pulling the Monte Carlo into victory lane, Junior climbed triumphantly atop the car, holding a beer aloft before Tony Jr. tossed Wilson to him for a few more celebratory arm pumps. Tossing the ball aside, Junior did his traditional highflying leap into the mosh pit of happy crew members.

"I'm glad I could be the guy to win the race," Junior told the NBC viewers. "And carry that American flag around there. That made me feel good."

He then gave a shout-out to his buddies, instructing them to, "Have the beer cold. It might be late, but I'll be there!"

"Wilson seems to be good luck," he laughed when asked about his new companion. He then described how he "was pattin' him on the head with ten to go!"

With his victory lane duties complete, we hopped in a van for a ride to the media center. As the emotions of the day started to set in, Junior was asked how it felt to win.

"This feels different than any of our other wins. I mean, we love winning, but it felt odd to celebrate. I watched the Formula One guys last week in Europe, and when Juan Montoya won, they didn't spray the champagne. My dad told me never to do any more burnouts after we won the Winston last year because it hurts the engine, so as I was coming around to head into pit lane, I thought about the big American flag we had in our pit area, and I asked them to bring it to me and I did a lap for the fans.

"It was neat to see the fans' reaction. I mean we've all been sad the past couple of weeks, and it was neat to see the NASCAR fans show their spirit and their patriotism just like the baseball fans or football fans have done. It does make me proud that I'm American, and I feel honored that I was the one to win on a day like today. I mean, it didn't matter who won, it was healing to be here and it was special to be together and feel like the NASCAR family was together for the country. The fans presented me, and all of us drivers, with some real inspiration out there."

Dale Jr. donated $75,000 from the win to the Speedway Children's Charities. "My sister and I wanted to do something," he explained. "We talked about it, and we decided we'd donate some money for the children. I mean, you sit on your couch and watch and you feel helpless. We wanted to do what we could to help."

After discussing the bigger picture, he was asked how it felt on a personal level to win again after Daytona.

"We *won* that race at Daytona," he said emphatically. "I'm still bitter about it, that it was tainted. It was a big moment for me and for a lot of people close to me."

What was he thinking in the closing laps?

"I was worried when that last yellow flag came out. You don't know how many times I have lost races on deals like that, but we got a good restart and held 'em off. I learned some things from Andy Pilgrim and the guys on the Corvette team that I raced with. They taught me some things on restarts, like how to short-shift without spinning the tires. So, even though I lost a little ground in first gear, by the time we were at top speed I had great momentum and I could get a great first lap on every restart.

"I felt bad for [Rudd]," Junior said, when told about a heated skirmish in the garage between Rudd and Rusty Wallace. "It cost him the race, or a chance to win. I looked up to him for many years. It was almost like I was pulling for him as much as I was myself during the race. My brother-in-law, Ray Holm, changes tires on his car.

"There's so much grip, hopping and bouncing the car with so much traction, I was happy to let Ricky lap people and fight traffic. I was happy to just keep him in sight and make a charge at the end. I didn't take too many risks until late, and I drove harder the last fifty laps."

Dale Jr. led five times for 197 laps, the third time during the season he had led the most laps.

"I knew we were gonna be good, but I didn't know we'd be *that* good. But, I never felt like we had it in our hands until I saw the checkered flag."

How was his meeting with Cal Ripken?

"He is just cool. Just the coolest guy in the place, ya know. Whether he wants to be or not, he's a great role model. A great athlete to look up to. He does his job and then he goes home to his kids and his family and I think he's someone we can all appreciate."

To close the news conference, Junior was asked about his new good-luck charm.

"I think Tom Hanks is good in about any movie, but I think that *Cast Away* is awesome. I guess because I felt like I've been on a deserted island since my dad died in February. You know, I'm surrounded by people all the time, and thousands of people at the track, but I feel all alone, ya know. I said that to some of the people close to me, and they thought it would be fun to surprise me with it in the car. Now that we've won with it, maybe it brought me some luck, so we may have to have that ball in there from now on."

chapter 43

a boomerang that doesn't come back

Kansas City, Kansas

The night before practice opened at Kansas Speedway, Dale Jr. made a sponsor appearance for Remington, signing autographs at a giant Cabela's hunting and fishing store adjacent to the track. The line of autograph seekers was immense, and the store manager was grateful for the boost in customers. After the session was complete, he told Dale Jr. to "Choose anything you like in the store." Though Junior wasn't a big hunter or outdoorsman like his father had been, he did love high-tech toys, and his eyes widened when he spotted an intricate crossbow. With components crafted from carbon fiber, the elaborate and complex weapon looked more like something from Junior's favorite video games than something used for hunting or target practice.

The following afternoon, Junior regaled the Eurys and crewmen such as "Two Beer" with tales of his new medieval weaponry.

"Hey," he yelled at me. "Go get that crossbow from my bus."

As I walked toward the motorcoach lot, I began to worry. With the 9/11 attacks so fresh in everyone's mind, security at the track had been stepped up. Coolers and other bags, for example, were no longer permitted inside the gates. Guards were stationed at each entrance, searching anything that appeared even the slightest bit suspicious. Now, Dale Jr. expected me to walk through the garage with an ominous and lethal weapon?

I wasn't thrilled at the prospect of being detained by authorities as a national security risk, so Junior's coach driver Shane Mueller and I created an elaborate covering, using towels and several blankets to wrap the weapon, trying our best to disguise its shape.

Carrying the crossbow in my arms like a delicate bundle, I sauntered past several security guards and through the gate. In the garage area, my heart rate racing, I walked quickly to the car, where the team was preparing to qualify. Dale Jr. unwrapped the weapon, showing it off like a proud papa as the crew ooh'd and aah'd, taking turns holding it.

The post-race hoopla from Dover hadn't reached near the fever pitch as the Daytona win, but the team took deep satisfaction in quieting the critics and skeptics. *Volleyball* magazine called for more details about the team's lucky charm, and the DEI sales and marketing staff began a dialogue with executives from Wilson Sporting Goods, who saw a spike in interest after the win.

Business throughout the country had slowed dramatically since the attacks, yet the requests for Dale Jr. continued to roll in. He received an invitation to appear in a music video with southern rapper Bubba Sparxxx and hip-hop producer Timbaland, but Junior's schedule wouldn't allow him to make a cameo. Junior also made initial contact with Adidas, his favorite shoe and sportswear company. (His initial request was only for free shoes; later in the decade, the company would sign a massive sponsorship deal with Dale Jr.) He had also heard from several movie producers, anxious to cast Junior in a film role as his schedule allowed.

Attendance at the amusement parks owned by Anheuser-Busch had dropped to a trickle after the attacks, and they invited Dale Jr. to bring all of his buddies to hang out for a day at Busch Gardens in Tampa, Florida, showing the public it was safe and secure to return.

In the test session earlier in the month, Junior had taken a liking to the new Kansas Speedway.

"I really like it," he explained. "I think the Chicago track was poorly designed: the transitions to and from the banking are terrible there, but this place is much, much better. It's very wide and very smooth, so I hope that means we can race in more than one groove on Sunday."

As is the case with nearly every new track, the fresh asphalt likely meant single-file racing as cars utilized the superb grip to stay in the inside lane. Ty Norris cautioned Dale Jr. about the single groove as he started the race on the outside of row 11.

"Be careful this first lap," Norris said. "I'll try to get ya down [into the inside line] as soon as we can, so be patient."

As the field raced into turn one, Junior was lucky to avoid a four-car crash.

The yellow came out again on lap 9, and Junior poked fun at one of his old Busch Series rivals, Todd Bodine. After a contentious crash in 1999, Junior angrily called Bodine a "cue-ball-headed fool" on national television. Now, the two found themselves bouncing off of each other in the Cup Series.

"I'm doin' some dirt-trackin' there with Cue Ball," Dale Jr. laughed. "If I wasn't in the back avoiding guys brake-checking each other, we'd be good. It was getting slick up there [in the high groove]."

"Yeah, the four guys running up there are all in the garage, wrecked," replied Norris.

As the race progressed past the 100th lap, Dale Jr. moved into the top 10, and then, by staying out longer on a tank of fuel, took the lead on lap 120.

"Don't fuckin' run me out of gas!" he yelled, mindful of the problems earlier in the year.

"That's five bonus points right there," Tony Jr. reminded him.

When Bill Elliot's Dodge engine suffered a comprehensive failure, NASCAR was slow to put out the yellow flag.

"Turns three and four, NASCAR!" Junior yelled with anger. "Fuckin' shit on the track! In the groove until right before start/finish line!"

When the yellow finally flew four laps later, the team chose to take fuel only, placing them in third place. With so much oil on the track, the cleanup process took longer than usual. Cruising at a tortoise pace bored Dale Jr., prompting a stream-of-conscious monologue.

"Watch this restart," Dale Jr. said. "I hope it don't end in a thud. They aren't putting the Speedy Dry where they need it . . . (pause) These goggles are the tightest I've ever had . . . (pause) This car drives pretty good . . . (pause) Everybody in that pit needs to say 'Hell yeah' to Tony Sr. *Helllllll yeah!* You boys are getting with it!"

"I wonder how many people have turned over to football by now?" Norris asked.

"I'll bet they all have turned over," Junior replied. "These caution flags are endless. I'm bored out here."

259

"Do you want to know the Redskins' score?" asked uncle Danny.

"No!" Junior yelled. "I don't want to hear any scores. I am in a great mood out here, and I don't want anyone to ruin my good mood. Maybe I can use this time for something productive, like brushing up on my rapping skills or something."

"How's Wilson?" asked Jeff Clark.

"He's hangin' in there," reported the driver. "I think he's asleep. These cautions are boring."

After several more laps, Dale Jr. had a question for his cousin.

"Hey, Tony Jr., what do you call a boomerang that doesn't come back?" he asked.

"A stick!" Tony Jr. replied immediately.

"Hahhhhh! You musta dated the same girl I did!" Dale Jr. laughed. "How many laps is this race?"

"Two hundred sixty-seven laps," Tony Jr. replied.

"Is that all? Hell, it's almost over," Dale Jr. said. "We got a fast car, so we need it to be long like Darlington."

"One to go before the restart," Norris reported.

"Oh, yeah, I almost forgot why we're here," Dale Jr. said.

When the race returned to green-flag speeds, Dale Jr. seemed content to run third behind Rusty Wallace and Johnny Benson. As Junior approached to pass, the engine in Benson's car blew up in a plume of smoke and debris. Dale Jr. steered wildly on the slick track, somehow avoiding Benson and the wall.

"Whoa! The save of the day there, boys! Save of the day," he said. "If we can avoid that, we can avoid anything. Let's put some tires on it. Four tires. Whatever tires you want. The car is really, really good."

Dale Jr. restarted fourth and seemed content to run there, saving the car for the final push to the finish. On lap 224, Junior broke the radio silence.

"Bad vibration! I don't know what it is," he reported.

"Bring it in here if you need to," Tony Jr. said.

"It's getting worse," Junior said as he crossed the line on lap 228.

As he turned into the first corner, the right front tire gave way, sending Junior hard into the outside wall.

"You all right, Junior?" Norris asked.

"Yeah," he said. "I banged my foot on the pedal."

~

After being released from the care center, he explained what had happened.

"I hit hard, and it's a damn shame because that was a great car," he said. "It would almost drive itself. I never really pushed hard, I was just kind of hanging in there until the last segment of the race. My left foot is kind of sore because I really hit the brake pedal hard when it hit the wall, but otherwise I'm OK.

"I'm sorry for Tony Jr. and the guys that prepared that car. It was awesome, and I think the new Kansas track was great. It will get better and better when we come back in the future. I was having fun out there."

The Bud team would end the day in 33rd position.

As the race continued, Dale Jarrett hit the wall hard on lap 247, knocking him unconscious. As a precaution, he was airlifted from the track but was released later that night with a concussion and broken rib.

Jeff Gordon, Jarrett's rival for the championship for much of the season, won the race, extending his points lead to a nearly insurmountable 222 points over Ricky Rudd. Rookie Ryan Newman was second in the crash fest while Rudd finished third.

The focus of the day should have been Gordon winning the inaugural race at a new track. Instead it became a farce as NASCAR unveiled a strange victory lane contraption made of PVC pipe. An inept attempt to prevent drivers from climbing on the roof of their car after a victory, the piping was placed against the window of the car as soon as it pulled to a stop. Looking like a junior high school science project gone awry, the two-dollar device was a misguided response to post-race infractions incurred when a winning car measured less than the legal height because a driver had leaped on the roof. After being coached on victory lane celebrations by NBC, winning drivers were again forced to mute their joy.

chapter 44

blaise

Concord, North Carolina

As the drivers were introduced before the UAW-GM 500 at Lowe's Motor Speedway, whispers began to circulate along pit lane that NASCAR was going to delay the start of the race. As the drivers strapped into their machines, we learned President Bush was going to address the nation.

The track fell silent before the President announced bombing had begun in Afghanistan, leading to choruses of, "USA! USA!" from the massive assemblage.

The delayed start only aggravated the frayed nerves in the Budweiser camp. It had been a horrible week, and they were all anxious to get the race started.

Blaise Alexander, a promising 25-year-old racer, had been killed in a crash at the speedway Thursday evening in a 100-mile support race sanctioned by the Automobile Racing Club of America. Alexander and Kerry Earnhardt were racing for the lead with four laps to go when their cars collided, sending Earnhardt's car upside down and Alexander's machine head-on into the front-stretch wall. Alexander, who was wearing a foam neck collar, not a HANS or similar device, died instantly of a skull fracture similar to the injuries that killed Kenny Irwin, Tony Roper, Adam Petty, and Earnhardt. Uninjured in the crash, Kerry Earnhardt was able to crawl free from his car.

The death cast a pall across the garage and served as another cold, vivid reminder of the need to continue developing stronger safety measures at all levels of the sport, not just the top tiers of NASCAR.

The car the Bud team planned to race had been reduced to rubble in the Kansas crash, forcing them to bring an untested chassis. The team struggled to find balance in the car during practice, then suffered a further setback with a blown engine in the final practice session. Before the race, the team gambled with a setup the Eurys had tried during a recent test session, but the agitated driver and team had no idea how their car would perform. The race was their opportunity to immerse themselves enough to forget Alexander's death for a short time.

Starting ninth, Dale Jr. took it easy, testing the handling before he started passing cars, eventually moving past Joe Nemechek in dramatic fashion for third place.

"Just use some patience here. Patience," Norris insisted.

"Patience, my ass. This is a badass race car!" was Dale Jr's reply as his confidence grew each lap.

Running second, Dale Jr. pulled in for four fresh tires under caution on lap 47. In the rush to take the lead, three lug nuts were left loose on the left rear wheel. Rather than risk a crash, the team called Dale Jr. back to the pits on lap 52. With the lugs now snug, Dale Jr. restarted in 36th place.

"OK guys. There's gotta be a way to get back up to the front," said a determined driver. "We have a kick-butt car here, but if we're going to get back up there to race these boys, I need your help. Whatever it takes—pit strategy or something—we're gonna do it."

"We will," said Tony Jr. "I promise you. We will."

It took Dale Jr. less than 60 laps to move into 17th place. But, fighting with so much traffic meant he was losing ground to the leaders. Suddenly, a crash in front of Dale Jr. provided the scariest moment of the day on lap 112.

"I just had something come through the front of the car!" a frantic Dale Jr. reported. "It came through the right side, so we need to check the nose and see what it was."

"Let's go," Tony Jr. urged his crew. "Let's make a patch for that right now."

"Dale Jr., it looks like the nose is intact," said Norris, who used high-powered binoculars to get a closer view of the damage.

"I don't know where it came from, but a big piece of lead—half a foot long—came flying through here!" Dale Jr. replied with alarm.

During the next pit stop, the team assessed the damage. The debris had somehow entered the cockpit through a crush panel behind the engine, creating a hole as it exited through the sheet metal on the right side of the car. The damage was minimal, but the crew was horrified to think of the consequences if something that heavy impacted Dale Jr. at high speed.

"Dale Jr., it left a hole the size of a baseball," Tony Jr. reported. "But it's by the jack post, so the car is OK."

The team continued to adjust the car with quick pit work, and Dale Jr. climbed into sixth place after a speedy stop on lap 169.

"Yeah! Good job!" Junior cheered. "But no medal yet. That's up to you guys at the end."

The crew upheld their share of the burden, recording three sub-14-second stops. Running fifth in the late stages of the race, Junior dueled frantically with Wallace, passing the No. 2 car for good with less than 25 laps left, only to see Ward Burton pass them both.

As the laps counted down, Norris made sure his driver was focusing on the car ahead, the No. 99 of Ward's brother, Jeff.

"You have five laps to go," Norris said. "You're catching that 99. That's fourth place right there.

"You're catching him," Norris reminded on the next lap. "Go get him. Four to go!"

Dale Jr. closed to Burton's rear bumper and made his move on the final lap. As Junior swept past the No. 99, the crew cheered for a great comeback to a fourth-place finish. Sterling Marlin and Tony Stewart dominated for much of the race, but Marlin pulled away late to take his second victory of the 2001 season. Stewart was second, followed by Ward Burton in third.

"My fingers are numb," Dale Jr. said as he held out shaky hands to show Tony Jr. "I was gripping the wheel hard all day. My hands feel raw from wheelin' the daylights outta that car.

"We were able to run with anyone except the 20 [Stewart] and the 40 [Marlin]," Dale Jr. said.

After winning, Marlin's crew ran to greet their driver on his cool-down lap. Bringing two American flags, they wanted Marlin to hold one aloft on a victory lap, as Dale Jr. had done at Dover. But NASCAR's Victory Lane Police prevented Marlin from taking the lap, insisting he drive straight to the winner's circle for the national TV audience. When the silver car arrived, NASCAR again put their rickety PVC contraption on the window to prevent Marlin from climbing on the car.

The outcry soon came from fans upset at NASCAR for preventing the patriotic victory lap on a day when the country had gone to war. In response, NASCAR said there had been a "miscommunication" with the team, but failed to explain further.

chapter 45

a foot race
with crutches

Martinsville, Virginia

Dale Jr. celebrated his 27th birthday Wednesday, or, as he put it, "sittin' on the porch, drinkin' cold beer." Because of his busy schedule of appearances, it wasn't the blowout he had hoped for, but he was happy to relax for a while with friends. It would be downhill from there as an older and wiser Dale Jr. made the trek several hours north to Martinsville, Virginia, for the second race of the season at the half-mile bullring.

Junior likened the rough racing to a boxing match with his favorite fighter, Arturo Gatti, the former light welterweight and super featherweight world champion.

"The track is so small, you're running so close together and it's so hard to pass cleanly that it's a miracle if you finish five hundred laps with a car that is intact," he explained. "Last year, I was like Arturo Gatti, just stepping in and swingin' hard, very aggressive and brutal. We crashed so often we decided to go to a more defensive strategy, holding back and being consistent. That plan worked a lot better."

Friday afternoon, Dale Jr. surprised even himself when he qualified second best.

"I dunno how we did it!" he laughed. "I just hit the marks, I guess. All the testing we've done really paid off."

But a steady rain washed away any chance to race on Sunday, and the race was rescheduled for Monday morning.

At the start, Dale Jr. played it cool, running third behind Jeff Gordon and Ricky Craven. On lap 45, he passed Gordon for second place and closed in on Craven. After he slid sideways in turn two, Norris encouraged him to keep charging but to be careful with the car.

"Great job so far," Norris said. "Just run your rhythm, buddy. Keep it going, keep it rolling. Just be easy on the nose of the car when you get there [to Craven]. Real good job. Just keep your pace."

Junior's concentration was so complete he didn't utter a word on the radio for the first 100 laps.

By then, Junior had dropped to seventh as his tires gave up. The nose was clean, but the rear bumper had been caved in on a restart.

Junior held his spot until a pit stop on lap 170 dropped him to 19th. He managed to gouge his way back into the top 10 when the team gambled on lap 207, taking two tires instead of four. The strategy didn't pay off, as Junior fought with the car, falling 22 positions in less than 50 laps.

By the halfway point of the 500-lap race, Junior began to suspect his problems were more than old tires.

"I think the right rear shock is broken!" he yelled as he tried to stay on the lead lap.

By lap 276, Junior was struggling in 32nd, one lap down, when a bump from Casey Atwood sent the Bud car spinning in turn two. Although Junior was able to drive away, the team brought him in for three pit stops during the caution period, trying to diagnose how the car had gone from very fast to pure evil.

"Dale Jr., both rear wheels are pulling, so it's not an axle," Tony Jr. reported.

The angry driver remained silent for several laps before answering.

"There's somethin' bad wrong," Dale Jr. said. "I can't drive it. I can't go into the corner like that. I don't care what you say!"

Trying to stay out of the way of the leaders, Dale Jr. spun again on lap 379, adding insult to injury. He was now 33rd, three laps down and embarrassed to be so slow.

"This is like running a foot race with crutches," he spat after refiring the car.

"You're doing a good job of hanging onto it," Norris said, trying to keep Junior's head in the game for the final laps. "Keep at it. Some of these guys are getting antsy, so we'll pick up positions when they start hitting the walls."

The Bud team managed to gain six positions, completing 496 laps in 27th place.

The likable Craven, who had recently returned to racing after two years of inactivity due to head injuries, earned his first Winston Cup victory in a spectacular duel with Dale Jarrett, who was nursing a broken rib from his Kansas crash. Craven, driving the Tide car for team owner Cal Wells, beat Jarrett by a margin of 0.141 second after the duo ran the final lap door-to-door, bouncing off each other several times.

chapter 46

are we gonna win?

Talladega, Alabama

The return to Talladega marked the anniversary of Big E's last victory, and Dale Jr. wanted nothing more than to match his father's feat. A few extra dollars were also on the line, as the team was eligible to win the Winston Million bonus. Twice before they came close, but the bounty had eluded them.

"We plan to carry that big wad of Winston's cash home with us," Junior said confidently in the days before the race. "If you wanna win a restrictor-plate race, you gotta deal with us. Our engine guys work year-round on it and our aero package is great too."

The team brought their best weapon, the chassis that had been so dominant at Daytona. After that victory, the team cut the body off the chassis (Dale Jr. claimed the sheet metal from the entire right-hand side of the car, mounting it on the wall of his new garage) and replaced it with a sleek new body. The team replaced or massaged nearly every component on the car. They had a million dollars of motivation, but what drove them in the days since July was proving their Daytona victory was legitimate.

The day before the teams arrived at Talladega, NASCAR announced a new regulation making it mandatory for drivers in the top three series to wear an approved head-and-neck restraint system. The last two Cup holdouts, Tony Stewart and Jimmy Spencer, would wear the HANS device in a race for the first time. Stewart had fought the mandate, citing his claustrophobia as reason for him not to use a device.

Since the Dover victory, it seemed Wilson received as much attention as the team or driver. Action Performance announced the production of a diecast replica of Dover's winning car with a mini Wilson ball as a bonus. The lil' round guy had taken on a life of his own, but Anheuser-Busch executives felt the volleyball was receiving too much exposure, so Wilson was taken out of the car. But the team was unwilling to give up their good-luck charm entirely so they mounted the ball, now smudged with oil and grime, on the pit box the morning of the race.

Dale Jr. started sixth and took the lead for the first time on lap nine. He led 33 of the first 50 laps, all run under green. His teammate Waltrip and previous Talladega winner Bobby Hamilton seemed to be the only cars with the speed to pass the No. 8.

Junior's strategy was simple: dominate the EA Sports 500 by leading as many laps as possible. Keeping the car in front of the pack gave him the best chance to win by running ahead of any massive crash. The drivers had avoided The Big One in the April Talladega race, but the prospect of another 188 laps without a major incident seemed slim.

The frantic three- and four-wide racing usually meant a very busy day for the spotter, but with the No. 8 in front, many laps passed without much chatter. After not hearing from the driver for more than 15 laps, Norris checked in.

"Junior, everything cool?" he asked.

"Yup," came the reply.

The second yellow flag of the day didn't come out until lap 131 for debris on the track. The Bud team made a stop on lap 132, with 56 laps remaining. It would be a stretch to make it that distance on one tank of gas, and the team dove into their fuel mileage computations.

"Are we really this good," Dale Jr. asked while leading, "or is everybody else just chillin'?"

"They're chillin'," reported Tony Jr. "But we're pretty good."

Meanwhile, the fuel figures continued to come up short: the best-case scenario showed the car would run out of fuel on the last lap of the race.

The break they needed came on lap 150, when the yellow flew for the third time.

"We're gonna get a splash," Tony Jr. told his driver. "Then we're gonna whoop their asses."

As the Bud car came to pit lane for three gallons of fuel, 12 lead-lap cars stayed on track, putting Junior 13th on the restart. For the first time, Dale Jr. would have to fight through traffic.

"I want you guys to know you gave me a great car," Dale Jr. said. "I don't know if I can get back up there, but I'm gonna do my best."

"We're better than them twelve boys in front of ya," Tony Jr. insisted.

Placing the nose of the Bud machine squarely on the bumper of Jeff Burton's Ford, Dale Jr. pushed the No. 99 through the rabble and into the lead in less than 10 laps. Waltrip had been leading, but suffered an overheating engine before dropping out of the race on lap 168 when his engine expired. Two laps later, Dale Jr. swept past Hamilton to take the lead. With his best drafting partner gone, Junior was on his own.

Tension began to ratchet up as the laps counted down. Drivers who had laid back much of the day were now charging hard. With 10 laps remaining, Junior led the top five in a single-file line as they tried to separate from the pack.

Stewart emerged three laps later after riding in the back all afternoon, mounting a charge with his teammate Labonte as the duo pointed their Pontiacs forward in the outside line. Stewart and Dale Jr. had spent so much time together at Daytona in February, discussing how the two could work together to help each other. Because of the huge wreck that sent Stewart tumbling in that race, they weren't able to put any of their plans into action. Now, would Stewart and Junior work together to the finish?

That question was answered in turn two, as Junior moved up the banking to block Stewart, who pulled a brilliant move by faking high then moving quickly to the inside of the No. 8. As the two raced side-by-side, the entire field began to close in. With less than five laps to go, there are no friends, and the field was now racing three-wide, 10 rows deep.

Labonte took the lead on lap 184 with a muscular push from Mark Martin. Stewart soon pulled into second, pairing the Joe Gibbs teammates as Hamilton also got past the No. 8.

"We've got to get some help," Junior yelled from fourth place. "It doesn't look real good right now!"

With two to go, Junior somehow forced his way inside Hamilton, putting him ahead of his fastest challenger, then pushed past Stewart as well.

Out of turn four, Labonte pulled ahead by more than 10 car lengths. Ordinarily, that would be good for Labonte, but on a restrictor-plate track, it allowed Junior to muster a massive head of steam for a slingshot move. With Labonte trying to block, Dale Jr. made contact as he rocketed to the inside. The flagman waved the white flag.

Stewart pulled behind his teammate for a split second, but seeing the momentum Junior was carrying, he left Labonte's draft to slide onto the Bud car's bumper.

"The 20's comin' with you! The 20's with you!" Norris said with surprise. "Protect the bottom."

In turn two, Labonte and Hamilton made contact as both cars slid near the wall. Neither lifted off the throttle, pushing them four-wide as they swept onto the backstretch.

As if a massive land mine had detonated, Labonte and Hamilton touched, sending the champ's green No. 18 car flipping upside down into the wall. Johnny Benson's car took a wicked turn, smashing nose-first into the outside barrier. The rest of the pack piled into the wall and each other at sickening speeds. The Big One had been avoided until the final lap, but it struck with a vengeance, damaging or destroying nearly 20 cars.

In front of the chaos, Stewart swung boldly to the outside of Dale Jr., taking the lead by a nose into turn three. Trying to take every ounce of side-draft from each other, the two scraped together as they battled. Running third, Burton was now in position to choose which driver would win the race. If he chose to draft with Stewart, Tony would easily burst past Dale Jr. But recalling how Junior had pushed him to the lead less than 20 laps before, Burton pulled the No. 99 onto the back of the Bud car. It was enough of a push to send Junior into the lead as the trio rounded turn four.

"Are we gonna win?" Junior screamed as the finish line came into view. "*Yeah*! I'm gonna win!"

"Yeaaaahhh!" screamed Tony Jr. "This one is for everyone who doubted the Daytona win!"

"Easy around the corner!" Norris interrupted. "Easy around the corner, there's a big crash. Slow it down."

"You guys are awesome!" Junior said, before reminding the team about NASCAR's emphasis on accurate post-race inspections. "Nobody jump on the car."

After creeping slowly through the debris field, Junior asked for some help.

"Does anybody see that Wells Fargo truck?" he asked, referencing the armored car that appeared whenever a driver won the Winston bonus. "I'm lookin' for the truck! A million bucks? Wild, isn't it?"

Meanwhile, Labonte climbed from his race car, which was still resting on its roof. The other drivers also walked away with no serious injuries.

Pulling into victory lane as the masses chanted, "Earn-hardt! Earn-hardt!" Junior stood on the window sill, pumping his arm triumphantly as "Winston bucks" (printed in a mythical "million-dollar bill" form) flew through the air like confetti, raining down on the driver, team, and car.

"I guess we proved that it wasn't no fix over at Daytona," Dale Jr. said in awkward, stumbling grammar to the TV audience.

"A great day, and I won a million dollars for a fan," he said, referring to Carrie Richter of Conneaut, Ohio, who also won a million dollars in the sweepstakes.

Bill Weber of NBC reminded him of his father's win the year before.

"I'm really excited about that," Junior said. "He won this same race last year under the same circumstances. We've done some crazy things this year. Winnin' at Daytona, winnin' after the terrorist attacks, and now winnin' this race just like my daddy did. It's crazy, man, I don't know what's goin' on!"

A jubilant team sprayed Budweiser and champagne, emptying any container of liquid within reach. After exhausting all they could find, the crew pushed the car toward post-race inspection, while Dale Jr. and Pops were taken in a van to the press box, located above the start/finish line.

"I guess I owe about half of this million dollars to Jeff Burton," Junior laughed. "He helped me all day.

"We got to beating and banging at the end," he said, explaining some of his aggressive moves that reminded many of his father. "I had to run into the side of the 18 [Labonte] and the 20 [Stewart], but they would have done the same thing . . .. I paid a lot of attention to my dad for a lot of years, so I think I had some sort of idea what he was doing. Then, racing against him last year, I learned a lot more. He was always teaching me lessons by leaving me behind out there. I think it's a lot easier to know what he was doing than it is to actually go out and do it."

The pressure of living up to those lessons wasn't lost on Dale Jr.

"If we didn't win, it would have been my fault," he said. "No matter how fast the car is, you have to be spiteful or uncaring in those last laps. I

273

ran into Bobby [Labonte] at the line on the white flag lap, and I thought I might have wrecked him, but I had a great run and my momentum was carrying me past him no matter what direction he was going."

As Junior addressed the media, a line of angry team owners and drivers streamed to the NASCAR hauler, protesting the rules that created the tight packs and inevitable crashes. The crash on the final lap had damaged several million dollars' worth of race cars.

"I thought, 'Man, we might win this,'" Junior said when asked about his view of the huge crash. "But, as soon as I'm looking at cars spinning in the mirror, the No. 20 was outside of me. I could feel the wind. I could feel his car pulling my car toward him."

As word spread that Dale Jr. was in the media center, sitting near the large windows towering above the grandstands, the crowd grew. Fans screamed, yelled, and pounded the glass loud enough to interrupt the questioning. Some of the fans waved signs, including one asking for Junior's hand in marriage. Every time he turned to look toward the window, the clamor grew louder.

"It felt great to win," Dale Jr. said, explaining the sense of redemption after so many critics questioned his Daytona win. "It feels good to make those people sleep in the bed they made."

While Junior's mood after the Daytona win had been pure joy and relief, this triumph seemed to make him deeply introspective as he pondered matching his father's final victory one year before.

"It will take many, many years for me to accomplish the things my dad did," he began with seriousness in his voice. "All those years I've been hearing about how he was the best at these kinds of racing. He never really sat down and told me what to do. It's cool to do things that my father had done, like winning the Winston. I had watched him win that race a few times, so it meant a lot to me when I won it to say, 'I did that too.'"

As a student of the sport, Junior understood he was now building his own history, his own legacy.

"When I was a little kid, I'd look back through all the books and old racing magazines, and I'd look at the winners and all the statistics of the races my dad raced," he said, before taking a thoughtful pause. "Now when I win, I feel like it's a mark in the books of the sport forever. If I'm lucky, I know it will be many, many years before I come close to what my father has done, but each thing I do is a step toward that. It's not a goal of mine, but it's a step in that direction to be known as one of the good drivers."

Dale Jr. reflected on his bloodlines, with a father and grandfather voted among the top 50 drivers of NASCAR's first 50 years.

"I wanna be in that book when the next one is written. I want to go down as one of the best. And maybe one day when I have a son, he can look back in the books and see how his daddy has done in 2001."

After leading the race 11 times for 67 laps, Dale Jr. moved into sixth place in points with five races remaining. With the bonus, the victory paid the team $1,165,773. In four restrictor-plate races during the season, Dale Jr. had two wins, a second, and a sixth-place finish, giving him the best record of any driver in those races. It was Dale Jr's fifth career win in 70 starts.

As much as Dale Jr. and the team felt vindicated, things were about to take an unfortunate turn. Two hours after the win, NASCAR's Jim Hunter, vice president of corporate communications, released a statement to the media.

"The No. 8 car failed inspection. The car did not meet the minimum height requirement of fifty-one inches. The car missed by one-eighth of an inch. NASCAR will review the situation and answer with a penalty."

The Bud car had passed all of the prerace measurements, but after 500 miles of bump drafting, the springs had compressed, resulting in the car being one of five entries to fail the post-race inspection.

In NASCAR's strange world of risk and reward, the sanctioning body has very rarely taken away a victory, no matter the infraction. Since the earliest days of the sport, the France family always believed the fans should go home knowing who had won that day's race, even if violations were found after the victory lane ceremonies had concluded. The team's victory and payday would stand, but headlines the following morning focused more on the violation than the dominating win.

"Junior Wins Weird One in Illegal Car" screamed Speedvision.com. The hometown *Charlotte Observer*'s headline read, "Earnhardt Jr.'s victory on hold." As much as the cash looked nice on the bank statement, the team was frustrated to see another victory tainted.

The following day, NASCAR announced a $25,000 fine to crew chief Tony Eury. The penalty was approximately two percent of the winnings, but the damage in public perception had been done.

chapter 47

driving the 3

Avondale, Arizona

"When I was at home playing Matchbox cars, I was driving for Richard Childress," Dale Jr. said. Now he was going to have the chance to drive for Childress in real life.

The biggest news of the weekend at the one-mile oval near Phoenix took place off the track, when Dale Jr. unveiled a pair of Busch Series paint schemes he would race in 2002. The first was a gorgeous blue-and-white Oreo paint scheme he was scheduled to drive at Daytona in February for Richard Childress Racing. The second was a hideous yellow-and-white Nutter Butter paint scheme he would drive at Charlotte in May.

That he was driving for Childress was big news, but the biggest news of all focused on the car number: 3. It would be the first time the number was carried in any of NASCAR's top three divisions since Earnhardt's death.

The Nabisco sponsorships was initially intended for Big E, who had driven with Oreo sponsorship in the Budweiser Shootout, but Junior agreed to step in for the two races. The cars would be built and prepared by RCR, but his race-day crew would be the DEI Budweiser team.

"To have the opportunity to work with Richard Childress is something I've thought about and wondered whether it would ever happen," Junior said, recalling a time as a youngster when he told Childress he'd be his test driver someday. "With the circumstances, I'm probably going to be driving the 8 car for years and years, but here's a chance for us to work together."

Junior was quick to remind everyone No. 3 had been his number too, and that he carried it to two Busch Series titles. The choice for him to drive No. 8 in the Cup Series was in honor of his grandfather Ralph, who used the number through his career. (Big E's number was also 8 when he made his Cup debut in 1975.) Many had pushed for NASCAR to retire the No. 3, but the sanctioning body never did so.

Junior didn't want the number retired unless they also retired Richard Petty's No. 43. Besides, Junior might have a son or daughter someday who would want to use the No. 3. No matter what number the cars carried, he was excited about working with a man who had such a huge role in his father's career.

"I'm sure Richard Childress is curious after watching me grow up all these years, exactly what kind of person I am to work [with] and what kind of a driver I am," Junior explained. "It's an opportunity for us to know a little bit more about each other that we obviously wouldn't have learned in the past."

Coming so late in the season, the long trip west to Phoenix seemed to be the breaking point for many exhausted team members. Tempers within the Bud team flared as they struggled in practice and qualifying. Things brightened temporarily when Sammy Hagar came by to speak with Dale Jr. The rocker wasn't there to promote his solo career or his work with Van Halen, but to draw attention to his new brand of tequila, thrilling the crew when he presented them with a case of his Cabo Wabo–brand intoxicant. They debated breaking open the bottles right there in the garage, but cooler heads prevailed.

The crowded garage area and an immense number of autograph seekers made it tough for the crew to get to and from their hauler, which frustrated Dale Jr. Rather than complain to NASCAR directly, he used a passive-aggressive move he had seen his father utilize.

Junior walked slowly from the car to the back of the NASCAR hauler where the sanctioning body's executives worked during race weekends. He took a seat near the back door of the hauler, and began signing autographs. As the crowds grew larger and larger, the officials were unable to exit the back door of their hauler, giving them a small taste of what the Bud team fought each weekend.

Starting deep in the field, Junior's race was hampered by intermittent interference and poor reception on the team's two-way radio. Even switching to the backup channel didn't help matters, so the team and driver were forced into short bursts of chatter when the car was on the front stretch.

Junior still managed to gain 15 positions in the first 50 laps. When he became mired there, the pit crew came to his rescue, making a blazing stop on lap 134, propelling Earnhardt Jr. into the top 10 for the first time. Once he was among the lead pack, he was able to stay there until debris from a crash on lap 203 bounced off the track into the radiator of the Bud car.

Junior immediately came to pit lane, but the engine stalled and would not refire. On a blast furnace–hot Arizona day, the crew pushed it down pit lane until it finally came back to life. Somehow, the overheating engine managed to produce enough power to keep Junior on the lead lap, though it sounded more like a sewing machine than a V-8 Chevrolet. Eventually, other drivers began reporting the car was dropping fluids. This was followed shortly by a complete engine failure on lap 287.

"It's heartbreaking," Dale Jr. told a couple of reporters who left the air-conditioned media center to speak with the Bud driver. "We had some debris damage the radiator and the engine just wouldn't last in this heat. I guess I had something like twenty laps of warning. I could tell it was beginning to heat up and smoke a little bit, but it was pretty clear we had a problem when everyone blew past us pretty easily."

Jeff Burton won his second race of the season and his second consecutive race at Phoenix, topping the field at the Checker 500. Mike Wallace scored a career-best second-place finish, while Ricky Rudd finished third.

The early exit dropped Dale Jr. to seventh in the Winston Cup point standings, falling one spot with four races remaining.

chapter 48

the host chillin'
the most

Rockingham, North Carolina

A fter the race, Junior and I took a short flight to Los Angeles, where he appeared Monday on "The Tonight Show with Jay Leno." Junior was hesitant about the appearance, even after Leno called him at home shortly after his father's death. Junior told him he'd like to at least win a few races so he'd have something to discuss other than his father. After the Talladega win, the time was right to book his appearance.

Waiting backstage in a drab greenroom, he watched TV nervously while I availed myself of the voluminous fruit tray. Leno came in to say hello before the show began, reviewing his notes and putting Junior at ease. Joining Dale Jr. on the guest list that evening was John Travolta (who blasted in and out of the studio for his segment) and the band Alien Ant Farm.

Junior's segment went well, as he expertly told the tale of his youthful speeding tickets.

"I got four speeding tickets by the time I was eighteen," he told Leno. "And each one of the troopers who pulled me over told me he had given my dad his first ticket."

When pressed about being single, Junior lamented the lack of selection at the racetrack, before jokingly suggesting he would be happy to invite single ladies to the track as his guest.

The tongue-in-cheek remark resulted in an avalanche of calls, faxes, emails, and letters to my office from willing invitees. A number of moms (and grandmothers) submitted their daughters for approval. I was quoted by the Associated Press stating, "We appreciate the interest, but we're not sure we can keep up with the demand. I don't think he knew the impact of what he was saying. Now he's got hundreds of prospective Mrs. Earnhardts calling."

After the Leno appearance, he began working on his next column for NASCAR.com. While most of his recent columns had been nostalgic looks at his father or the sport, Junior went an entirely different direction for November. With the offseason quickly approaching, he anxiously awaited the chance to throw several of his now-famous parties. As a public service of sorts, Junior wrote a lengthy opus on his rules and guidelines to create the perfect party.

It included hilarious advice, such as preparing for your New Year's Eve party by setting "all of your clocks at different times so you can enjoy a few extra kisses from the hottie next to you," as well as guidelines for parking, toilets, and making sure a sufficient dance floor was in place. He liked to close each column with a funny signature, and this one concluded "the host chillin' the most, Dale Jr."

Our procedure for submitting the columns was simple: Junior wrote the material and emailed it to me. Before I sent it to *Winston Cup Scene* magazine or the website, I edited his work, correcting spelling errors or glaring grammatical errors without changing the essence of what he had written. While I liked his ideas, I felt this column was too lengthy, so, to make it more concise, I changed the paragraphs into a numbered list of 12 rules.

I sent it in and forgot about it until it appeared on the website a week later. Dale Jr. saw the changes I had made and became more angry with me than at any other time.

"Why did you fuck with what I wrote?" he yelled.

"I thought it was too long," I answered defensively.

"Well, don't change my shit ever again!" he said.

The Bud car carried a special decal at Rockingham, promoting the release of the new album by the band Smash Mouth (most known for their 1999 hit, "All Star"). As part of Budweiser's effort to link their sports and musical sponsorships, it was a perfect union, and the band played a special Charlotte concert Friday night and then came to the racetrack that weekend as guests of Bud and Dale Jr.

Though the Rockingham track was similar to Darlington in the way it eviscerated tires, Earnhardt Jr. and the team looked forward to showing what they could do after the February race ended with the Bud car in the wall after only three corners. The No. 1 Pennzoil team had a superb Rockingham setup that carried Park to victory in the rain-delayed event following Earnhardt's death. Park and Junior could drive similar setups, but with Kenny Wallace now in the driver's seat, would the two teams be able to mesh like before?

Some of that concern went away in qualifying as Wallace drove the yellow DEI machine to the pole position. Happy for his new teammate, Dale Jr. went to the ceremony after qualifying, personally presenting the Budweiser Pole Award to Wallace.

At the green flag, Dale Jr. once again suffered a collision on the first lap, but this time he was able to continue. Not so lucky was Kyle Petty, who bounced off of the Bud car and into the wall.

Under caution, Junior quietly explained what happened.

"I didn't think he was comin' down like that," he said, followed by a long pause. "But, I guess I thought wrong."

When the racing resumed, Junior made it look easy, riding the low line through the corners, passing cars with ease. While most of his competitors lost grip and slid into the high line in the corners, Junior passed his way to fourth.

After the initial yellow flag involving Petty's spin, the race settled into a rhythm and stayed green for the next 170 laps. Unfortunately for the Bud team, they made a pit stop three laps before the caution on lap 177, trapping them nearly a full lap behind the drivers who had yet to pit.

Dropping as low as 24th place due to the bad timing, Dale Jr. hoped for more yellow flags to help him push back through the field. Unfortunately, there were no caution periods on the remaining laps, and Junior fought his way to 15th place at the finish.

Joe Nemechek, recovered from the injuries suffered earlier in the season, earned his second career Winston Cup victory with a dominating performance. Nemechek led 196 of 393 laps in the Pop Secret 400, and beat Kenny Wallace across the finish line by more than six seconds. Wallace matched his career-best Cup finish, and was trailed by Johnny Benson in third.

"How about Kenny!" Junior exclaimed on the cool-down lap.

When asked about his new teammate after the race, Junior was happy to sing his praises.

"He's a good guy who stepped in after Steve was injured," Earnhardt Jr. explained. "It's not an easy situation for anyone. But Kenny has a great attitude and he's fun to be around and he's helping to keep the Pennzoil team on track. It's a great finish for them and for DEI."

"We were great early on," Junior said about his own race. "But the car went away after that first pit stop. I was outta control the rest of the day. This track is so difficult because it just chews up the tires, then you hang on for dear life until your next pit stop. You have cars that are laps down coming in for fresh tires and then they come back out a second or more per lap faster and they just blow past you like you're standing still. It takes a lot of concentration to keep from knocking the wall down each lap."

chapter 49

what's it going to take?

Homestead, Florida

After the Talladega victory, Gary Nelson, NASCAR's Winston Cup director, approached Junior with a simple question: what's it going to take to get him to wear a full-face helmet?

Dale Jr. had long respected Nelson, who had been a crew chief for many years before becoming a NASCAR executive. After Junior suffered through several horrid outings early in the 2000 season, Nelson encouraged the rookie to relax and just be himself. Two days later, Junior won the race at Texas.

"I want to wear one," Junior said, telling Nelson how he had worn one while driving the Corvette, but explained his father's reaction when he wore one in his stock car at Daytona. "Man, my daddy felt so strongly about open-face helmets that I feel bad putting a full-face helmet on."

His father's defiant views had echoed through his head for months, holding him back from making the change. But, prompted by Nelson's point-blank question, Junior finally went to Tony Eury and Teresa, getting their thoughts and blessings on making a change. To the relief of many who worried about him, Junior decided the time was right to make the switch. As practice began at Homestead, he pulled on the black full-face helmet he had worn briefly at Daytona. With the Hutchens Device attached, he climbed into his race car.

Dale Jr. was also the focus of a news conference Friday at the track, unveiling a new 2002 sponsorship with Drakkar Noir cologne. The brand saw sponsorship of Earnhardt Jr. as an opportunity to reinvigorate their sales. The sponsorship was also a strong complement to the Budweiser backing: while Bud placed Junior's image in bars, restaurants, and convenience stores across the land, the Drakkar effort would expand his reach into department stores.

In the aftermath of 9/11, the country had also been gripped by fears of anthrax. In the weeks after the terrorist attacks, the deadly powder had been mailed to a series of politicians and media outlets, killing five people. In response, Teresa insisted much of the mail directed to Dale Jr. remain unopened.

Since the Leno appearance, the onslaught of ladies trying to gain Junior's attention had only grown. But with the anthrax fears connected to the U.S. Postal Service, one enterprising young lady from the Pacific Northwest took a different approach. Midway through Friday-morning activities at the track, FedEx envelopes were delivered to Dale Jr., Kenny Wallace, Michael Waltrip, and several others. The identical contents of each envelope included a note of instruction to please deliver the enclosed documents to Dale Jr. The young lady included an 8x10 glamour photo, and a lengthy letter explaining how her grandmother encouraged her to write about the many ways she was the ideal girl for him. Though she didn't receive a reply, it was certainly a novel approach to getting his attention.

In Saturday's Busch race, Kevin Harvick secured the 2001 series championship. His win made Richard Childress the first team owner to win a title in NASCAR's top three series (Cup, Busch, and the Craftsman Truck Series), and brought back fond memories for Dale Jr. and much of the team, who had celebrated two Busch Series titles here in the same fashion.

When Sunday's race began, the Budweiser bunch hoped their fond memories and two days of grueling test sessions at the Homestead track would pay dividends. They did not.

Dale Jr. remained inside the top 20 for the first 25 laps, but the handling on the Bud car became so evil he was forced to make an unscheduled pit stop on lap 29, believing a tire was flat. The stop for four new tires and a series of adjustments dropped them to last place, one lap behind. The team caught a break when a caution flag came out on lap 83, allowing them to circle back onto the lead lap.

As agonizing as their struggle had been, it took a backseat during the next caution flag when a horrible pit accident injured three crewmen from the No. 28 Robert Yates–owned team of Ricky Rudd. Under caution,

Ward Burton made contact with the car of Casey Atwood on pit lane, which sent Burton's car into the crewmen and a NASCAR official.

Seeing the ambulances and commotion in Rudd's pit concerned Dale Jr., whose brother-in-law Ray Holm was a rear-tire changer for the team.

"Hey, what happened with the 28 and the 22 cars?" Junior asked.

"Somebody ran into the 22 and he hit a couple of crew members on the 28," Tony Jr. explained.

"Are they OK? How bad?" Junior asked. "Was Ray-Ray involved? Tony Jr., can you see him from there?"

"I can't see him, but we believe he's OK," Tony Jr. told him. "It looks like it was the jackman and the front-tire guys."

"You let me know how those boys are, and tell me if you see Ray-Ray," Dale Jr. insisted.

Rudd's front-tire changer, Bobby Burrell, was airlifted from the track with head injuries; the jackman, John Bryan, suffered a concussion and strained knee. Tire changer Kevin Hall suffered bruises and lacerations, and Kenny Lawson, a NASCAR official, was also hit but suffered no major injuries.

(In 1990, the cars of Ricky Rudd and Bill Elliott had collided on pit lane, killing Elliott's rear-tire changer, Mike Rich. The crash led NASCAR to institute pit-lane speed limits that made it much safer for the over-the-wall team members. The 2001 Homestead crash, which luckily did not involve a fatality, led to a new rule making it mandatory for over-the-wall crew members to wear helmets on pit lane.)

Tony Jr. assured Dale Jr. that Holm had not been hit, much to Junior's relief. The remaining laps were a game of catch-up, as Dale Jr. tried to climb from last place. He was able to claw back to finish 15th for the second week in a row.

The last time Bill Elliott had driven into a Winston Cup victory lane, it was behind the wheel of a Budweiser-sponsored car in September 1994. Since then, Elliott had started 227 races without a win, but he returned to the winner's circle with flair, as he passed his young teammate Atwood with five laps remaining to win the Pennzoil 400. It was the first win for Evernham Motorsports.

Michael Waltrip, whose season had been a massive struggle since his season-opening win, fought hard to slip by Atwood in the final laps, grabbing second place.

Just as he had been happy for Kenny Wallace the week before, Junior was thrilled to see Waltrip finish so well.

"Good for Michael!" he said. "That team has struggled, but after a few personnel changes, they've really been good lately. During one of the yellow flags, I was right behind Michael and I wished I could have talked with him on the radio. I could tell he was really running good, and I'll bet he was having fun and must have been in a really good mood."

chapter 50

i got a little emergency here

Hampton, Georgia

We stayed in Miami after the race to shoot two Budweiser commercials for 2002. The first spot featured a racing action script, inspired by an answer Junior had given on a NASCAR questionnaire in 2000.

"What would be the one thing you'd add to your race car in the future?" it asked.

"Music!" Junior replied, repeating it for emphasis. "Music! Someone get me some *music!*"

The first commercial, a 30-second spot dubbed "CD," opens with Dale Jr. racing hard while a Foo Fighters–esque soundtrack blares. The commercial takes a funny and surprising turn when the background music suddenly begins to skip. In the midst of the race, Junior pulls off his glove and ejects a CD out of the stereo in the dashboard of his race car. A quick polish doesn't cure the skipping disc, so Junior pounds the dashboard with his fist. When the player still won't respond, he solves the problem by slamming his car hard into the back of another. The music begins playing again, Junior smiles broadly, and it all ends happily.

After a lengthy day of shooting at the Homestead track, we traveled a short distance north in Junior's motorcoach to Fort Lauderdale, where the second commercial would be shot the following evening.

The film crew took over large chunks of a quiet neighborhood to shoot the spot called "Victory Lap." The commercial was part of

Anheuser-Busch's extensive effort to encourage designated drivers, and was tentatively slated to debut during the 2002 Super Bowl telecast.

The script called for Dale Jr., as the designated driver, to chauffeur his passenger in a street car painted to look exactly like his race car. The passenger sends Junior on a circuitous route, yelling and waving at his friends and neighbors as he's being driven by a NASCAR star. Junior finally asks, "Dude, where exactly do you live?" "Oh, right back by the bar," is the answer.

The commercial costarred Ed Helms, a young comedian and actor. Before Helms would appear on "The Daily Show" and "The Office," or take his memorable missing-tooth role in *The Hangover*, he and Junior spent nearly 12 hours inside the car, giving them ample time to laugh and joke between takes.

As dawn approached, the final scene called for Helms to flirt with several sexy women as Junior drove him slowly down the block. The production had taken longer than expected, and the race was on to film the final segment before sunrise. As the production ran past its original schedule, one of the women in the scene was visibly upset between takes because she was going to be late for her flight to a major photo shoot. When he discovered Natasja Vermeer, a Dutch model and actress, needed to get to the South Carolina coast for her modeling gig, Dale Jr. did what any chivalrous star with a private plane would do: offer to fly the stunning starlet to her destination.

After filming was complete, we headed to the airport and climbed aboard one of DEI's planes. As soon as the engines spun to life, Junior was fast asleep, worn out from the overnight filming. While he slept on his opportunity to chat up the lithe blonde model, I was left to keep her company until she was delivered to her chosen locale.

The superfast Atlanta Motor Speedway loomed next on the calendar. After two 15th place finishes, driver and team looked forward to running up front again and solidifying their points position at a track where they had always been among the fastest.

Dale Jr. ran a harrowing qualifying lap of more than 192 miles per hour and was thrilled when it held up for his second pole position of the season.

"I saw the lap Mark [Martin] made and I said, 'That's a great lap. What a stud,'" Dale Jr. explained in the post-qualifying news conference.

"Then we go out and beat his time by almost three-tenths, so I dunno *what* that makes me!" he laughed. "We coulda been a little better, but I felt like we had a great lap.

"That was just wild fast. I shut the car off after that lap. I'd had enough. I didn't want any more," he laughed, when asked why he took only one qualifying lap. "That's fun, but at the speeds we're going, that is one helluva ride. I mean, this track is faster than Daytona or Talladega, and it really gets your heart pumping."

Feeling good about the qualifying lap, Junior sat for an extended period, answering a wide array of questions. With the season so near an end, it seemed the perfect time to reflect on the tumultuous year.

"It's been a good year," he said. "I don't dwell so much on what happened several months ago so much as I do two weeks ago. So my mood changes from week to week, because of performances two weeks ago. My mood right now is I'm frustrated with the way we ran at Homestead and wherever we were before that. But we won Talladega. That was exciting and great and that already kind of wore off. I feel like, as a driver, I kind of planted my feet a little more firmly in the soil, so to speak.

"I think my worries and curiosities about our company and its ability to progress after my father's death have kind of been resolved. I feel real confident in Teresa and I feel like she wants to be there. I was curious as to whether she wanted to deal with it. I grew real confident in her ability to stand and stick it out. She's really excited about being a female team owner. That's kind of intriguing to her. She likes those kinds of challenges, so I feel good.

"I think it's going to be awhile before we see Teresa at the track. She's wanted to come, but I'm not sure she knows what she'll be in for when she gets here. I don't know whether she expects it to be a big deal to the rest of the world or not. I think when she's comfortable, she'll be back."

Dale Jr. spoke about his continued maturation.

"I'm still not quite where I want to be off the racetrack . . .. There's a lot of decisions to make and associations and relationships to make. I'm still learning. I don't know if you ever get to the point where you make all the right decisions, but I'm getting better at that.

"I don't think that I've had to change, or unconsciously changed, my personality for anybody. Even our association with Drakkar. I asked them before we started, 'You know who I am, how I act, and what I do. Is that

289

what you all want? Because you're not going to dress me up in a tuxedo every time we do an appearance.' I try to make sure everybody understands that."

Finally, he was asked about his interest in an ownership role at DEI.

"Hardly any at all. I was kind of curious, excited, worried, timid, all those things about it when my dad was killed, about what was going to happen. As the months and months went on, if I was to take on any part of ownership or whatever, it would be no more than a label. I didn't have anything professionally to provide to the company. I couldn't be anything more than a face on the title, so to speak, because I just didn't have the smarts and the intelligence yet to really lead anything or be in control of anything of that magnitude."

Starting from the pole, Dale Jr. took off early, leading the race for a total of 171 laps and setting a torrid pace. His poise behind the wheel shone more than ever before, as his occasional flights of fancy on the radio were replaced with determined concentration. Harvick had won the previous Atlanta race in an emotional finish, but no one wearing a red Budweiser uniform had forgotten how close they had come to a victory of their own that day.

The middle and late stages of the race were spectacular, as Earnhardt Jr. dueled with Jerry Nadeau, Bobby Labonte, and Tony Stewart on the ultrafast, multigrooved track. It seemed Junior could take the lead whenever he wanted and he assumed the top spot seven times throughout the race. Running in the high line, only inches from the wall, he found he could rocket off the corner and down the straight.

Despite his pace, Dale Jr. did experience some problems in the cockpit. During a yellow-flag period beginning on lap 121, he reported a runaway water bottle that had broken free of its mount.

"Hey, this water bottle is flying around in here. Can I just throw it out?" he asked Tony Jr.

"Uhhhhh, well, wait. Let's check with an official first," Tony Jr. recommended. "We don't want NASCAR penalizing us for throwing shit on the track."

"Let me know, 'coz it's just rolling all around," Dale Jr. said.

"OK, they say you can throw it out at the end of the pit lane here when you come by next lap," Tony Jr. reported.

"If we win this race, Action [Performance] can produce a special diecast with the flying water bottle accessory," laughed Norris.

"All right, but let's make sure it doesn't happen again, 'coz if that would have hit me on the arm I don't wanna know what would have happened at these speeds," said Dale Jr.

It seemed one of those days when everything worked well, with the pit crew consistently turning blazing pit stops. As the race slowed for the fifth caution of the day on lap 263, the Bud team prepared for their last stop. They responded with another four-tire change in less than 14 seconds. It was an ecstatic bunch that sent their car back on track in the lead.

"All right, babe," Tony Jr. yelled. "It's up to you to bring it home!"

Their joy was short-lived. Dale Jr. keyed the microphone one lap later with a distress call.

"All right, I got a little emergency here. A medical emergency," he said. "I have a big ol' chunk of metal in my left eye. I tried to get it myself but I can't. As soon as this race is over, I need to get it out as soon as possible. Make sure someone is there to take it out as quick as they can. Make sure that happens."

As the race restarted, Junior tried to hold the lead while driving with one eye open. Norris helped him remain calm and tried to guide him through traffic as best he could, while I raced to find a mobile EMT team along pit lane. I arranged for someone to be positioned in our pit area in case the situation worsened and Junior needed to pull in before the race ended.

With less than 50 laps remaining, Junior held on the best he could, eventually seeing six cars zoom past him in the final laps.

Nadeau, whose only career win had come in this event the year before, led the field as he crossed under the white flag. But Nadeau's car ran out of fuel, and Bobby Labonte swept past to win the NAPA 500. Sterling Marlin and Harvick also got by Nadeau, who coasted across the line in fourth.

"I'm really sorry guys," Dale Jr. said as he crossed the line in seventh place. "I was trying my best at the end, and I was really struggling. I was just hoping I wasn't gonna wreck myself or especially anybody else. Somehow, we hung on there."

"All right, Dale Jr.," Tony Jr. said. "We've got some medical staff ready to go at the hauler. Take it easy and roll on in here. They'll take care of you."

As he pulled to a stop, Earnhardt Jr. gingerly pulled off his helmet and climbed on a cart for a quick trip to the care center inside turn two. Doctors irrigated his left eye and were able to remove a tiny slice of metal.

Holding an ice pack over the eye, Junior quietly agonized about another race win that had slipped through his fingers. More importantly, though, there was no serious injury to the eye.

As the medical cart drove us back to the garage, Jeff Gordon and his Hendrick Motorsports team were celebrating. By finishing sixth, Gordon locked up his fourth Winston Cup championship. At the time, only Earnhardt and Richard Petty had won more Cup titles.

Despite gaining 10 bonus points for leading the most laps, Dale Jr. dropped one spot to eighth in the standings, while race winner Labonte vaulted past Junior and Rusty Wallace. As it had been all season, positions 2 through 10 were extremely tight, and Gordon was the only driver to lock in his points position before the finale. Dale Jr.'s finish at Loudon could place him as high as 6th or as low as 10th in the final standings.

"I was driving as hard as I could all day," he told the guys when we arrived back in the garage. "That was great fun running with those guys. Our car was tight in the middle, so I'd run the high line. We could hold 'em off most of the time when they'd try to go low. We could get a run on 'em off the turns and keep the lead down the straights. Damn, that was fun."

chapter 51

we were junk

Loudon, New Hampshire

It had already been a brutal, long season, and due to the changes in the schedule caused by the terrorist attacks, the season stretched past Thanksgiving. What Junior needed more than anything was time with his family, and he was able to enjoy at least some of the day Thursday before the entire NASCAR air force flew to New Hampshire early Friday morning.

The one-day show at Loudon was reportedly scheduled for Friday to allow two extra days for NASCAR to run the race in case of snow. Many worried the late November return to the northernmost track on the schedule was going to be a frigid struggle, but the day arrived with surprisingly moderate temperatures.

There was a single brief practice session in the morning, and the starting lineup was determined by the point standings at the time of the originally scheduled race. In the earlier race at Loudon, Dale Jr. had started 29th and wound his way to a top-10 finish. Starting eighth would be a significant improvement.

Having secured his fourth Winston Cup title the week before, Gordon rocketed away from the pole position, dominating the race. Expecting cold temperatures, Goodyear brought tires designed for low temps, which caused problems for the Bud team almost as soon as the race began. Dale Jr. pushed hard, causing his right-side tires to blister.

"It's really, really bad now," Dale Jr. reported, less than 50 laps into a race in which he was seemingly losing a position with each lap.

"If it's really bad, just bring it in and we'll fix it," Tony Jr. replied. "There's no sense in taking a chance on injuring yourself by trying to do too much here."

"There must be something wrong with this set of tires," Dale Jr. said. "I got a bad vibration in the right front. It's so bad it feels like something is bent. We got something serious goin' on here."

"OK, we'll change the air pressures," Tony Jr. said.

"You gotta give me more than that! I don't wanna be sideways like this anymore," Dale Jr. yelled. "It ain't no fun."

When the second yellow flag of the day came out on lap 51, the team stopped twice for a series of adjustments.

"Let's make some big changes here," Tony Jr. said. "We may as well park it if it keeps drivin' the way it is right now."

Restarting 39th after the two stops, Dale Jr. continued to fight for traction. When the next yellow appeared on lap 97, the team made four more stops to adjust the right front shock and the right front camber (the angle at which the tire meets the pavement). While the wholesale changes helped the car, Dale Jr. was forced to come from 41st place, two lap behind the leaders.

"OK, we still got a chance at a decent finish here," Dale Jr. said, unconvincingly. "Let's keep after it and pass these guys. We can come back."

The remaining 200 laps were a game of catch-up, as Dale Jr. somehow sliced through heavy traffic to gain 17 positions.

As forgettable as the day was for the Bud crew, it was a particularly memorable finish. Robby Gordon pushed Jeff Gordon out of the way to take the lead on lap 284. Jeff had been dominant all afternoon, and angrily retaliated by slamming into Robby's car, earning the champion a one-lap penalty.

Robby Gordon held on to earn his first NASCAR win, driving the No. 31 car for Richard Childress Racing. Gordon, who had replaced Mike Skinner after the Dover race, grabbed the first victory for sponsor Lowe's Home Improvement. (It was the final race for Lowe's with RCR—they had committed to join Hendrick Motorsports the following year with rookie driver Jimmie Johnson.) Gordon donated his winnings to a charitable fund for New York firemen.

Despite a nightmarish day, Dale Jr. persevered to finish 24th, three laps behind. It was enough of a comeback to secure eighth place in the final point standings, a huge improvement over a 16th place finish the year before.

"We were junk to begin with, but once we made those changes, we could at least run competitive times with the leaders," Junior explained as the team packed the hauler for the final time in 2001.

"The last fifty laps were crazy!" Junior laughed. "We had some pretty damn good racing going on there. I didn't know who was even on the same lap as we were, or if I was racing lead-lap cars, but everyone was racing hard. I knocked in the nose of the car racing the 01 [Jason Leffler], and now it looks like one of those cool muscle cars in the sixties with the sloped nose."

Junior asked for a points rundown to see how his season had ended.

"Damn! I really wanted to catch that Miller car," Junior said, noting Rusty Wallace finished the season 21 points ahead of him. "But, I'm happy with eighth."

chapter 52

one day soon

New York, New York

Fueled by adrenaline and sorrow, Dale Jr. and his team made it through the season.

It was a year of three dramatic and emotional victories, and a huge improvement in consistency. In stark contrast to their rookie season, the team finished strong, with wins at Daytona, Dover, and Talladega. Only two drivers (Gordon and Jarrett) won more races than Dale Jr., whose winnings for the year topped $5.8 million. After finishing 16th his rookie year, Earnhardt Jr. finished the 2001 season 8th in the standings.

Though three wins in a season were considered a success, it meant 35 (often heartbreaking) losses for Dale Jr. and his fans. In return for the immense support he received wherever he went, Junior did his damnedest each week to give them something to cheer for or brag about at the water cooler on Monday morning. In recognition of his mettle, *The Sporting News* awarded him the Toughest Driver award for 2001.

Dale Earnhardt Inc. had also thrived. Despite losing its leader at Daytona and one of its drivers at Darlington, DEI was the only company in Winston Cup with three race-winning teams during the season.

Junior's offseason plans meant he was finally able to shoot a music video with Matthew Good (which turned out to be a rollicking trip from Memphis to Las Vegas). He was also honored to carry the Olympic torch in Charlotte as it traversed the country toward Salt Lake City for the 2002 Winter Games.

But first, Dale Jr. was required to travel to New York the final week of November for the annual NASCAR banquet honoring the 2001 champion, Jeff Gordon. As a top-10 finisher, it was the first time Earnhardt Jr. was onstage at the Waldorf Astoria, accepting more than $400,000 from NASCAR and Winston for his points finish.

Though New York could be a snarled mess during the holiday season, it was a welcome escape for many of the drivers. Unlike most elsewhere in the country, in New York Dale Jr. and the other drivers could go out without being recognized or bothered. One of the traditions the night before the banquet was partying at the infamous dive bar, the Hogs & Heifers Saloon. It was a chance to relax without pretensions, have a few beers (or a *lot* of beers), and kick back.

But amid the great time, Junior's mind was elsewhere.

"I really don't want to accept that award," he told me, referring to an honor being given posthumously to his father the following morning. As much as he hated accepting awards for his dad, no one else named Earnhardt would be in New York City until later in the day, so it fell on his shoulders.

The Myers Brothers breakfast at the Waldorf is the traditional venue to present a number of NASCAR awards that aren't a part of the larger banquet that evening. One of these honors was the Myers Brothers Award, recognizing a lifetime of work within the sport as selected by the National Motorsports Press Association. The NMPA chose to honor Earnhardt for his considerable body of work during his storied career.

Junior's breakfast was getting cold, sitting in front of an empty seat. As the awards ceremony neared, I went to his room several floors above the ballroom. It wasn't uncommon for me to wake Dale Jr. at the track, but this morning, several minutes of knocking produced no response. Finally, I heard rustling.

"I'm not going down there," he said, without opening the door.

I went back downstairs without him, as David Poole, president of the NMPA, delayed the announcement of the award.

I spoke quietly with Ty Norris, explaining my difficulties. Norris went to the room and after what seemed like an eternity, walked back into the ballroom with Dale Jr., looking pale with bloodshot eyes. Poole could finally announce the selection of Dale Earnhardt for the Myers Brothers Award of 2001.

Dale Jr. walked to the podium to a standing ovation. The room was filled with industry leaders—drivers, team owners, and sponsor executives—who were certainly cheering in recognition of his father but also in honor of Junior's strength after the tragedy.

"Accepting awards for my father is probably one of the toughest things I do, or have ever done," he said honestly. "I know no matter what I say it would never be as good, or never be as cool, or never be as smooth as what he might say."

After the ceremony, he was adamant it would be the last time he'd accept an honor on his father's behalf. From now on, any award he accepted would be his own.

That night at the champion's banquet, Garth Brooks sang the tear-jerker "The Dance," before bringing Teresa Earnhardt to the stage. It was Teresa's first public appearance since her brief Las Vegas media conference, and she accepted the Most Popular Driver award for her late husband. The award was selected each year by fan voting, and surprisingly, it was the first time Earnhardt had won it.

Later in the evening, Dale Jr. strode to the podium to deliver a speech he had written several nights before. Because he had refused to share it with NASCAR in advance, he spoke without the aid of a teleprompter. His speech was occasionally halting, but sincere.

"This year, I battled for wins with the champions of our sport, and after each race I missed my father's approval very much," he said. "Whether they know it or not, many of the drivers filled that void. Tony Eury did double duty as well, offering fatherly advice at any moment."

Dale Jr. credited his team with giving him superb machines throughout the year.

"Our race cars practically drove themselves sometimes," he said, before going for the laugh. "But I still maintain the argument that I believe I'm worth five spots."

Dale Jr. went through his list of acknowledgments and thank yous (including hilariously mispronouncing my name), before recognizing the series sponsor, Winston.

"Thanks for everything," he said. "Especially the million-dollar bonus."

As he concluded, he predicted good things for himself and his team.

"One day soon, the Bud team will headline this joint, and they'll help me write that speech."

The 2002 season was less than 90 days away. Would it hold heartache or joy? Would it begin with another eerie dream? No matter what the future held, it would be Dale Jr.'s first full year without his father. He was ready to stand alone, carrying the Earnhardt name into battle.

thanks and acknowledgments

There are two people at the very top of my **THANK YOU** list: Dale Jr. and my mom for being supportive for so many years.

This project could not have been completed without the generous work of Bill Kentling, Kristi Boyer, and Mike Davis. Thanks to Lee Klancher of Octane Press for providing a publishing framework for the project.

Thank you to all of the superb people I've worked with at Anheuser-Busch, including (but certainly not limited to) Tim Schuler, Steve Uline, and Brad Brown. Big "attaboys" are extended to Harold Hinson, Mike Snell, Joe Glynn, Pam Surbaugh Mariani, Tim Patek, and Webster Spaulding.

My appreciation goes to Nancy Wager and Judy Kouba Dominick from Chevrolet for providing interview transcripts through the years, as well as many of the good folks from the former DEI: Ty Norris, Tony Eury, Tony Eury Jr., Steve Crisp, and Steve Hmiel. Thanks, also, to many of the fine people I've worked with in recent years, including DeLana Harvick, Dr. Jack Cathey, and Darrell Waltrip.

There are so many fine people in the media world who have become friends and/or created superb material that was an essential part of the research for this book. I'm certain I'm forgetting someone, but thanks go to (in alphabetical order): Jay "Jayski" Adamczyk, Erik Arneson, Ben Blake, Holly Cain, David Caraviello, Liz Clarke, Monte Dutton, Robert Edelstein, Lewis Franck, Jenna Fryer, Andy Hallberry, Mike Harris, Ed Hinton, Chris Jenkins, Clare B. Lang, Dustin Long, Dennis McCafferty,

Ryan McGee, Jeff MacGregor, Rick Minter, David Newton, Andy Parsons, Jim Pedley, Jim Peterson of Dale Jr.'s Pit Stop, Wendy Plaut, Bob Pockrass, the late David Poole, Nate Ryan, Ralph Sheheen, Marty Smith, Marty Snider, Lee Spencer, John Sturbin, Touré, Jim Utter, Matt Yocum, and John Zimmermann.

And, lastly, thanks to everyone who has continually badgered me, asking, "Hey, when are you going to write another book?" Well, kids, here it is.

jade

dale earnhardt inc., 2001

Mooresville, North Carolina
Dale and Teresa Earnhardt   Team owners
Ty Norris   General manager/No. 8 spotter
Steve Hmiel   Technical director
Richie Gilmore   Chief engine builder

no. 8 budweiser chevrolet winston cup team

Name	Shop Duties	Race-day Duties
Tony Eury	Crew chief	Pit strategy
Tony Eury Jr.	Car chief	Front-tire changer
Brandon Blake	Mechanic	Mechanic
Jeff Clark	Engine tuner	Jackman
Brian Cram	Mechanic	Driver comfort
Scott Daniels	Pit setup	Tire catcher
Kevin Eagle		Gas man
Danny Earnhardt		Front-tire carrier
Barry "B" Hoover	Mechanic	Signboard
David Lippard		Catch-can man
Karen Massencup		Scorer
Sonny McCurdy	Truck driver	Gas-can handler
Dean Middlemiss	Fabricator	Pit setup
Shawn Nettleton	Tires	Tires
Jon Neumeyer	Mechanic	
Kevin Pennell	Mechanic	Mechanic
Tom Ryan	Fabricator	Tire catcher
Bill Snyder		Rear-tire carrier
Dan Stillman	Brakes/suspension	Tire catcher
Bill Sutphin	Mechanic	
Dave Urckfitz	Fabricator	
Steve Wolfe	Mechanic	Rear-tire changer

In the Red

You can learn much more about this book on the Web, with photos, videos, and more:

Octane Press: octanepress.com/book/red
Twitter: @InTheRed2001
Facebook: In the Red
Tumblr: inthered2001.tumblr.com

~

About the author, Jade Gurss:

Twitter: @JadeGurss
Facebook: facebook.com/jade.gurss
fingerprint inc.: fingerprintonline.com